Y0-ATI-773

Mannin Revisited

Twelve essays on Manx culture and environment

Mannin Revisited

Twelve essays on Manx culture and environment

Edited by

Peter Davey
David Finlayson

Associate Editor: **Philippa Tomlinson**

Front cover illustration: "Live to learn to live"
Douglas Secondary School Roll of Remembrance, by Archibald Knox,
reproduced by kind permission of Schoill ard Noo Ninian
(St Ninian's High School)

Scottish Society for Northern Studies
2002

Published in Scotland by:
The Scottish Society for Northern Studies
c/o Department of Celtic and Scottish Studies
University of Edinburgh
27 George Square
Edinburgh EH8 9LD

ISBN 0 9535226 2 8
Copyright 2002, Scottish Society for Northern Studies
and individual contributors

All rights reserved. No part of this publication may be reproduced, stored in a retrieval system or transmitted in any form, in any quantity or by any means electronic, mechanical, photocopying, recording or otherwise without the prior written permission of the Society and appropriate contributors. Multiple copying of any of the contents of the publication is always illegal.

The Scottish Society for Northern Studies is pleased to acknowledge the generous support of Manx National Heritage towards this publication.

Printed by:
Nelson Press Co. Ltd.
Nelson House
Kingswood Grove
Douglas, Isle of Man IM1 3LY

Contents

Preface
Peter Davey and David Finlayson … … … … … … … … … …   i

Changing Landscapes of the Isle of Man
Richard C Chiverrell … … … … … … … … … … … … … …   1

Manx Sculptured Monuments and the Early Viking Age
Ross Trench-Jellicoe … … … … … … … … … … … … … …   11

Manx Place-Names: an Ulster View
Kay Muhr … … … … … … … … … … … … … … … … … …   37

Emerging from the Mist: Ireland and Man in the Eleventh Century
Seán Duffy … … … … … … … … … … … … … … … … …   53

Watch and Ward on the Isle of Man: The Medieval Re-occupation of
Iron Age Promontory Forts
Andrew Johnson … … … … … … … … … … … … … … …   63

At the Crossroads of Power and Cultural Influence: Manx Archaeology
in the High Middle Ages
Peter Davey … … … … … … … … … … … … … … … … …   81

A Brief Encounter: The Duke of Atholl and the Isle of Man 1736 - 1764
Ros Stott … … … … … … … … … … … … … … … … … …   105

Manx Farming Communities and Traditions. An Examination of Manx
Farming Between 1750 and 1900
Chris J Page … … … … … … … … … … … … … … … … …   115

Manx Folklore - a Changing or Continuous Tradition?
Yvonne Cresswell … … … … … … … … … … … … … … …   137

'The Devil once a Fiddler Made': the Connection between Manx,
Scottish and Norwegian Fiddle Music
Fenella C Bazin … … … … … … … … … … … … … … … …   151

The Isle of Man - In the British Isles but not Ruled by Britain:
A Modern Peculiarity from Ancient Occurrences
Sybil Sharpe … … … … … … … … … … … … … … … … …   161

Securing the Future for Manx Gaelic
Philip Gawne … … … … … … … … … … … … … … … … …   173

Contributors

Fenella C Bazin: Acting Director of the Centre for Manx Studies; Director of Post-graduate Studies.

Richard C Chiverrell: Lecturer in the Department of Geography, University of Liverpool.

Yvonne Cresswell: Curator of Social History at Manx National Heritage since 1987. Research interests include: Manx folk life, Arts and crafts designer, Archibald Knox; Civilian internment on the Isle of Man during World War I. She is currently researching the development of Manx folklore through the 20th century.

Peter Davey: Reader in the School of Archaeology, Classics and Oriental Studies at the University of Liverpool and Director of the Centre for Manx Studies in the Isle of Man.

Seán Duffy: Head of the Department of Medieval History, Trinity College, Dublin.

Philip Gawne: Manx Language Development Officer (Manx Heritage Foundation and Manx National Heritage), one of the founders of Mooinjer Veggey.

Andrew Johnson: Sixteen years as Field Archaeologist for Manx National Heritage. His principal interest is in upland archaeology, particularly from the perspective of seasonal settlement and land use and ranges around the Irish Sea and through the Western Isles of Scotland.

Kay Muhr: Senior Research Fellow of the Northern Ireland Place-name Project in the Department of Irish and Celtic Studies, Queen's University, Belfast. Currently Chairman of the Ulster Place-name Society and Vice-President of the Society for Name Studies in Britain and Ireland.

Chris J Page: Southern Area Site Manager and Cregneash Farm Manager at Manx National Heritage.

Sybil Sharpe: Many years lecturing/researching in law at U.K. Universities; has published extensively in law journals and has produced three books on aspects of public law. Since moving to Man she has embarked on a study of Manx constitutional history and, in particular, the relationship between Tynwald amd Westminster.

Ros Stott: Member of staff at the Centre for Manx Studies where she does research into the eighteenth century history of the Isle of Man.

Ross Trench-Jellicoe: Honorary Research Fellow in the History Department at Lancaster University, completing a corpus of Manx sculptured monuments from the Early Middle Ages.

Preface

This small volume in the "occasional " series of the Scottish Society for Northern Studies (SSNS) was triggered by the very pleasant and rewarding four day conference held in Port Erin during April 2000. We are particularly grateful to Dr Andrew Foxon of Manx National Heritage for his assistance in organising the conference.

Though at the southern end of the SSNS conference range, Man's Norse connections are very well established through the Medieval History of Man and the Isles down to the modern bishopric of Sodor and Man. Completely encircled by, and easily accessible from Scotland, England, Wales and Ireland the history of Man was bound to be turbulent.

The twelve chapters of the volume can be roughly divided into three sections. The first chapter sets the geographical scene by considering in some depth the geological structure and history of the island. The second chapter gives a fairly detailed account of the quite remarkable array of Manx sculptured stones while the third chapter looks at Manx placenames from the slightly unusual view-point of Northern Ireland.

The next group of four chapters covers the history of Man. The first looks at the influence of Ireland on Man in the eleventh century. The next considers the promontory forts situated round the coasts of Man and speculates on an iron-age origin followed by a medieval re-use. There follows an extended discussion of the medieval history of Man in the light of recent archaeological excavations and finally we have an account of a brief but fairly recent (18th century) episode when Scotland again exerted an influence on Man in the person of the Duke of Atholl.

The final group of chapters discusses Farming, Folklore, Manx music and perhaps more controversially, the relation of Tynwald to Westminster. The final chapter gives an account of the quite remarkable recovery of Manx Gaelic from effectively zero to two percent participation of the Manx population. Scotland take heed!

While not one of our twelve authors is based in present-day Scotland, the Scots connection comes through strongly in almost every chapter. We are most grateful to them all for the time and effort expended in preparing and correcting the manuscripts.

Our special thanks are due to Philippa Tomlinson for her hard work in the technical editing and publication management fields and to Georgiana Mazilu for her work in the preparation of figures and illustrations.

Peter Davey
David Finlayson

Changing Landscapes of the Isle of Man

Richard C Chiverrell

Introduction

The Isle of Man is a small mountainous island in the northern Irish Sea basin. The island comprises two upland areas that reach 621 meters at Snaefell separated by the low-lying central valley. There are further lowlands in the south east and the extensive northern coastal plain (Figure 1). The Isle of Man is a fault-bounded block of Cambrian, Ordovician and Silurian slate formed by crustal extension and doming during the late Jurassic and early Cenozoic (Quirk and Kimbell, 1997). Devonian and Carboniferous lithologies form the bedrock geology of the lowlands. Two million years ago climates cooled heralding the onset of the Quaternary - a recent geological epoch associated with high magnitude climate changes from ice ages (glacials) to warm periods (interglacials). During the glacials of the Quaternary successive advances of substantial ice sheets sculpted the landscape of the British Isles. The Isle of Man lies directly in the path of ice sheets advancing from mountains in Scotland and the Lake District, southwards across the Irish Sea, and so would have been covered and sculpted by the erosive power of successive glaciations. During interglacials climates improved to conditions similar to, or warmer than, that encountered in Britain today. Each ice sheet is akin to a large scouring pad advancing across the landscape removing sedimentary evidence of previous events. Consequently as the last Ice Age, the Devensian (80-11.5 kyrs ago)[1] produced an ice sheet that extended far into the southern Irish Sea, covering the Isle of Man, the recent sediments on the island only reflect land-forming processes during and after the Devensian. Early research held that the uplands were an ice-free nunatak during the Devensian (Wirtz, 1953; Cubbon, 1957; Thomas, 1976), but recent estimates of ice thickness indicate that the island was covered during the Devensian glacial maximum (Bowen, 1973; Boulton et al. 1977).

The Quaternary geology of the Isle of Man divides into two suites of deposits – local upland sediments and lowland sediments composed of lithologies foreign to the

---

[1] 1 kyr = one thousand years

Island (Kendall, 1894; Lamplugh, 1903). The foreign deposits consist of a mixture of diamict floor, drumlin field, ice-marginal moraine, ice-disintegration topography, ice-front alluvial fan, subaqueous fan, sandur and proglacial lake sediments deposited almost exclusively on the northern coastal plain. The uplands are covered with an extensive and almost ubiquitous cover of till composed of locally - derived slate, with the thickest deposits (up to 20 metres) on the floors of the main valleys and substantially thinner sequences on steeper slopes and interfluves. Soon after the ice retreated from the island the extensive cover of glacial till was rapidly reworked by periglacial slope processes producing thick sequences of soliflucted till (Thomas, 1985; Dackombe and Thomas, 1985; 1989). The Devensian climate began to warm sharply around 15 kyrs ago, but the transition from glacial conditions to the current warm period (the Holocene) was punctuated by short-lived cooling of the climate, particularly between 13-11.5 kyrs ago before the onset of the Holocene 11.5 kyrs ago. Landforms and sediments set into or overlying the glacial and periglacial deposits reflect land-forming processes during late glacial and Holocene times. Understanding the Manx landscape requires an appreciation of a considerable variety of geomorphological (land forming) processes responsible for the development of the natural landscape.[2]

Devensian glaciation of the Isle of Man

Ice covered the island during the main advance of the Devensian ice age, which commenced after 30 kyrs ago. Ice sheets expanded from Scotland and Cumbria forming a large ice body that at its zenith between 28-22 kyrs ago extended into the south Irish Sea. There is no morphological evidence that ice formed on the Isle of Man, with the smoothed and sculpted upland landscape produced by a large 1000-750 metre thick ice sheet consuming the entire island (Dackombe and Thomas, 1989). During the advance of the icesheet thick sequences of glacial sediments were deposited on the northern coastal plain abutting against the 300 metre high, north facing, faulted escarpment (Figure 1). Further glacial sediments were deposited in the south of the island on the Plains of Malew, where the sediments are sculpted to form drumlins. Drumlins are oval shaped low hills composed largely of glacial sediments smoothed by the flow of the ice. Ice marginal moraine ridges form at the snout of glaciers owing to the tectonisation of pre-existing sediment, the pushing of debris by thrusting ice and through the simple accumulation of debris along the ice margin. Across the northern plain of the Isle of Man there is a series of east-west orientated linear ridges composed of glacigenic sediment that are almost certainly ice marginal moraines or ridges produced by oscillations of the glacier snout as the ice retreated. South of the Bride Hills these retreat or recessional moraines take the form of low amplitude linear ridges.

In places, fluctuations of the ice margin have produced more substantial ridges. The Bride Hills are a suite of ridges aligned east-west across the island. The sediments exposed on the coast at Shellag Point are highly deformed by glacio-tectonism, having

---

[2] The landscape history of the island has attracted considerable attention during the past five years, which will culminate in the publication of *A New History of the Isle of Man Volume 1 - Evolution of a Natural Landscape* (Chiverrell and Thomas, 2001b). The volume synthesises the wealth of recent research on the Pre-Quaternary and Quaternary geology and geomorphology of the Isle of Man.

been folded and thrusted by the glacier during a minor readvance of the Devensian ice sheet. North of the Bride Hills coastal cliff sections reveal a stacked sequence of glacial tills deposited during and after the ice advance which is responsible for the glaciotectonics. These sediments are believed to be contemporaneous with glacial sediments and landforms at Orrisdale and near Peel. During this readvance the Devensian ice margin was aligned along the west coast of the island as far south as Peel and northwards to the Orrisdale ridge, before veering north-east to the Bride Moraine and offshore into the Vannin Sound (Figure 1a). There are further ice marginal sediments north of Orrisdale exposed in the cliff sections at Jurby. These sediments and landforms were deposited during further northward retreat of the ice margin to the Jurby ridge (Figure 1b). Unlike the earlier glacial sediments, which were deposited in a terrestrial environment, the Jurby succession is subaqueous and was produced by an ice margin dipping its snout into a large ice marginal lake. The dimensions of this lake are unclear, but it was substantial given that there are several metres of glaciolacustrine sediment exposed on the west coast near Killane, beneath Ballaugh Curragh and on the east coast at Dog Mills.

Deglaciation of the Isle of Man

During the later stages of the Devensian the ice margin had already advanced to and retreated from maximum limits. Recent interpretation of the glacial landforms suggests that the ice margin was at the Bride-Orrisdale limits by 18-16 kyrs ago, and so although the uplands and south of the island were ice free the island continued to experience a cold climate until 14.5 kyrs ago. Organic sediments in former kettle hole basins date the timing of the ice margin clearing the island. Kettle hole basins at Jurby Head and Kirk Michael were produced when dead-ice buried within glacial sediment melted and collapsed leaving shallow basins filled with water. Radiocarbon dating of organic sediments from the base of these basins indicates the ice had cleared the island by circa 16.0-15.0 kyrs ago. There are no *in situ* glacial sediments in the Manx Uplands, the hill-slopes and valleys are covered with a mantle of slope process sediments. The thickest deposits occur on the valley floors, and have been incised into by subsequent fluvial activity leaving valley side solifluction terraces (Figure 2). The slope processes responsible for soliflucted till deposits in the upland valleys took place during cold periglacial conditions immediately after deglaciation. Periglaciation is the modification of landscape under a non-glacial cold climate (Ballantyne & Harris, 1993). Frost heave structures and ice wedge casts in the upper layers of glacial sediment pay further testimony to a period with a periglacial climate after deglaciation. Substantial alluvial fans surround the Manx Uplands issuing from the main valleys (Figure 1), and were formed by deposition of vast quantities of sediment as the rivers incised into the soliflucted tills that choked the valleys. The timing and duration of alluvial fan formation on the coastal plain provides a chronology for the main phase of fluvial incision in the Manx uplands. Organic sediments overlying and underlying alluvial fan gravels at Glen Balleira and Ballaugh constrain alluvial fan formation to between 18.0-11.5 kyrs ago. In the uplands, river terraces and alluvial fan surfaces are set into the soliflucted till, and are contemporaneous with the fluvial incision and formation of lowland alluvial fans.

Pollen and beetle fossil records provide further information about the Manx landscape immediately after deglaciation. Organic sediments in kettlehole basins at Kirk Michael and in depressions (pingos) formed by periglacial ground-ice on the Ballaugh alluvial fan (Figure 1c) have yielded pollen diagrams that identify the vegetation changes between 15.0-11.5 kyrs ago (Mitchell, 1965; Dickson *et al.* 1970; Chiverrell and Thomas, 2001). Grasses and sedges, with low frequencies of the open ground herbs sorrel, mugwort, saxifrages, pinks and plantains dominate pollen spectra. Gradually as the climate improved after 14.5 kyrs ago sporadic shrub pollen grains occur, with juniper, crowberry, willow and birch more abundant between 14.5-12.5 kyrs ago. There is a short-lived retrogressive phase where birch, willow and crowberry decline and the open ground herbs are more abundant, which signifies a cooling of the climate between 12.5-11.5 kyrs ago. Beetles provide more precise climate data when present in fossil records, because there are a number of species with specific tolerances of temperature. Consequently subfossil beetle remains have been used to quantitatively reconstruct changes in climatic conditions at the end of the last ice age. Beetle records from the Kirk Michael and Jurby Head kettlehole sediments identify a rapid 10 degree warming of mean summer temperatures circa 14.5 kyrs ago, conditions which persist until between circa 12.5-11.5 kyrs ago when there was a sharp downturn in mean summer temperatures of 10 degree centigrade (Joachim, 1978). In the British Isles the warm period is called the Windermere Interstadial and the subsequent downturn in temperatures is called the Loch Lomond Stadial. The Loch Lomond Stadial ended with a 10 degree warming of mean summer temperatures circa 11.5 kyrs ago and marks the beginning of the current warm period, the Holocene. The vegetation colonisation during the Windermere Interstadial stabilised the landscape of the Isle of Man, with soil development and a cover of open ground herbs and dwarf shrubs. This stabilisation reduced rates of erosion and sediment transfer in the uplands, and so the solifluction activity ceased and much of the fluvial incision probably occurred during the Windermere Interstadial and Loch Lomond stadial. The incision that occurred in upland catchments contributed substantial quantities of fluvial gravel to the mountain front alluvial fans that flank the Manx Uplands.

After the Ice Ages

The Holocene period began 11.5 kyrs ago with a rapid warming of climate. Evidence of the character of the early post-glacial landscape of the Isle of Man is derived from organic sediments in the major peat basins. Pollen data from organic sediments at Ballaugh Curragh, Curragh-y-Cowle, Pollies and the Lhen Trench (Figure 1c) identify the colonisation of the island by vegetation after the last ice age (Innes *et al.* unpublished). Heath-land dominated by dwarf birch, crowberry, heather, juniper and herb-rich grasslands are gradually replaced as woodlands return to the island. Birch woodland expanded 10.7-10.2 kyrs ago, with hazel and pine arriving slightly later 10.2-9.0 kyrs ago as a boreal forest community became established on the island. The Irish Elk *(Megalocerus giganteus)* survived in this developing boreal forest until 10.6-10.2 kyrs ago, according to ^{14}C dates on what is the most recent specimen recorded anywhere in the world (Gonzalez *et al* 2000). Holocene Irish Elk on the Isle of Man were also of smaller dimensions than their counterparts in Ireland in the late glacial period. The boreal forest declined and was succeeded by mixed deciduous woodland as oak and elm returned to the island 8.5-8.1 kyrs ago with hazel continuing to thrive as an understory shrub. Alder joined this mixed deciduous woodland around 8.1-7.7 kyrs ago. The vegetation changes after this point reflect the impact of people on the landscape. During the Mesolithic and Neolithic these impacts take the form of minor reductions in woodland pollen reflecting small scale and temporary clearances. Substantial clearance and cereal cultivation is recorded during the late Neolithic and intermittently throughout the Bronze Age. More substantial clearances affecting the uplands and the northern and central lowlands are recorded during the Iron Age, and witnessed the most substantial removal of woodland from the island. The sequence of vegetation changes ties closely to the detailed archaeological and historical records of human activity on the island, and demonstrates the considerable impact people have had upon the landscape during the late Holocene (Davey, 1999; Innes *et al.* unpublished).

Organic sediments on the northern plain of the Isle of Man also record the sequence of sea level changes during the Holocene. Marine waters influenced currently terrestrial sites at Lough Cranstal, the Lhen Trench and at Phurt, and so are indicative of higher sea levels. Sea level rose rapidly from a low of 55m below OD during the late Devensian as the climatic conditions improved during the Holocene. On the northern coastal plain the raised cliff-line and beach at the Point of Ayre and associated fresh and brackish water lagoonal basins are indicative of higher sea levels 9.0-8.4 kyrs ago. Recent unpublished research has identified further evidence for changes in sea levels on the Isle of Man, with seven regressive and four transgressive sea level changes at Phurt and the Lhen Trench between 7.7-4.4 kyrs ago (Innes *et al.* in prep.). Holocene palaeoclimate data is not abundant on the Isle of Man, with the changes in bog surface wetness recorded in the peat sediment on Beinn-y-Phott providing one of the few proxy archives of climatic fluctuations. The Beinn-y-Phott peat stratigraphy records shifts to a wetter climate after 3.3-2.9 kyrs ago during the Bronze Age, before 2.4-2.2 kyrs ago during the Iron Age and before 1.3-1.2 kyrs ago during the early Medieval Period (Chiverrell *et al.*, 2001). These wet shifts occur at similar times to those recorded in peat sequences elsewhere in the British Isles and provide further evidence for regional climate change.

Alteration of the landscape by people and continued climatic fluctuations albeit on a smaller scale than occurred during the Devensian imply the Manx environment has been changing throughout the Holocene. Rivers have carried out the most significant land-forming processes during the Holocene, and Manx rivers like the Sulby, Neb and Auldyn have produced a suite of river terraces (Chiverrell *et al.* 2001). River terraces are former floodplains abandoned as rivers incise; rivers typically either deposit sediment aggrading the floodplain or incise leaving former floodplain as terraces. Environmental controls on river systems include human activity within the catchment, climate changes or high magnitude events (floods), and these affect whether rivers incise or aggrade. The higher terraces in the Manx uplands date to the late Devensian and are composed of very coarse gravel. During the early Holocene rivers continued to occupy these terraces and were unable to cope with the calibre of material and incise, and so they were either aggrading or quiescent systems. There are younger terraces incised into these early surfaces, but these formed after incision during the last 3000

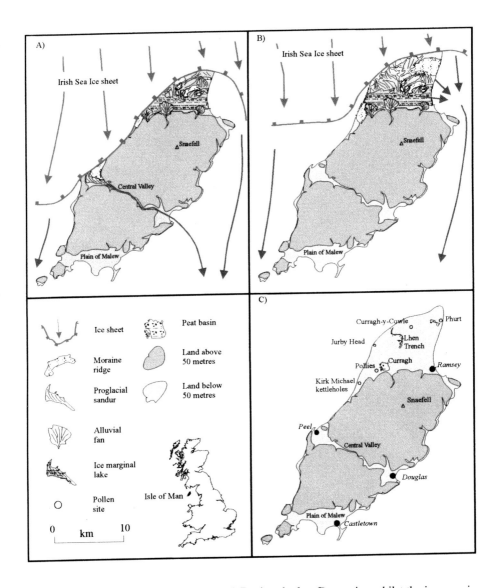

Figure 1: Landscapes of the Isle of Man. a) During the late Devensian whilst the ice margin was at the Orrosdale/Bride limits; b) During the late Devensian whilst the ice margin was at the Jurby limits; c) the locations of late Devensian and Holocene palaeocological sites.

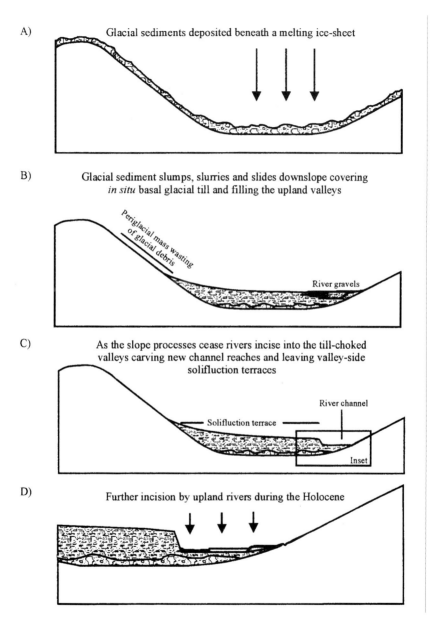

Figure 2: Landscape changes in the valleys of the Manx Uplands. A) on deglaciation 18-16 kyrs ago; B) during the cold periglacial conditions after deglaciation 16-14.5 kyrs ago; C) during warm and cooler conditions 14.5-11.5 kyrs ago; and D) during the Holocene (10-0 kyrs ago).

years of the Holocene. During this time period the rivers have produced between one and and three younger terraces. Increased scale of human activity is the most likely trigger for these phases of increased fluvial activity, given that the fluvial incision is coincident with substantial woodland clearances. However there have been shifts to wetter climatic conditions during the late Holocene and it is possible climate may be triggering fluvial incision. The most likely hypothesis is that fluvial incision has occurred in response to the combined efforts of people and climate.

Synthesis

The rolling uplands and gently undulating lowlands of the Isle of Man reflect the cumulative effects of land-forming processes during and since the last ice age. The drift mantled and smoothed upland hill-slopes are only broken by cliffs flanking the reaches incised by fluvial activity. The fluvial incision has left valley side terraces of solifluction deposits and suites of river terraces. The river terraces reflect the adjustment of river systems during the late Devensian and environmental changes during the Holocene. The lowland landscape is almost entirely an artefact of the last ice age, with the key components of a glaciated terrain characterising the northern plain and the plain of Malew. The evidence for post glacial landscape change is limited to sequences of organic sediments at Ballaugh Curragh and the Lhen Trench, and the Ayres coastal succession. It is the evidence of glacial activity and the glaciated landscape that has always and continues to attract the attention of geologists and geomorphologists, because the island is "an unrivalled field for the study of the conditions that ruled in the northern part of the basin of the Irish Sea during the glacial period" (Lamplugh, 1903).

Acknowledgements

The author gratefully acknowledges financial assistance from the British Geological Survey (NERC), Manx Heritage Foundation, the Gough Ritchie Trust and Manx National Heritage during recent research on the Isle of Man. I am also indebted to the Manx Government for providing the MANNGIS digital mapping data; Juan Bridson for assistance with the MANNGIS data; and Peter Davey and Geoff Thomas for critical readings of an earlier version of this paper.

Bibliography

Ballantyne C K and Harris C, 1993, *The Periglaciation of Great Britain.* (Cambridge University Press, Cambridge).

Boulton G S, Jones A S, Clayton K M and Kenning M J, 1977, 'A British Ice-sheet model and patterns of glacial erosion and deposition in Britain'. In *British Quaternary Studies,* pp 231 - 246, (Oxford University Press).

Boulton G S, Peacock J D and Sutherland D G, 1991, 'Quaternary'. In *The Geology of Scotland,* pp 503 - 542. Craig G Y (ed). (The Geological Society, London.)

Bowen D Q, 1973, 'The Pleistocene succession of the Irish Sea'. *Proceedings of the Geologist's Association.* 83, 249-273.

Chiverrell R C, Davey P J, Gowlett J A J and Woodcock J J, 1999, 'Radiocarbon dates for the Isle of Man'. In Recent *Archaeological Research on the Isle of Man,* pp 321 - 336, Davey P J (ed). (BAR British Series 278, Oxford.)

Chiverrell R C and Thomas G S P (eds.) 2001, *A New History of the Isle of Man: Volume 1 Evolution of the natural landscape.* (Liverpool University Press).

Chiverrell R C, Thomas G S P and Harvey A M, 2001, ' Late-Devensian and Holocene landscape change in the uplands of the Isle of Man'. *Geomorphology.*

Cubbon A M, 1957, 'The Ice Age in the Isle of Man'. *Proceedings of the Isle of Man Natural History and Antiquarian Society,* 5, 499-512.

Dackombe R V and Thomas G S P (eds.), 1985, *Field Guide to the Quaternary of the Isle of Man* p 122. (Quaternary Research Association, Cambridge).

Dackombe R V and Thomas G S P, 1989, 'Glacial deposits and Quaternary stratigraphy of the Isle of Man'. In *Glacial deposits of Great Britain and Ireland,* pp 333 - 344. Ehlers J, Gibbard P L and Rose J (eds.) (A A Balkema, Rotterdam).

Davey P J, 1999, *Recent Archaeological Research on the Isle of Man.* (BAR British Series 278, Oxford).

Dickson C A, Dickson J H and Mitchell G F, 1970, 'The late Weichselian flora of the Isle of Man'. *Philosophical Transactions of the Royal Society, London,* B 258, 31-79.

Gonzalez S, Kitchener A C and Lister A M, 2000, 'Survival of the Irish elk into the Holocene'. *Nature,* 405, 753-754.

Joachim M J, 1978, *Late-glacial Coleopteran assemblages from the west coast of the Isle of Man.* (Unpublished PhD Thesis, University of Birmingham).

Kendall P F, 1894, 'On the glacial geology of the Isle of Man'. *Yn Lioar Manninagh,* 1, 397-437.

Lamplugh G W, 1903, 'The Geology of the Isle of Man'. *Memoir Geological Survey of Great Britain,* p 620.

Mitchell G F, 1965, 'The late Quaternary of the Ballaugh and Kirk Michael districts'. *Quarterly Journal of the Geological Society, London,* 21, 359-381.

Quirk D G and Kimbell G S, 1997, 'Structural evolution of the Isle of Man and central part of the Irish Sea'. In *Petroleum Geology of the Irish Sea and Adjacent Areas,* Meadows N S, Trueblood S P, Hardman M and Cowan G. (eds.) (Geological Society of London Special Publication 124, pp 135-159).

Thomas G S P, 1976, 'The Quaternary stratigraphy of the Isle of Man'. *Proceedings of the Geologist's Association,* 87, 307-323.

Thomas G S P, 1985, 'The Quaternary of the Northern Irish Sea basin'. In *The Geomorphology of Northwest England,* pp 143 - 158, Johnson R H (ed.) (Manchester University Press).

Thomas G S P, 1999, 'Northern England'. In *A revised correlation of Quaternary Deposits in the British Isles,* Bowen D Q (ed.) (Geological Society Special Report No. 23. pp 91-98)

Wirtz D, 1953, *Zur Stratigraphie des Pleistocans im Westen der Britischen Inseln. Nues Jahrbuch Geologies und Palaeontologie,* 96, 267-303

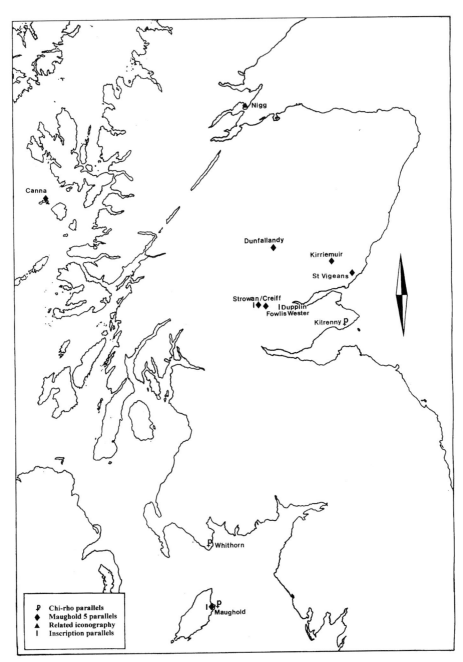

Key Scottish parallels for Manx sculpture.

Manx Sculptured Monuments and the Early Viking Age

Ross Trench-Jellicoe

Introduction

The corpus of Manx sculptured monuments carved within a loose date bracket stretching from the fifth to the twelfth century is still little understood. Mann, by nature of its central geographical position in the Irish Sea and British Isles, stands at an insular crossroads and is open to receive influences from the landmasses which immediately surround it and on occasion from yet further afield. Dependent upon which area is dominant at any given moment, the Isle of Man lies open to fresh cultural input which is then absorbed into the local tradition and modified. Sometimes the external influence is so strong or unprecedented that the native culture seems almost overwhelmed before eventually reasserting itself.

Background: The development of Manx sculpture studies

By the 18th century only four Manx sculptures were recorded and then only for the antiquarian interest of their runic inscriptions (Gibson 1722). In the 1820s the published number had already risen to nine (Oswald 1823, 502-8), while by 1841, Kinnebrook, the first author to devote a book solely to the topic, illustrated thirty pieces. J. G. Cumming listed forty four in 1857 by which time new finds were becoming regularly reported (Cumming 1857a; 1857b; 1865a; 1865b; 1865c; 1866). The doyen of Manx sculpture studies, P.M.C. Kermode, whose interest spanned well over half a century, recorded eighty two items in his first catalogue of 1887, a number which rose to include one hundred and seventeen in his magnum opus of 1907 and increased by a further forty four to one hundred and sixty one monuments by the time of his death in 1932 (Kermode 1910-11; 1911-12; 1915-16; 1920-1; 1928-9). Today the total stands at a little over two hundred monuments and fragments.

The intellectual framework

Kermode was the first scholar seriously to attempt an overall understanding of the events that had produced the sculptured series. He divided them into two main groups the 'Celtic' and the 'Scandinavian' (Kermode 1907) and he numbered each item within a running order which he believed represented a chronological list (*ibid*, 1907). Both these analyses were very much the product of a ninteenth-century scholarly world view and, although a useful approach in its day, may now be seen both as simplistic and inappropriate. Labels such as 'Celtic' and 'Scandinavian' are unhelpful, given that only peoples and their language may be defined as Celtic while the unsuitability of the term Scandinavian is highlighted by the fact that ninth- and tenth-century incomers did not raise Christian monuments before reaching the British Isles, becoming converted and adopting insular traditions of commemoration. If any label is appropriate it must be 'Manx', for the monuments seem all to have been carved here although it is perhaps possible that the stone on which a very few of them were carved may have reached Mann from elsewhere. Subdivisions may be seen most usefully in terms of Early and Late Manx.

Numbering monuments in a chronological list presents its own problems. Kermode did not shie away from the difficulties posed by numbering his corpus. In each new catalogue (Kermode 1887, 1892, 1907, 1924) the accommodation of fresh discoveries produced a renumbered sequence. The current sequence, his fourth attempt inherited by Manx National Heritage (Kermode 1924), is a procrustean bed, too inflexible to happily or meaningfully accommodate the fifty plus discoveries that have come to light since 1924 and is unable to adjust to changes in current perceptions of dating and connections. The present monument identification system is a mess, hallowed only in having been used for three-quarters of a century but still unknown outside Mann where Kermode's 1907 list remains the basic reference.[1]

Whatever, the influences exemplified on the monuments seem to have been derived from a great variety of sources both insular and beyond, ultimately from the whole length of the Mediterranean region and across Northern Europe. This is no less than we should expect to a greater or lesser extent, given the diverse and eclectic nature of culture received by Mann over at least the last three millennia. What is also certain is that those incoming influences were moulded and finished in a native tradition, forging older and more recent influences to produce a unique blend of available motifs.

The arrival of Christianity on Mann

Fifth-century ancestors of the Manx were not naturally Christian and, like other insular cultures, were subject to the introduction of Christianity, along with its cultural baggage. The earliest evidence that I have considered, four ogham inscriptions carved

---

[1] In the forthcoming British Academy corpus of the sculptured monuments of the Isle of Man, it is proposed to adopt a system identifying the monuments using a neutral parish and site label which will also have the benefit of being open-ended. This new numbering system has been used here, for instance Maughold 5:96(67) indicates the British Academy corpus designation of parish church number, 5, followed by :96 - the Manx Museum numbering and finally Kermode's 1907 number (67).

on pillars and boulders, found in the south of the island, show no explicit Christian evidence (Kermode 1907, nos 1- 4) although they are today believed likely to have been carved within a milieu of defined Irish, early-Christian settlement. There can however be no doubt that the sixth-century formulae of the southern, Santon inscription (incorporating horizontal terminal 'i' in each word) - *MONOMENTI AVITI*, 'of the monument of Avitus' (*ibid*, no 34) and also a bi-lingual inscription, from the site of Knock y Doonee in the northern parish of Andreas are explicitly Christian. The latter is incised in Latin and Old Irish, in Roman capitals and ogham script respectively, and may be translated in its Latin form, *AMMECAT[I] FILIVS ROCAT[I] HIC IACIT*, as 'of Ammecatus the son of Rocatus lies here' (Kermode 1910-11, 444-50). Both represent contact with South-west Wales or Cornwall and demonstrate the continuity of the influence of continental trade and Christianity on those communities (Thomas 1971). The introduction, probably also during the sixth century, of simple primary crosses, incised onto unshaped monuments and unprepared surfaces, represents the first explicit sign of Christianity. Significantly, once established, a tradition may continue over a long period and should make us wary of assigning every example of a primary cross to the Early Middle Ages. Only contextual archaeology can confirm the dating. Such monuments and examples recovered early last century were not subjected to current, more rigorous standards of excavation with the result that fewer than a dozen primary and simply decorated slabs, recently recovered from the sites of Keeill Vael, Michael (Trench-Jellicoe 1983) and St Patrick's Isle, German (Trench-Jellicoe, 2002), can be meaningfully stratified. All were recovered from what appear to be secondary and probably tenth-century re-use contexts. Otherwise only the slabs produced by the excavations at Cronk yn How, Balleigh, Lezayre (Bruce & Cubbon 1930) approach this level of scientific archaeology.

Difference between Manx and other insular sculpture traditions

The tradition of sculptural form and style seems to have developed differently and at a different pace in lands surrounding Mann. Church furniture apart, Northumbria initially produced fairly small incised and false-relief shaped slabs before creating the High Cross form at Hexham, Bewcastle and Ruthwell, by the mid-eighth century (Cramp 1984; Bailey & Cramp 1988; Allen and Anderson 1903, part 3). The Scots of Dal Riata, mainly under the auspices of the Columban *familia*, also produced small slabs before developing their quintessential monuments, the relief-carved crosses of St Oran, St John and St Martin on Iona (RCAHMS 1982) and at the related Islay sites of Kildalton and Kilnave in the middle to second half of the eighth century (RCAHMS 1984). Pictish Christian sculpture (Allen & Anderson 1903, part 3), perhaps borrowing its initial forms at the beginning of the eighth century from Northumbria or more probably from the earlier Ninianic tradition of South-west Scotland (Trench-Jellicoe 1998), tended to enlarge the slab as time went on, eventually creating during the ninth century, large examples, some quite huge - the Pictish equivalent of the High Cross, encapsulating a page of manuscript in stone - before adding, sparingly, the free-standing cross to their repertoire towards the end of this period (Henderson 1999). Ireland, following Iona,

Figure 1: Maughold fragment of an altar frontal with *chi-rho* and *omega*.

Figure 2: Maughold slab with encircled hexafoil, crosses and three inscriptions.

seems to have developed the high cross form only in the ninth century before which the smaller slab was in vogue (Lionard 1961; Harbison 1992).

Early literacy at Maughold monastery

On Mann, as in Wales (Nash-Williams 1950), the small incised slab seems to have remained the traditional monument well into the ninth century, even at the Manx monastic centre of Maughold where they seem to have drawn inspiration from nearby South-west Scotland (Trench-Jellicoe 1980; 1998) and perhaps also, in a limited way, from Northumbria (Kermode 1907, nos 25, 117) as well as Ireland (*ibid*, no 28). Away from this centre, primary cross slabs and similar monuments displaying some embellishment of the simpler form – the addition of bar terminals and trifucation of the terminals – together with simple outline crosses seem to have been the order of the day (*ibid*, nos 5-14). Maughold (and Ronaldsway, Malew, if it can be shown to be pre-ninth century (Neely 1940; Laing & Laing 1980-9)) alone show sophistication. At Maughold, sculpture is distinctively monastic in style with evidence of a fragmentary altar frontal currently incised only with the remains of a double-encircled cross of arcs with an attached *chir-ho* monogram and a Greek letter W, *omega*, carved to the upper right, which, almost certainly, originally balanced with a Greek letter A, *alpha*, in a lost section to the left (Kermode 1907, no 21) (Figure 1). Also at Maughold is a multiply-inscribed small slab with a triple-encircled hexafoil, the circle containing a damaged text (*ibid*, no 27) cryptically recording (I believe) '[in the name of] Jesus Christ' that ARNEIT was not only a priest and bishop in the island but also an abbot (Trench-Jellicoe, in preparation). Beneath the main motif stand two further inscriptions flanking crosses incorporating a later form of the *chi-rho* monogram. One message asks us to be aware of the cross as the image of Christ (*CRUX XPI/IMAGENEM*) and the other is carved 'in the name of Jesus Christ' (*IN IHV XPI/ NOMINE*) (Figure 2). This level of literacy and sophistication is unlikely to be encountered elsewhere other than at a monastic site. It is possible also to imagine that most Irish monasteries of the eighth century were not much more sculpturally sophisticated than Maughold and that it is only after this date, as Mann seems to drift apart culturally under the influence of Viking pressures, that the more status-conscious free-standing monuments began, typically, to be erected on Irish monastic sites (Edwards 1990).

Vikings on Mann: How did the arrival of the Vikings affect Mann?

It was by such a community that a Viking presence was first encountered on the Isle of Man. The process of Viking-age land-taking and pagan burial practice has been explored in general by David Wilson (1974; 1989-97) and site-specifically by David Freke (Freke, 2002) but little is known of the mechanisms by which pagan incomers were brought to Christianity. Questions demand answers and blanks need filling. Did the extent of Viking settlement overwhelm earlier Manx Christianity? Was the monastery of Maughold disabled in a similar way to that recorded in the Annals which laconically note the commencement of disruption in Britain (AU s.a. 794.3, 796.7) and amplify the report in Ireland (AU sa. 797.2), at Lindisfarne (ASC 793) and on Iona (AI 795, AU s.a. 801.9, 806.8)? Was their effect similar to the alien pressure which caused Abbot Cellach of Iona, in the year 807 (AU s.a. 806.4), to remove most of his remaining monks to Kells and to rebuild the monastery at his new site? Was the local monastic community murdered during greedy attacks in search of accumulated loot or did monastic Maughold rather wither and die, unable to sustain itself, robbed of its supporting estates by land-hungry Vikings? How did the Manx of the Viking Age eventually come to produce such a distinctive and lavish series of large slab monuments (and eventually their own version of the high cross (Kermode 1907, nos 108, 109)) apparently out of the blue? Most sensibly we might ask why and how a fair number of high-quality sculptures were carved and how they relate to other sculptures found at various sites. There are no native written records to help us understand this period, no dedicated annals or chronicles appear for another two and a half centuries (Broderick 1979) and the Isle of Man passes virtually unnoticed from generation to generation for centuries in the written records of surrounding lands. But we do possess the monuments themselves which we can use as documents in an attempt to comprehend the religious, social and political history of this period on Mann.

A Pictish-style sub-group

Amongst the more sophisticated members of the group that Kermode designated 'Celtic' are small numbers of similar, apparently related monuments, sometimes confined to a single site, interrelated by tricks of design or repeated motifs (Trench-Jellicoe 1999a). One of the more puzzling of these sub-groups is focussed on Maughold and includes half a dozen items reminiscent of the distinctive look of Pictish sculpture and displaying traits found on slabs on the eastern side of Scotland - east of Druim Alban. Isolated far out in the Irish Sea with no necessary discernible connection manifest in between (links particularly absent amongst sculpture along the Irish Sea littoral of South-west Scotland) it is difficult to explain this phenomenon on Mann. Most of the monuments are larger than those hitherto examined at Maughold although certainly not all of them are so. Some display monastic features and the composition of the stone used suggests that a few, at least, came from the same quarries close to Maughold used by eighth-century sculptors rather than the better quality materials from further afield used by tenth-century Manx carvers.

Maughold 5:96(67)A - the Saints' Slab

The foremost sculpture amongst this small group is a fairly large, worn and damaged slab of lighter blue slate (Kermode 1907, no 67). It was recovered in the late 1850s (Oswald 1860, 206-7) from a secondary context where it had been re-used, lying face downwards, acting as a stair tread, in an external flight leading up to Maughold church gallery, a structure which is thought to have been built around 1717 (Radcliffe & Radcliffe 1979, 46). The ringed cross which fills the only carved face is plain but the lower quadrant panels each contain parallel but not identical mirrored registers of

Figure 3: Maughold 5A decorated with clerics, horsemen and beasts.

iconographic decoration (Figure 3). The upper registers contain two seated clerics facing each other across the cross shaft. In the middle register two lively riders steer towards the cross while the bottom register contains asymmetrical representations of quadrupeds, probably intended to represent hound and lion. The beast to the left stalks up the shaft, head partly lowered, with lithe body, expanding chest and a long tail trailing behind, curling at the tip. The beast to the lower right is similar in form but walks with his back to the cross shaft, head turned backwards looking along his back towards his long rising, S-curved tail which terminates in a bob. Apart from the turned head the beast is reminiscent of the lion in the Book of Durrow (Meehan 1996, 62; fol 191v). It is noticeable that the elements effect a diminuendo as they descend from the large clerics above to the small beasts beneath, evidence here of a hierarchy of size reflecting significance and in which the dominant cross symbolizes Christ and His Salvation.

The clerics (Figure 4), who represent Christ in His earthly kingdom, are thus the next most important element to Christ, honouring and touching the cross to confirm the point and they clearly act in concert as a single complementary unit across the shaft register. The riders beneath come hierarchically next in the design and also represent a unitary composition, each horse, portrayed as if rising, touches the cross shaft with its leading limb and both rider and mount gaze forward towards the cross (Figure 5). Their function is less straighforwardly explained than that of the clerics above: they either represent Everyman (that is the viewer) travelling the world at large and, as such, symbolically journeying through life subservient to the clergy above who instruct and who intercede on their behalf. Alternatively, they perhaps represent the dispersal of the 'Good News' of the Christian message. Although that explanation appears less likely in this context, it may have formed part of the original model (Trench-Jellicoe 1999b, appendix 2). The viewer seems impelled to recognise that this group, like the clerical figures above, accepts and acknowledges Christ's salvational message signified by the dominant Cross. The lowest register must also, it seems, be considered as one unit in which both beasts are detached from the cross shaft and locked in a predatory interaction in which the beast to the left (Figure 6) stalks that to the right who watches over his shoulder (Figure 7). Such a scene represents the lower orders of creation – disassociated (because turned away) from Christ's saving grace but symbolically it is likely also to represents human susceptibility and the lower sensibilities of mankind. The beast to the left portrays the *modus* of sin while that to the right represents the human predicament, needing continually to be aware that s/he is under siege to ever-present sin, which awaits an opportunity to creep up unexpectedly and betray the human soul. The portrayal is fortunately not unique, similar animal scenes exist on programmed monuments elsewhere in insular sculpture.

On aggregate the message carried by the iconography of this cross can be seen to instruct the viewer how the Christian message should be perceived and its importance for the individual's salvation on several levels: through intercession, acknowledgement and care of the soul, all under the prominent symbol of Christ's saving grace. Interestingly, however, the designer did not leave its interpretation to chance and although the salient evidence is now damaged to the point of illegibility, the surface originally included three or perhaps four inscriptions, fragments of letters from two of which yet survive. Two of the inscriptions were placed symmetrically on either side of

Figure 4: Maughold 5, left cleric with damaged inscription on cross-shaft.

Figure 5: Maughold 5 – mounted rider.

Figure 6: Maughold 5 – left quadruped.

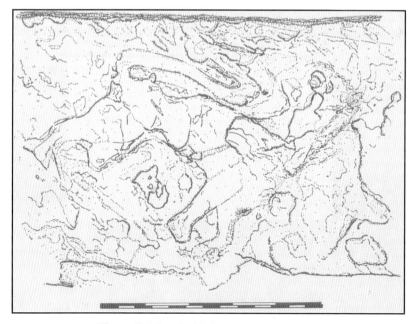

Figure 7: Maughold 5 – right quadruped.

the shaft at the top of the flanking panels above the heads of the clerics. That to the left is now completely lost although the deeply incised ruled guide lines for the lost lettering are visible. In the right panel more remains and the message bespeaks sophistication, being carved on three lines, in two different scripts (Figure 8). The upper lines contain a smaller, cursive script of which four or five fragments and almost complete letters remain. The lower line contains tall serifed minuscule letterforms of which eleven vertical elements survive. Nothing of the sense of the inscription is recoverable but the presence of two different scripts indicates that not only was the monument's iconography conceived in hierarchical terms but that the written information was also structured in a hierarchy of scripts, a method of working normally only reserved for contemporary luxury manuscripts. The remaining inscription is carved onto the cross shaft in between the clerics. While it must be suspected that this was originally a multi-lined composition laid out within a frame, it is possible that what we are looking at represented just two separate lines of script each within a cartouche. Only the left part of the upper line now remains legible, where three sections of a delicate and stylish capital letter S with narrow serifed terminals survive. To the right is a short central section of a vertical line and to the right again a very short vertical section of a third letter. Some curves and lines below, also perhaps sections of a couple of letters, appear on the badly damaged surface. The identified letter, *S,* seems to be the initial letter of a syntagma and the three letters together may guessingly represent *SCS.* If so, they may originally have had an abbreviation bar above to indicate they formed the contraction of *SANCTUS,* an appropriate designation in this context for the seated figures to left and right. The form of these letters appears most similar to the upper script above the right cleric.

The production of this cross slab at Maughold marks a sophistication of practice on several levels. For apparently the first time on Mann we have a large slab, carved in relief with a ringed cross, bearing explicit iconography and with labelling of some of that iconography, which invites the expectation that the viewer is literate. This highlights a huge jump underscoring a considerable advance in technique and understanding in the use of sculpture. But what was the source and what the stimulus for the new message?

Scottish sources for the Maughold Saints' Slab

The manifestation of such an important development should make us initially look to the countries round about to seek the source. The most suitable area, providing a raft of comparable features, is Scotland. Eastern Scotland changed its name and the concepts of nationality underlying that name towards the end of the ninth century from Pictland to Alba (Broun 1999; Herbert 2000) and that change itself is probably part of the wider pattern of adjustment in the British Isles which eventually produced large relief sculpture on Mann. As I have tried to demonstrate in a recent paper (Trench-Jellicoe 1999b), the upheavals caused by Viking contact with Britain brought about significant change as a response. The Columban community on Iona is recorded moving its administrative headquarters to Kells in 807 (AU s.a. 806.8) but sculptural evidence in Scotland indicates that part of the *familia Iae* also went eastwards, settling for a period in Pictland, probably on monastic sites in the regions of Fortriu, Athol and Circinn (mainly Perthshire and Angus), where they seem to have set up a mission

Figure 8: Maughold 5 – lower right panel inscription in two scripts.

headquarters with the express purpose of converting the pagan Viking settlers and eventually recouping their patrimony in Western Scotland (Trench-Jellicoe 1999b). Some time was to pass before this mission was able to make an appreciable impact but probably by the middle of the ninth century their main outposts were being re-established on Iona, on Canna (*ibid,* 617 - 18) and at other sites including Maughold. As the whole of the British Isles came under siege by turns during the ninth century it must have become clear to the well-organised and now mission-orientated Columban *familia,* that the challenge of reclaiming their own *paruchia* could also be widened into other areas of Viking settlement and thus be seen as a contingent opportunity. Recorded Columban exploits in Iceland are one example (Jennings 1998, 33) but the Irish Sea province was closer to home and also a logical extension of the movement in Western Scotland. Later in the century and into the following century Southern Scotland and Northern England and further afield would surely have come within their ambit.

In the light of these observations, slabs with similar iconography to that discussed at Maughold occur on sites in Perthshire and Angus. Although the overall programme may differ, the upper section of the back of a slab from Dunfallandy, south of Pitlochry (Allan & Anderson 1903, part 3, 286 - 9), carries a representation of facing, seated clerics, similar to those in the Manx scene. Here they flank a small cross mounted between them in a low socket which also frames sufficient space to incorporate the rider's head in the panelled scene below (Figure 9). A slab recovered in the 1920s at Fowlis Wester (Waddell 1932), the second of four monuments from the site, also has a pair of seated clerics flanking the cross shaft, portrayed as at Maughold. This scene is complex in that it has an angel suspended above one seat while the other figure is flanked, unusually in insular art at this date, by stylised desert trees (Figure 10). This monument, like Maughold's, is carved on one face only. Other examples, such as the seated, facing figures on the front of St Vigeans no 7, and those standing on Kirriemuir 1C, Angus (Allen & Anderson 1903, part 3, 268 - 9, 227), and framed in the upper pediment of a slab at Nigg, Easter Ross (*ibid,* 75 - 83; Henderson 2001, 120 - 6), show the clerics receiving a loaf of bread from the beak of a bird or breaking it in the *cofractio* manner mentioned by Adamnán in his *Life of St Columba.* Such scenes may be paralleled in copies of early icons still preserved at the monastery of St Anthony in the Egyptian desert (Dalrymple 1997, 420 - 3, illus) and are readily recognised as portraying the meeting of Saints Paul and Anthony, a vignette illustrating a passage from St Jerome's *Life of St Paul, the Hermit* (Waddell 1936, 48 - 9) in which a half loaf is the gift of God, delivered each day by a raven, to feed St Paul and becomes doubled so that he may also feed his guest. The central loaf also symbolises the body of Christ in the Eucharist and the dominant cross that replaces it in the scenes at Maughold, Dunfallandy and Fowlis Wester is yet another symbol for Christ's salvation. Maughold may therefore be seen as an outlier of this specifically Pictish, ninth-century iconography. Moreover Saints Paul and Anthony were regarded in the early church as the founders of monasticism and this is also particularly relevant for their presence at Maughold in the early Viking Age.

The representation at Maughold of the lively rider, with the horse portrayed as if rising, is also derived from a specifically Pictish model of a high-stepping horse, found

Figure 9: Dunfallandy, Perthshire – reverse, saints flanking a cross.

Figure 10: Fowlis wester 2 – saints flanking a cross.

ubiquitously throughout eastern Scotland (Allen & Anderson, part 3) and, as we have seen, juxtaposed at Dunfallandy with Saints Paul and Anthony. The lowermost scene with two quadrupeds on the Maughold slab is a version of a scene otherwise found in the lowermost cross arm panel, immediately above the three shaft panels on the east face of the a'Chill Cross, Canna (Trench-Jellicoe 1999, appendix 2) where a gracile predatory quadruped stalks a thick-set lion with bobbed tail who, similarly to the Maughold beast, looks over its shoulder (Figure 11). I have elsewhere dated the a'Chill Cross to the middle of the ninth century (*ibid,* 617) and considered it specifically in the context of Viking conversion iconography in the Western Isles (*ibid,* appendix 2). Although both lie within a similar milieu, it is stylistically certain that the Canna monument predates by a generation, the production of the Maughold Saints Slab. This Manx slab should be viewed as a multi-valent monument, bearing layers of meaning in its iconographic programme which underscore the importance of belief in the Christian message and warning the viewer of the consequences of rejecting it.

Perhaps the most signficiant parallel in Scotland for the Maughold slab is the monument at Fowlis Wester but connections with other Strathearn sculpture also exists. The Market Cross at Creiff, a few kilometres to the west of Fowlis, is believed originally to have come from the nearby valley site of Strowan (Hall *et al.* 2000). Here, the form of the ringed cross is closely similar to that carved on the Maughold slab and in the middle of the cross shaft is preserved a badly damaged panel containing the remnants of a rare inscription (Forsyth & Trench-Jellicoe 2000, 166-8) (Figure 12). This is paralleled only in the Perth region by a panel on the nearby and important Dupplin Cross (Forsyth 1995) which is almost certainly a product of royal patronage. It is likely that all these monuments date to the second half of the ninth century. Further it is inconceivable that two cross monuments such as Fowlis Wester 2 and Strowan/Creiff, standing a few kilometres apart should not themselves be related in some cogent way and both be understood to have influenced complementary elements of iconography and literacy present on the Maughold slab. It seems most probable, therefore, that Maughold was in receipt of conversion iconography, displaying links with other Columban programmes derived from a monastic source in the Strathearn area and such evidence should link Viking evangelization on the Isle of Man with a Columban mission based primarily in Pictland. Maughold became, in all probability, an outreach mission base for the conversion of Mann in the mid to later ninth century.

Other Pictish-style monuments at Maughold

The Saints' Slab does not stand alone at Maughold in demonstrating Pictish links although it is undoubtedly the most convincing example. Amongst other monuments, Maughold 14:53(29)A (Kermode 1907, no 29, P1 XI), also carved in distinctively coloured orange stone won from pre-Viking quarries, shares a feature only encountered in Pictland, a cross form known as the quadrilobate cross,[2] found otherwise in the British Isles only on a restricted group of ninth-century monuments in Perthshire, Angus and Kincardine.[3] Another particularly Scottish cross type, executed using a

---

[2]The quadrilobate form of cross-ring was first formally identified by RBK Stevenson (1958, 42). Unlike a standard ring which encircles the crossing, quadrilobate types have a narrow, individual circle completing each arm pit.
[3]A non-exhaustive list of quadrilobate crosses would include Fordoun, Aberlemno 2, Eassie, Meigle 1, Meigle 5, Rossie Priory, (Allen & Anderson 1903, part 3, figs 217, 227, 231, 310, 314, 322).

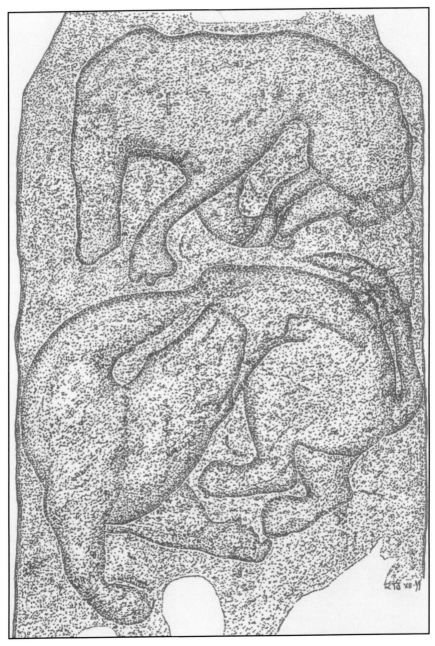

Figure 11: Canna, E face – stalking beasts.

Figure 12: Crieff, Perthshire – main face with damaged inscription panel on the shaft. Courtesy of Perth Museum & Art Gallery, Perth-& Kinross Council, Scotland.

compass and with a broad ring, all framed within a rectangular double-outlined panel, is found both on Maughold 26:51(23)A (Kermode 1907, no 23, Pl IX) and at an outlying keeill site at Ballavarkish in the most northerly Manx parish of Bride. Both monuments were carved in a similar slate probably at a slightly later date than those stones previously examined. From their form it appears they served as altar frontals. The Ballavarkish slab fragment (Bride.Ballavarkish 1:52(-); Kermode 1911 - 12, 69-74) is particularly interesting for two reasons. Firstly it seems likely that Ballavarkish keeill stood on the way leading to a point of embarkation from the northern tip of the island for the short sea crossing to Isle of Whithorn and beyond (Trench-Jellicoe 1980, 202-3) and secondly, the carved front of the monument is embellished with a series of graffiti inscriptions which in all probability represent a record of personal prayer asking for safe passage whose carving was perhaps executed over a period of time. Six incised names including Lugni, Diprui, Condilici, Mailorei and perhaps Bred or Bren, seem to represent Old Irish forms. Most signficantly, one of them, Mailorei, records himself as *'SCRIBA'*, 'scribe', an office sufficiently significant in the monastic hierarchy at other sites to warrant recording amongst obits appearing in the Irish Annals (Figure 13). All bar one of the names is preceded by a cross (Kermode, *op cit*), each of a different design which almost certainly represents an individual signature. This is of great interest as the scribe possesses the most elaborate and imposing cross. Further, apparently also associated with a cross, is a lightly-cut ogham graffito, carved in the left cross arm. This is a significant feature which holds implications for dating in a late Manx/Picto-Albanach context. We cannot divine how soon after the altar frontal was erected the graffiti were added but it almost certainly lies within a later ninth- to tenth-century bracket and this evidence may serve to confirm that Maughold continued to function as a monastery into the tenth century.

Conclusions

What is highlighted by the evidence explored here is the existence of a period of approximately a hundred years which lies within the earlier phase of the Viking Age, between the Early Manx phase and those later monuments showing evidence of Viking influence in motif or design. It spans a time of conversion when it is difficult to detect any overt Viking influence and motifs and methods are drawn from pre-existing insular iconographic programmes and abstract design which were modified and developed to suit current requirements.

Little is known of how the site first developed at Maughold or of its early connections although some relationship with Ireland may be suspected to form the background of Armagh's transparent attempt during the late seventh- and early eighth-century to frame a claim to suzerainty over the religious life of the island. This may be hypothesised from the lengthy Chapter 23 of Muirchú's *Life of Patrick* (Hood 1978, 9, 21, 72-4, 93-4) which sketches a tale of confrontation between Maccuil, an Ulster brigand, and St Patrick, his conversion and a penitential journey in which, manacled, he is carried in a skin boat without oars, thus at the mercy of the elements, to "the land assigned to him by God" (*ibid*, 94), to Evonia which here equates with Mann (*ibid*, 94).

Figure 13: Ballavarkish, Bride – graffito inscription "MAILOREI SCRIBA."

who, having recovered a key from the belly of a fish to release him from his gyves, train him in the faith so that he may eventually succeed them to become both prelate and bishop (*ibid,* 94). The story appears to be a blatant attempt to legitimise a direct hierarchical connection between Mann and the Coarbs of Patrick and, although it must be viewed in terms of the politics of power in eighth-century Armagh, some early link may underlie the claim however tenuous, contrived and miraculous the tale. Even if we lacked early, sculptural evidence (Trench-Jellicoe 1998), from this story we may extrapolate that Maughold not only existed and functioned as a monastery but had already become an important, and presumably the focal, site on Mann by the mid seventh century although no direct evidence for a specific Irish connection is indicated by the sculpture on the Maughold site. Armagh's pretensions had certainly been overtaken by events by the second half of the ninth century when, within a radically changed insular polity, Mann and particularly Maughold appears to become a cog within another major, international organisation.

Although it is still difficult to draw together all the relevant evidence for influences on the Isle of Man and particularly Maughold in the mid to second half of the ninth and early tenth century it is significant that the island was in receipt of purposive and directed influence from a centre in Pictland, probably in Strathearn, which encapsulated what appears to be a deliberate iconography of conversion developed, in this case by the Columban mission. But it is also worth recognising that this was likely to be only one of several foci in Scotland responsible for implementing the planning of a central mission control of a highly organised Columban *familia* perhaps masterminded from Dunkeld (Bannerman 1999, 73-5, 91-4; Broun 1999) although the surviving sculptural remains from that site are neither plentiful nor notable (Allen & Anderson, 1903, part 3, 317-19). Sculptural evidence indicates that another centre, responsible to the mission for a section of the Western Isles was present in Angus (Trench-Jellicoe 1999b, 618-25) and sculptural links should also make us suspect that yet another mission station existed for Northern Scotland and the Northern Isles, possibly established at Rosemarkie but more probably at one or more centres along the coastal ridge of Easter Ross between Nigg and Tarbat. Thus, working in concert with other centres, Maughold was in receipt of a range of shared iconography and presumably also susceptible to an accompanying programme of conversion as part of an overall drive to christianise pagan incomers.

This early phase of the Viking Age seems to have lasted until a time when the laity had absorbed at least the fundamentals of the faith, permitting time for accompanying relevant social adjustments in the status of the religion amongst the incomers, and allowing sufficient concurrent time to elapse for the synthesis of alien artistic influence with the native product to create the production of a confident and appropropriate new decorative style to emerge in sculpture on Mann. The new vibrant, full-blown Late Manx style, blending a limited iconography and a restricted range of abstract ornament from disparate external sources with elements we can now see were already present in a native tradition originally brought into Mann from Scotland. This development paralleled a layered process similar to that encountered in areas of Scandinavian settlement in Northern England which produced a parallel series of Anglo-Scandinavian monuments during the tenth century.

Nevertheless on Mann, the first century of Scandinavian presence, spanning the ninth and early tenth century, witnessed a steady sculptural development in its own right before the advent of the tenth-century synthesis which probably took place in a secular milieu of socially-aware local chieftainly commissions rather than in an ecclesiastical environment (Trench-Jellicoe 1999a). This manifestation may be traced amongst small groups of sophisticated, decorated monuments that Kermode (1907, 1 - 37) included in his 'Celtic' dustbin but which can today be seen to belong within the earlier phases of the Viking Age. Such observations allow us to sub-divide the Late Manx group into an initial and a later phase, the latter sculptures substantially encapsulating those Manx monuments which Kermode (1907, 38-70) designated 'Scandinavian'.

Postscript

Continuing work in both Mann, Western and Northern Scotland on this intervening group, carved within the Viking Age but apparently showing only insular traits, offers an exciting prospect for understanding a wide range of political, social and religious developments in the Irish Sea province at a time of few written records.

Acknowledgements

I wish to thank Mark Hall, Andrew Johnson, Douglas MacLean, Basil Megaw and David Wilson for their help and comments.

Bibliography

Abbreviations

AI   *Annals of Innisfallen,* MacAirt S, 1983, (ed.)
ASC   *Anglo Saxon Chronicle,* Plummer C, (ed, on an edition by J Earle) 1892:
        Two of the Saxon Chronicles Parallel (Oxford).
AU   *Annals of Ulster,* MacAirt S and MacNiocaill G, (eds) 1983, (Dublin).

References

Allen J R & Anderson J, 1903, *Early Christian Monuments of Scotland,* 3 parts (Edinburgh) reprinted (with intro by I B Henderson) 1993 (Balgavies).

Bailey R N & Cramp R J, 1988, *Cumberland, Westmorland and Lancashire North-of-the-Sands* (The British Academy Corpus of Anglo-Saxon sculpture, vol 2, London).

Bannerman J, 1999, 'The Scottish takeover of Pictland and the relics of Columba' in Broun & Clancy 1999, 71-94.

Broderick G, (ed) 1979, *Cronica Regum Mannie et Insularum: Chronicle of the Kings of Man and the Isles* (Douglas).

Broun D, 1999, 'Dunkeld and the origin of Scottish identity' in Broun & Clancy 1999, 95-114.

Broun D & Clancy T O, 1999, *Spes Scottorum: Hope of Scots, Saint Columba, Iona and Scotland* (Edinburgh).

Bruce J R & Cubbon W C, 1930, 'Cronk yn How: an Early Christian and Viking site, at Lezayre, Isle of Man' *Archaeologia Cambrensis* 85, 267-308.

Cramp R J, 1984, *County Durham and Northumberland* (The British Academy Corpus of Anglo-Saxon Sculpture, vol 1, London).

Cumming J G, 1857a, *The Runic and Other Monumental Remains of the Isle of Man* (London).

Cumming J G, 1857b, 'On a newly recovered runic monument on the Isle of Man at Kirk Braddan' *Archaeological Journal* 14(55), 263-6.

Cumming J G, 1865a, 'On the ornamentation of the runic monuments of the Isle of Man' *Archaeologia Cambrensis* 12, 156-67.

Cumming J G, 1865b, 'Runic inscriptions of the Isle of Man' *Archaeologia Cambrensis* 12, 251-60.

Cumming J G, 1865c, 'On some more recently discovered Scandinavian crosses in the Isle of Man' *Archaeologia Cambrensis* 12, 460-5.

Cumming J G, 1866, 'Notes on the stone monuments of the Isle of Man' *Archaeologia Cambrensis* 12, 46-60.

Dalrymple W, 1997, *From the Holy Mountain: a journey in the shadow of Byzantium* (London).

Edwards N M, 1990, *The Archaeology of Early Medieval Ireland* (London)

Forsyth K, 1995, 'The inscription on the Dupplin Cross' in Bourke C (ed), *From the Isles of the North, Medieval Art in Britain and Ireland: proceedings of the Third International Conference on Insular Art held in the Ulster Museum, Belfast, 7-11 April 1994* (Belfast), 237-44.

Forsyth K & Trench-Jellicoe R, 2000, 'The inscribed panel' in Hall *et al.* 2000, 166 8.

Freke D J (2002), *Excavations on St. Patrick's Isle, Peel, Isle of Man, 1982-1988: Prehistoric, Viking, Meadieval and later.* Liverpool University Press, 463 pages.

Gibson E (ed) 1722, *Camden's Britannia, Newly Translated into English with Large Additions and Improvements* (London).

Hall M, Forsyth K, Henderson I B, Scott I G, Trench-Jellicoe R and Watson A, 2000, 'Of Markings and Meanings: towards a cultural biography of the Crieff Burgh Gross, Strathearn, Perthshire' *Tayside and Fife Archaeological Journal* 6, 155-88.

Harbison P, 1992, *The High Crosses of Ireland: an Iconographic and Photographic Study* 3 vols (Romisch-Germanisches Zentralmuseum, Forschungsinstitut fur vorund frnhgeschichte monographien, band 17, 1, Bonn).

Henderson I B, 1999, 'The Dupplin Cross: a preliminary consideration of its art-historical context' in Hawkes J & Mills S, (eds) 1999: *Northumbria's Golden Age* (Stroud) 161-77.

Henderson I B, 2001, 'This wonderful monument': the cross-slab at Nigg, Easter Ross, Scotland, in Binski P & Noel W, *New Offerings, Ancient Treasures: Studies in Medieval Art for George Henderson* (Stroud).

Herbert M, 2000, 'Rí Éirenn, Rí Alban, kingship and identity in the ninth and tenth centuries' in S Taylor (ed), *Kings Clerics and Chronicles in Scotland 500-1297: essays in honour of Marjorie Ogilvie Anderson on the occasion of her ninetieth birthday* (Dublin).

Hood A B E, (ed & trans), 1978, *St Patrick, his writings and Muirchú's Life,* (Arthurian Period Sources, vol 9, Stroud).

Jennings A, 1998, 'Iona and the Vikings: survival and continuity', *Northern Studies* 33, 37- 54.

Kermode P M C, 1887, *Catalogue of the Manks Crosses with Runic Inscriptions* (Ramsey).

Kermode P M C, 1892, *Catalogue of the Manks Crosses with the Runic Inscriptions* (Ramsey).

Kermode P M C, 1907, *Manx Crosses, or the Inscribed and Sculptured Monuments of the Isle of Man* (London), reprinted 1994, (includes as appendices: Kermode 1910-11; 1911-12; 1915-16; 1920-1; 1928-9), (Balgavies).

Kermode P M C, 1910-11, 'Notes on the Ogam and Latin inscriptions from the Isle of Man and a recently found bi-lingual in Celtic and Latin' *Proceedings of the Society of Antiquaries of Scotland* 45, 437-50.

Kermode P M C, 1911-12, 'Cross-slabs recently discovered in the Isle of Man' *Proceedings of the Society of Antiquaries of Scotland* 46, 53-76.

Kermode P M C, 1915-16, 'Further discoveries of cross-slabs in the Isle of Man' *Proceedings of the Society of Antiquaries of Scotland* 50, 50-62.

Kermode P M C, 1920-1, 'Cross-slabs in the Isle of Man brought to light since December 1915' *Proceedings of the Society of Antiquaries of Scotland* 55, 256-60.

Kermode P M C, 1924, *List of the Cross-Slabs Arranged by Parish* (Douglas).

Kermode P M C, 1928-9, 'More cross-slabs from the Isle of Man' *Proceedings of the Society of Antiquaries of Scotland* 63, 354-60.

Kinnebrook W, 1841, *Etchings of the Runic Monuments in the Isle of Man* (London).

Laing L R & Laing J, 1980-9, 'The early Christian period settlement at Ronaldsway, Isle of Man: a reappraisal' *Proceedings of the Isle Man Natural History and Antiquarian Society* 9, 389-415.

Lionard P, 1961, 'Early Irish grave-slabs' *Proceedings of the Royal Irish Academy,* 61C.5, 95-169.

Meehan B, 1996, *The Book of Durrow, a medieval masterpiece at Trinity College Dublin* (Dublin).

Nash-Williams V E, 1950, *Early Christian Monuments of Wales,* (Cardiff).

Neely J H, 1940, 'Excavations at Ronaldsway, Isle of Man' *Antiquity* 20, 72-86.

Oswald H R, 1823, 'Notes of reference to the series of delineations of the runic and other ancient crosses in the Isle of Man' *Transactions of the Society of Antiquaries of Scotland* 2.2, 502-8.

Oswald H R, 1860, *Vestigia Manniae Insulae Antiquora* (Manx Society, vol 5, Douglas).

Radcliffe W & Radcliffe C, 1979, *A History of Kirk Maughold* (Douglas).

RCAHMS 1982, Argyll, vol 4: *Iona* (Royal Commission Ancient Historical Monuments Scotland: 22nd report, Edinburgh).

RCAHMS 1984, *Argyll, vol 5: Islay, Jura, Colonsay and Oronsay* (Royal Commission Ancient Historical Monuments Scotland: 23rd report, Edinburgh).

Stevenson R B K, 1958, 'The Inchyra stone and some other unpublished early Christian monuments' *Proceedings of the Society of Antiquaries of Scotland* 92, 33 - 55.

Thomas A C, 1971, *The Early Christian Archaeology of North Britain* (London).

Trench-Jellicoe R M C, 1980, A new *chi-rho* from Maughold, Isle of Man', *Medieval Archaeology* 24, 202-3.

Trench-Jellicoe R M C, 1983, 'The cross-slabs from Keeill Vael', appendix 2, Morris C D, 1983: 'The survey and excavations of Keeill Vael, Druidale, in their context' in Fell C, *et al.* (eds) 1983: *The Viking Age in the Isle of Man:* selected papers from the Ninth Viking Congress, Isle of Man, 4-14 July, 1981 (London), 126-8.

Trench-Jellicoe R M C, 1998, 'The Skeith Stone, Upper Kilrenny, Fife, in its context' *Proceedings of the Society of Antiquaries of Scotland* 128, 495-513.

Trench-Jellicoe R M C, l999a, 'Messages on a monument: iconography on a Late Manx fragment recently recovered from Bishopscourt' in Davey (ed) 1999: *Recent Archaeological Research on the Isle of Man* (British Archaeological Reports, British Series 278, Oxford), 183-98.

Trench-Jellicoe R M C, l999b, 'A missing figure on slab fragment no 2 from Monifieth, Angus, the a'Chille Cross, Canna, and some implications of the development of a variant form of the Virgin's hairstyle and dress in early medieval Scotland' *Proceedings of the Society of Antiquaries of Scotland* 129, 597-647.

Trench-Jellicoe R M C 2002, 'Early Christian and Viking-Age monuments' in D J Freke *Excavations at Peel Castle,* 1982-88, 282-290.

Trench-Jellicoe R M C, (in prep.), 'Evidence of literacy on sculpture: early documents from Maughold, Isle of Man'.

Waddell H, 1936, *The Desert Fathers: translations from the Latin with an introduction,* (London).

Waddell J J, 1932, 'Cross-slabs recently discovered at Fowlis Wester and Millport' *Proceedings of the Society of Antiquaries of Scotland,* 66, 409 - 12.

Wilson D M, 1974, *The Viking Age in the Isle of Man: the archaeological evidence* (C.C.Rafn lecture 3, Odense).

Wilson D M, 1989 - 97, 'The chronology of the Viking Age in the Isle of Man', *Proceedings of the Isle of Man Natural History and Antiquarian Society* 10, 359 - 72.

36

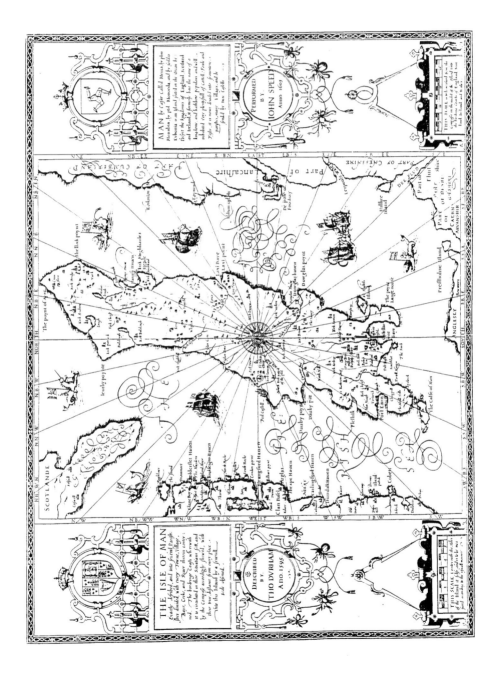

Manx Place-Names: an Ulster View

Kay Muhr

In this chapter I will discuss place-name connections between Ulster and Man, beginning with the early appearances of Man in Irish tradition and its association with the mythological realm of *Emain Ablach,* from the 6th to the 13th century.[1]

A good introduction to the link between Ulster and Manx place-names is to look at Speed's map of Man published in 1605.[2] Although the map is much later than the beginning of place-names in the Isle of Man, it does reflect those place-names already well-established 400 years before our time. Moreover the gloriously exaggerated Manx-centric view, showing the island almost filling the Irish sea between Ireland, Scotland, England and Wales, also allows the map to illustrate place-names from the coasts of these lands around. As an island visible from these coasts Man has been influenced by all of them.

In Ireland there are Gaelic, Norse and English names - the latter now the dominant language in new place-names, though it was not so in the past. The Gaelic names include the port towns of *Knok* (now Carrick-) fergus, "Fergus' hill" or "rock", the rock clearly referring to the site of the medieval castle. In 13th-century Scotland Fergus was understood as the king whose migration introduced the Gaelic language. Further south, Dundalk "fort of the small sword" includes the element *dún* "hill-fort", one of three fortification names common in early Irish place-names, the others being *ráth* "ring-fort" and *lios* "enclosure". In between are Belfast, now more important than Carrickiergus, meaning "approach to the sandbank ford", and Newry, another natural history name meaning "place of yew trees"- tree names also being a common feature of Irish placenames. The importance of saints in ecclesiastical names is shown by the saint's name Patri[c]k at Down (also *dún*), and Island Patri[c]k further south. It was probably this *Inis Patraic* "Patrick's Island" which was attacked by the Vikings in AD 798, but it has sometimes been understood as Peel i.e. St Patrick's Island of the Isle of Man.

Viking influence in the Irish Sea gathered in strength from the late 8th century. The east coast of Ireland also shows, between Rathlin and Dublin, three sea loughs which bear Norse or Norse influenced names: Olderfleet (now the entrance to Larne Lough),

---

[1] According to the conventions of name studies, Manx place-names in current use are not italicised, only word-elements in Manx (and other languages) and earlier spellings of names.

[2] Illus. (See page 36) John Speed's map of Man 1605, from Thomas Durham's survey 1595 (Cubbon 1974)

Strangford and Carlingford. The first name was understood by them as *Ulfrekr's fjorðr,* though "Ulfrekr" was probably a re-interpretation of the Irish river name *Ollarbha,* now the Larne Water which enters the lough at this point[3]. The others are *strang fjorðr* "strongcurrent fjord" and *kerlinga fjorðr* "hag's fjord" (PNI ii 6 - 8, PNI i 83). Scotland shows the district name Galloway, the "place of the foreign/Viking Gaels" colonised by the mixed Gaelic and Norse-speaking people of the Hebrides (Watson 1926 101, 173 - 4). Ulster however has apparently no Viking settlement names.

On the Isle of Man also the Vikings settled the land as well as using the harbours. Names on Man include the Norse names now spelled as Fleshwick, "green-spot creek" ON *flesvík* (Kneen 34); Jurby, "deer settlement, animal farm", ON *djúra-by* (*PNIM* ii 245); Point of Ayre, "gravel bank" from ON *eyrr* (*PNIM* iii 176); Ramsey, "wild garlic river" from ON *hrams-á* (*PNIM* iv 167); Laxey, "salmon river" from ON *laks-á,* the river noted for salmon fishing in 1668. As with Ramsey, and the Gaelic name Douglas, the name has been transferred to the settlement from the river (*PNIM* iv 326).

The parish names are shown beginning with *Kirk* "church", of Norse origin, but the spelling of the rest indicates a more authentic Gaelic pronunciation of the saints' names than the current English versions: *Kirk Mighhill* (Michael), *Kirk Bridge* (Bride), *Kirk Maghaul* (Maughold) - where the final -d from the Latinised form *Machaldus* does not appear. Similar names from Ulster (none unfortunately on the map) would be in Gaelic *Cill Mhichil, Cill Bhríde* "Michael's church, Brigid's church". The element *cill / keeill* was still used for church sites by Manx speakers (*PNIM* ii 77, iv 120). St Patrick appears in *Kirk Patrik of the peel* and again in *Kirk Patrack* at Jurby.

From the Isle of Man as mapped by Englishmen at the beginning of the 17th century we return to the Ulster view, as old as written literature in Irish.

Emain (Ablach) "Emain of the appletrees"

An Old Irish story in prose and verse describes a sea-voyage to the Otherworld by a legendary hero called *Bran* "raven" son of *Febal* (Meyer 1895). Bran's name links him with the north coast, since his father's name is that of the river Foyle *(Febal)* which passes *Srub Brain* "Bran's promontory" now Sroove at the most northern point of its estuary. However on the voyage Bran meets the Irish sea god Manannán who claims to be the real father of a historical royal prince of the *Dál nAraide* kindred of east Ulster, Mongán son of Fiachna (d.625) (AU 112 - 113).

The story begins dramatically with the appearance of a woman from "unknown lands" bearing a branch of apples. She offers it to Bran and in verse invites him to follow her:

> *Crób dind abaill a hEmain*   'A branch of the apple-tree from Emain
> *do-fet samail do gnáthaib*   I bring like those well-known' (*Immram Brain* §3).

The name *Emain* appears to belong to the land from which she comes, and yet it was well-known as the name of the traditional capital of prehistoric Ulster *Emain Macha,*

---

[3]Mac Giolla Easpaig, D. 2000. Unpublished article: "Scandinavian influence on the toponymy of Ireland," 39-43.

Emain "of the cultivated land", now Navan Fort west of Armagh. By the time this tale was written, that Emain, famous as the king's dwelling in the Ulster Cycle epic tales, was no longer held by the original *Ulaid* or Ulstermen. Relocating it in less circumscribed territory might be a way of salvaging their lost pride. The wonderful *Emain* (sometimes *Emnae*) of Bran's adventures in this tale is out at sea. The sea-god Manannán takes his name from the Isle of Man and it seems that *Emain/Emnae* can also be identified with his kingdom. Displaced (and Christian) Ulstermen, the story asserts, can still be sons of the gods, as the chief Ulster Cycle warrior Cú Chulainn was fathered by Lugh (Muhr 1996 55 - 6).

Bran's voyage is a story of wonders, but 6th-century history also asserts that the peoples of east Ulster were taking to the sea in search of new territory. The *Dál Riata* group of the north-east took themselves and the Gaelic language to north-western Scotland. Late in the century the Annals of Ulster record in Latin that the *Ulaid* (probably meaning *Dál nAraide* of the mid-east with *Dál Fiatach* of the south-east, or *Dál Fiatach* alone) attempted to claim Man. Since the annals were being written in Latin at this date the names are Latinised: (*AU* 88-90.)

AD 577 *Primum periculum Uloth in Eufania* "First expedition of the Ulaid to Man"

AD 578 *Reversio Uloth de Eumania* "Expulsion of the Ulaid from Man" (?)

The spelling of the genitive plural *Uloth* (later *Uladh*) shows this is a near-contemporary record, while the spellings *Eumania/Eufania* (the latter presumably recognising the lenition of *m* to *v*) represent the name *Emain* rather than *Man*. However a record four years later of the Scottish Dál Riata king *Aedán mac Gabrán's* victory in the battle of *Manu* (declined as a nasal stem, *Bellum Manonn*) reminds one that neither place-name is unique (*AU* 582), and that this time *Man[u]* refers to *Manaw Gododdin*, a British district name preserved in Clackmannan or Slamannan "stone, mountain of Manann" on the Firth of Forth in Scotland (Watson 1926, 103).

A century later an Ulster-Man connection is recorded in Muirchú's Life of Saint Patrick, (Bieler 1979 102 - 6 = Muirchú I 23) which includes the story of Patrick's meeting, in Ulaid territory (*in regionibus Ulothorum*), the wicked tyrant *Mac Cuill moccu Greccae,* who held court from a wild place in the hills called *Droim Moccu Echach.* Since it also appears to be near Lecale (*Mag Inis*) and the sea, *Droim Moccu Echach* "ridge of the descendants of Echu" is unlikely to be Dromore inland[4] and *Moccu Echach* are probably the descendants of Echu Gunnat, *Dál Fiatach* ruler of the Ards peninsula, who were overthrown by the Vikings in the 9th century. The Life tells how Mac Cuill attempted to discredit and kill Patrick, but was converted by his power and baptised, and told for penance to shackle his feet and throw the key in the sea, then set himself afloat in a small boat without rudder or oar and accept his fate from the wind and the sea. The wind blew him to an island called *Evonia,*[5] where he was taken in by the first two bishops to baptise and preach there. He learned the practice of his faith from them until he became (editor Bieler's translation and brackets):

---

[4]Pace Bieler index 257. Dromore inland is the cathedral town for the *Dál nAraide* group called *Uí Echach* "descendants of Echu" later Iveagh, see Muhr 1996b, *PNI* vi: *North-West Down / Iveagh*, pp.1,5,6; 104,106,108. Little is known of Mac Cuill's own group, the "descendants of Gréc".

[5]*in insolam Euoniam nomine* "at an island called Euonia"; *baptismum in Euonia* "baptism in Euonia".

Maccuill de Mane episcopus et antestes Arddae Huimnonn
"Maccuill bishop of Mane and prelate of Arde Huimnonn (the Isle of Man)".

Since it was stated explicitly in Jocelin's 12th century Life of Patrick (Colgan 1647 98), Maccuill has been identified with the Manx saint Maughold, Latin Machaldus, the eponym of Kirk Maughold parish in the east of the Isle of Man.[6] This tradition was also known in Ireland: *Mac Cuill a Manainn* "Mac Cuill from Man" (Ó Riain 1995, 59 §387). Maccuill's description here may consist stylistically of two parallel phrases meaning the same thing, *antestes* being a regular medieval Latin term for bishop (Latham 1965). Muirchu's Life does not use the name Man as an n-stem, but rather appears to adopt it as if it were declined like Latin *urbs*.

Bieler (text & index) and George Broderick (Broderick 1980-1) have identified the second part of *Arddae Huimnonn* with Man: without comment by Bieler, Broderick as a "scribal misreading of Manann", explaining that "the profusion of minims in this name, e.g. in *u, i, m, n,* in the Latin texts could in ms. very well be confused". To me it appears more like the *Emain/Emnae (Emonia)* name with the nasal declension usually found in Gaelic with Man. At any rate Muirchu's Life of Patrick appears to contain three different forms of the island's name: *Evonia* and Man with Latin declension, and one of these in a confused Irish form.

Early Irish *Ard* genitive *Aird* means "height" but *Aird* genitive *Ardae* is a feminine noun meaning "promontory", as in the Ards peninsula in Ulster (*PNI* ii, Hughes & Hannan 1992, 3). Muirchú's *Arddae* seems to be this genitive, and it is suggested that if *Man[e]* is Man then *Ard[dae] hUimnonn* is Maughold's particular part of it, "promontory of Man", designating Maughold Head, near the saint's church and burial place on the east of the island and in his parish. This headland was known by recent Manx speakers as *Kione Vaghal* [7] and *kione* was the regular word for headland. There is no evidence for *aird* "promontory" in modern Manx, but Broderick adduces the nearby place-names *Kerroo ny hArd* "quarter of the Ard", *The Ards/Ny Ardjyn QL*, and *Cashtal yn Ard* "castle of the Ard"[8] further inland as evidence for a wider area south of Ramsey once having been thought of as Maughold's promontory (Irish *aird*) as no great height *(ard)* is involved. *Cashtal yn Ard* is a chambered tomb spectacular enough to be associated in later tradition with the famous 11th-century king Godred Crovan of Man and the Isles.[9]

One other suggestion to avoid the apparent doubling of the place-name is that *di Mane* here might be a misreading of *de mare* "from the sea",[10] referring to the way the saint "bishop and prelate of Man" reached the island, his actual sea voyage parallelling conversion and baptism (Muhr 1999a, 201 - 2).

---

[6] *Mac Cuill* is an Irish name meaning literally "son of hazel", but recent research by E. Fitzaimons has shown that it may be used as a variant of Cailín or Mo Chae, the saint of Nendrum on Strangford Lough (pers comm).
[7]Thomas Christian of Ramsey, the authority for most of these names: *BUPNS* 2.3 15 n.12.
[8]*BUPNS* 2.3, 13, 15 n.15; *PNIM* iv 23-5; grid-refs SC 4689, one-inch sheet 87.
[9]*Cashtal Ree Gorree* "King Gorry's castle", Thomas Christian: *BUPNS* 2.3, 15 n.18.
[10]The reading in the Brussels ms, explained by Bieler 23 as "suggestive of an exemplar in insular script". *BUPNS* 2.3, 14 n.5 implies that *de mare* was either in the Book of Armagh or Broderick's own interpretation.

In more recent oral tradition, Patrick himself visited Man from Ulster by leaping the sea on his horse, which left its footprints at a well[11] and on *Sleau Innyd ny Cassan* "mountain of the place of the feet" at Peel,[12] and the horseshoe-shaped well at Maughold Head (Gill 1963, p.327). According to Gill, this well was dedicated to both St Patrick and the saint of the area, Maughold.[13]

The late 12th century bardic poem in praise of Raghnall, King of Man[14] also uses both names, and makes the mythological context of Emain clear: this place (or part) of Man is also compared to Tara, (Bhreathnach 1995) legendary seat of the high-kings of Ireland, descendants of Sadb:

Emain na n-aball cumra	Eamhain of the fragrant apple-trees
Teamair Mhanann cin mbebbla,	[is?] the Tara of Man without deceit,
as siat cuaine saer Sadbha	The noble progeny of Sadhbh are
abhla craebh n-uaine nEambna.	the green-branched apple-trees of Eamhain.

The etymology of *Emain* is undecided. Wagner suggested a meaning connected with water, "a stream",[15] while O'Rahilly suggested *isamonis*, which can be translated "holy mound", or Otherworld hill (O'Rahilly 1946 13; Toner 1988 34). As well as the prehistoric legendary capital of Ulster, a few other names in Ireland contain the element; and another island, the monastic settlement of Inchcolm in the Firth of Forth in Scotland, was once known as *Emonia* (Watson 1926, 104,131.) There the embarcation place of Porthaven (earlier *Portevin*) may preserve a version of the name, which is entirely lost in the Isle of Man.[16] The element Man has been given similar meanings, it has generally been connected with Latin *mons* "mountain", but the places in Ireland and Scotland so named are near water, like the hilly Isle of Man and its deity Manannán.

Land division on the Isle of Man

The Manx Traditionary Ballad edited by R.L. Thomson[17] gives a local history of the settlement of the island which was presumably preserved by oral tradition from the late 15th or early 16th century before being written down in the 18th.

Mananan beg va Mac y Leirr	Young Mannanan who was son of Ler (Sea)
Shen yn chied er ec row rieau ee	was the first who ever owned her,
Agh myr share oddyms cur-my-ner	but as I can best observe
Cha row eh hene agh Anchreestee.	he was nothing but a heathen. (v.3)

At length Patrick came and blessed the island and set up as bishop St German, who built chapels (*cabballyn*), one in every *treen balley*.

---

[11]Kneen 362, St Patrick's Well / Silver Well; PNIM 1, Sheading of Glenfaba (1994) 67: *Chibbyr Noo Pharick / Chibbyr Sheeant / Chibbyr yn Argid*

[12]Kneen 53 (in Kirk Christ Rushen, not yet published GB).

[13]*Chibbyr Vaghal, PNIM* iv Sheading of Garff (1999) 75. The story of Patrick's horse appears with another well, *Chibbyr Pharick* iv 266.

[14] "A poem in praise of Raghnall king of Man" *Baile Suthach Sídh nEamhna* ed. B. Ó Cuív, *Éigse* viii (1957) 283-301, p.289 §8.

[15]*Ériu* 28 (1977) 13; ZCP 38 (1981) 19 n.55.

[16]i.e. Gaelic *Port Eamhain/Eamhna,* Simon Taylor from Geoffrey Barrow pers. comm.

[17]*Études Celtiques* 9 vol IX fasc 2 pp 521-548, vv3,17.

Eisht haink Maughold Noo aynjee	Then came St Maughold to the island
As gheqv eh thalloo ec y Chione	and took land at Maughold Head
As hrog eh keeill as rollick mygeayrt	& built a church & a graveyard round it
Yn ynnyd by-vian lesh beaghey ayn.	the place where he wanted to live. (v.17)

As well as his own church foundation, Maughold is credited with establishing the Manx parishes or *skeeraghyn*, a term borrowed from Norse, the equivalent of English *shire*, also used as *sgìre* in Gaelic Scotland. The terms *keeill* and *rollick* parallel Irish *cill* "church", also often used in parish names, and *reilig* "graveyard". Early churches became the centres of parishes and the rest of the settlement pattern shows affinities with Ireland.

Keeill "church" plus the name of the saint to whom it was dedicated was the usual form in Manx of the church names, while the form *Kirk* + saint's name was used for the parish in English. Of course *kirk*, the Scandinavian equivalent of English church, means the same thing as *keeill* in this sense. The alternation of *kirk* and *cill*, anglicised *kil[l]*, followed by a saint's name occurs in Scotland, where it may arise from Gaelic-Norse bilingualism in possibly the 10th century (MacQueen 1956; Nicolaisen 1976, 108 - 11) and occasionally in the north of Ireland[18] where it is probably a borrowing from Scotland. The name of the six sheadings into which the island is divided seems to be entirely Norse: *settungr* "a sixth part". The sheadings are then divided into *skeerey*/parishes as mentioned above, usually three to a sheading. The next division is the treen, 4 - 6 to a parish, and the quarterland, 3-4 to a treen. Marstrander has suggested that treen (the same spelling in Manx) derived from the Gaelic phrase *tír uinge* "ounce land, land paying the rent of an ounce", a term also known in Scotland, but it seems more likely that it is simply Gaelic *trian* "third" (*PNIM* iv, §3 p.xiv). Quarterland is a translation of Manx *kerroo, carrow* "quarter", equivalent to Irish *ceathramh*.

Land division and settlement are closely linked, and Broderick (1978) noted the high proportion of treen and quarterland names which contain the Manx element *balley* (Irish *baile*) "homestead, settlement": 20 of the 93 treens and 217 of the 362 quarterlands. In the north and especially north-east of Ireland *Bally* is often prefixed to place-names in official documents in the early 17th-century to indicate that a particular name is a townland, the unit most equivalent to the Manx quarterland.[19]

In comparison northern Irish parishes are much more variable in size, from 6 to more than 200 townlands, not easily related to the secular division, known from evidence c.1600, of a *ballybetagh* "land of a food-provider". The *ballybetagh* was divided into 12-16 *ballyboes* (Irish *baile bó* "settlement of a cow", probably at one time "land paying the rent of a cow"), the land unit which most often underlies the English term townland. Townlands may also be grouped by 3s and 4s into quarters of a *ballybetagh*, and *ceathramh* "quarter" anglicised carrow also appears in townland names as quarters of these quarters.[20] The *trian* or third exists in names but is not

---

[18]Kirkinriola for Kilconriola "church of *Cú Riaghla*" McKay 1995, *PNI* iv *The Baronies of Toome,* 216; Kilmoyle "roofless church" Upper or Kirkmoyle townland, Ballymoney parish.

[19]Flanagan, D. 1978, "British" *BUPNS* 2.1 p.52. "bally is often prefixed indiscriminately to placenames in early 17th-century inquisitions, grants etc to indicate that the name represents a townland unit".

[20]Four-townland groups are common in church lands: Reeves, W. 1847. *The ecclesiastical antiquities*

usually a recognisable part of this system, while townlands may also be divided into *sessiaghs*, or "sixths", but which are usually three to a townland. The fact that, in both places, fractional subdivisions are used which are no longer etymologically exact argues for a long-established system of land division which has evolved through time – apparently within the Gaelic-speaking tradition, apart from the name given the sheadings. In Ulster terms, the townland is the equivalent of the Manx quarterland, while the (obsolete) Manx *treen* is the equivalent of the (obsolete) quarter of a *ballybetagh*.

Name-links between Ulster and Man

Carl Marstrander's map of Manx sheadings and parishes (Marstrander 1937, 404) illustrates this system and also the similar-if-not-the-same system of naming Manx parishes. Most of them derive from churches dedicated to a patron saint, often Gaelic. In Manx the names begin with *keeill* "church", Irish *cill*, regularly Englished as Kirk. Church names appear in Ireland alongside secular Gaelic names, like the parishes of Ballaugh, Jurby and Rushen on Man. Some of the saints may be peculiar to Man, but more work needs to be done on the saints mentioned in Ireland and Scotland, including their place-names, before* we can be sure. For Manx place-names we have George Broderick's very full and ongoing series, and from North to South the sheadings and parishes are:

Ayre	Kirk Andreas, Bride, Christ Lezayre (*PNIM* vol. iii)
Michael	Kirk Michael, Ballaugh, Jurby (*PNIM* vol. ii)
Garff	Kirk Conchan, Lonan, Maughold (*PNIM* vol. iv)
Glenfaba	Kirk German, Patrick (*PNIM* vol. i)
Middle	Kirk Braddan, Marown, Santan (*PNIM* vol. v)
Rushen	Kirk Christ Rushen, Arbory, Malew.

Although Bowen (1977, 147f) says there is no pre-12th-century evidence for most of these dedications, he divides the saints into four types: (1) Man only (2) found in the rest of the Celtic world (3) familiar Celtic saints (4) international saints. Dedications to the first two types are the most likely to be early, and these include *Conchenn* "doghead" (Megaw 1962-3) a name used as the Gaelic equivalent of St Christopher, "Lonan", probably Adamnán via *Cill Adhomhnáin*, Maughold who has been documented above; Braddan, Marown, and Santan, who seem most likely to be local Manx saints (*PNIM* iv 20-ln, v 21-2). Arbory is *Cairbre*, Malew is from Irish *Mo Lua*, a 6th century saint also commemorated in Gaelic Scotland, as a monastic founder on the island of Lismore (*PNIM* iv 21; Watson 1926, 292-3). There was formerly a pattern on the 4th of August at Laa Lau (*Lann [Mo] Lua*) (Flanagan 1969, 8), the ancient church of Ballinderry beside Portmore Lough in Co. Antrim, efficaceous for the cure of warts and "other diseases also". In current local tradition the cure was for insanity[21] and this was also the case at one of the saint's Scottish sites in Europie at the Butt of Lewis (Forbes 1872, 411). One wonders if a reverse Manx superstition were connected: Insanity in the parish of Kirk Malew was supposedly caused by drinking from a particular communion cup in Kirk Malew, until the use of the cup was discontinued (Gill 1963, p.287).

---

of Down, Connor and Dromore, pp.259-60; the quarters of Bangor *PNI* ii 145.
[21]Ordnance Survey Memoirs Ballinderry, eds A Day and P McWilliams vol 21 pp.54-5 (Belfast); local tradition from Kieran Clendinning of Lurgan pers. comm.

Ulster Irish influence can be traced in the personal names on the inscribed stones of Man. If the reading is correct, one written in ogam provides a direct link with the Conaille of Louth:

BIVAIDONA MAQI MUCOI CUNAVA[LI]: "Bivaidu of the Conaille" (Ogam, small broken stone, Rushen; the reading "Conaille" is from Marstrander p.425).

The Conaille apparently derived their name from the hero Conall Cernach of the Ulster Cycle tales. Christian inscriptions show the mixing of Gaels and Scandinavians through the names of the people involved:

MAIL BRIKTI SUNR ATHAKANS SMITH RAIST KRUS THANO... GAUT KIRTHI THANO AUK ALA I MAUN "Mael Brigte son of Athakan the smith erected this cross. Gaut made it and all in Man" (cross-slab, Michael)

Mael Brigte (later Maol Bríde) means "devotee of St Brigid". Brigid, born in Faughart in Co. Louth, was one of the best known Irish saints (Bowen's class 3), alongside Patrick and Columba/Colum Cille.

MAL LUMKUN RAISTI KRUS THENA EFTER MAL MURU FUSTRA SINE... "Mael Lomchon erected this cross for Mael Muru his foster-mother..." (cross-slab, Michael) (Kermode 1907, 74, 150, 198).

Maol Lomchon is "devotee of St Lomchú" and *Lomchú* "bare hound" appears to have been an east Ulster saint, from the reference to him on Jan 9th in several Irish martyrologies: *ó Cill Lomchoin i nUlltoibh* "from Lomchú's church among the Ulaid".[22] St Muru is associated with the church of Faughan in North Donegal, although a family descended from a *Maol Mura* "devotee of Mura" were associated with the church in Armagh (Muhr 2001).

The Norse influence on Man is a contrast with Ulster, which has no mixed inscriptions and as well as the names of the three eastern sea-loughs (each with a surviving Irish name, see above) has only the Copeland Islands or *Kaupmanneyar* "merchant islands", not named on the Speed/Durham map.[23]

The thoroughness of the Norse colonisation of Man can be shown by a wider range of elements than those already mentioned in discussing the map. Some of these are: *by* as in Grenaby QL "green farm" (*PNIM* iii 342); *dalr* "valley", Dalby TR (i 95) "dale farm", Cardle QL (TR *Cardall*) "mill river dale" (iv 70). Some of the hills are called *fjall*, Snaefell "snow mountain" (*PNIM* iii 464), Sartfell "black mountain" (ii 95), Barrule Malew "lookout mountain" and Barrule Maughold which is "stone-heap mountain" (iv 62,404); Lamblell QL (TR *Lambefell*) "lambs' hill". Other elements are *garthr* Amogary QL (TR *Amogary*) *Ámundar -gaðr*, "Ámund's enclosure" (*PNIM* iv 218); *hofuð* Howstrake QL (TR *Haustrake*) "headland path" (iv 398); *nes* "nose, promontory", Agneash QL (TR *Hegnes*) "edge promontory" (iv 217); *staðir* "farm" Clypse QL "rock farm" (iv 384).

The progression of languages through time can be seen in names which are translations. Ramsey "wild garlic river" from Old Norse *hrams-á*, seems to be connected with the name *Strooan ne Crawe*, Manx for "stream of the garlic", for the stream which forms part of the parish boundary (PNIM iv 158, 167). In other cases a

[22]Best & Lawlor 6, Stokes 12, Todd & Reeves 11.

[23]Mac Giolla Easpaig, D. Scandinavian influence Unpublished p.20-1

translation has been added to a name which was no longer understood: Rheaneash QL (TR *Rennesse*) "nose division" where the nose/promontory marked out by the name to Norse speakers needed clarification in Gaelic; Cronkaberry QL "hill of the *berg*"; Stronabeck "stream of the beck" (*PNIM* iii 261; iv 390 *recte* 389; iv 157). The same thing has happened between Gaelic and Gaelic in Cronk Crock, where the later pronunciation of "hill" has been used to explain the earlier (*PNIM* iii 363). A pronunciation similar to *Cronk*, the Manx form of Gaelic *cnoc*, has also been recorded in minor place-names derived from the lost Gaelic of south Co Down (*PNIM* iii 363; *BUPNS* ser.1 iii pt 3 (1955) pp.43, 47.) Finally there is translation between Gaelic and English, where the local word flatt from ON or N.English *flat* "flat piece of ground" has been used to translate Gaelic *faiche* "green": *Faai Veg Flatt* "little flatt flatt"; *Naie Flatt* "flatt flatt" (*PNIM* iv 106, 249).

The age of the Gaelic place-names has been much discussed. As we have seen, the island was referred to in Gaelic from the 6th century, and its supernatural guardian Manannán was still remembered in recent local tradition. Some church sites dedicated to unusual Gaelic saints may have borne these names from the same early period, which sent Irish saints like Colum Cille and Mo Lua to Scotland. However the Manx dedications to Patrick and Brigid seem likely to be the result of 11th century migration from Dublin and Meath, and Broderick agrees that most of the island's Gaelic place names were "formed since the end of the Scandinavian period", which makes them 13th-century and later (*PNIM* i 18; Introduction §6 p.xxiii.)

In Ireland it seems now to be accepted, from the names listed in the charters of Norman church foundations, that the land units and their Gaelic names were clearly a system before the Normans arrived in the late 12th century, and recorded some of them in grants to churches (e.g. Newry abbey, *PNI* i 1). Some people accept them as much older: "The enduring townland system did originate late in the early Christian period".[24] In the Isle of Man this has been said of the system but not of the names, the one earlier, the other later than the Norse settlement. Marstrander (1937) linked the early Christian *keeill* sites with the *treens*, and Broderick reports how Megaw (1978) has shown from the distribution of 9th-century Norse burial mounds in separate quarterlands that "the holdings which came to be known as quarterlands represent in general elements in a very early (ie pre-Scandinavian) land system".

It is appropriate then to explore how the Gaelic place-names of Man compare with those in Ireland, including how Manx quarterland names are different from townland names in Ireland. Differences may be due to age, or to language changes due to different conditions on the Isle of Man. The heritage of Gaelic place-name forms may include early linguistic features, or reference to aspects of the environment which no longer exist. Where not stated, references are to George Broderick's ongoing *Place-Names of the Isle of Man (PNIM)*.

Compounds of noun plus noun or noun plus prefixed adjective are generally considered to be old - Mooragh in Ramsey from *muir-mhagh* "sea-plain" (*PNIM* iv 196) can be compared with the parallel Welsh formation *morfa*; or Ulster *muirbholg* "sea-bag,

---

[24]Aalen, F.H.A., Whelan, K. and Stout, M. 1997 *Atlas of the Irish Rural Landscape*, p 22, although the caption to the Armagh townland map dates the system from "since at least the medieval period" p 21. One feels it is only place-name scholars, with their concern to collect all the earliest references to a name, who can answer the question about land-unit and name continuity - where the sources exist. Broderick lists 2 sources before 1200, and another 7 before 1600 (*PNIM* intro §4.1).

enclosed bay"(Muhr 1999b 8; *PNI* vii (Mac Gabhann) 198 - 200). Doolough, Dollagh "black lough" with initial stress is "a close compound of some antiquity" (*PNIM* ii 171, 239; Intro §7.8). Preposed adjectives where the noun following bears the stress are "a later development" (Intro §7.8). Arderry (*PNIM* iii 271, iv 362) is from "high wood, thicket", an etymology suggested for the house called the Argory in Co. Armagh. Manx *Breckbooilley* "speckled fold" occurs several times (*PNIM* iv 258, FN 421) but I have not met it in Ireland. Corvalley QL "conical hill farm, isolated farm" is not a current term in Manx but, as in Ireland, is "quite common in Manx placenames" (*PNIM* i 225, Introduction i §7.8.1). It appears in Ulster as Corbally, where the translation is also a puzzle: "the prominent townland /farmstead" "odd, noticeable townland" (*PNI* iv (McKay) 176; *PNI* vi (Muhr) 196.)

Typical Irish Gaelic place-name elements may be used similarly or differently in other parts of the Gaelic speaking world. The names of a number of Manx hills begin with *Slieau*, Gaelic *sliabh*, which is the common word for mountain in Ireland, as in Slieve Donard and many other of the Mourne mountains visible from the Isle of Man (*PNI* iii (Ó Mainnín) 151-170.) However this is not a common place-name element in Gaelic Scotland, occurring only in the south west nearest to Ireland, especially the Rhinns of Galloway, but also Islay, Jura and Arran which are also the area of earliest settlement by Dal Riada in the 6th century. In both these areas Nicolaisen considers that the names "may well be assignable to a pre-Norse stratum of Gaelic speakers" (Nicolaisen 1976, 39-45 esp. p.45); The distribution of *Sliabh* is currently being re-examined by Simon Taylor.

Inis, the Gaelic word for "island", appears in *Purt- or Bally ny Hinshey* "port/settlement of the island", the Manx name for Peel, where the original church and castle were built on the small island off shore (*PNIM* i 298). An alternative historical name was *Holmetoun*, the Norse equivalent or probable translation, *holmr* "islet" + *toun*, of *Bally ny Hinshey*. Dónall Mac Giolla Easpaig points out a parallel instance on the east coast of Ireland where Holmpatrick, a Norse translation compound influenced by Irish word order, is the name of the parish containing St Patrick's Island, which was called *Inis Pátraic* in 798.[25] However the antiquity of the Manx name may also be demonstrated by the meaning "island" for *inis*. As with the meaning of *holme* generally, (Mawer 1930, 38) *inis* (and its diminutive *injeig*, Scottish Gaelic *innseag*) in Man almost always now has the meaning "river meadow". Other words for field are not quite like Ireland: the regular one is *magher*, the original meaning of which was "plain", while others have been borrowed. Here Scottish Gaelic has kept the original word *achadh*, common in Irish place-names but replaced in speech by *páirc*.

The Manx equivalent of Irish *cabhán*, apparently only used in minor names, is translated not as in northern Ulster a "round dry hill" (*pace* Kneen 184), but by Broderick as "hollow, small valley", as in Coan Argid "hollow of silver", Coanmooar "big hollow" (*PNIM* ii 58), Con Shellagh, a beach, "willow hollow" (i 73); Conrhennie "bracken hollow" (iv 275, 386). This meaning is known further south in Ireland. Broderick lists *coan* and its variant *quane* under "Common elements in Manx place-names" (intro. §6) comparing Scottish Gaelic *cabhan, camhan*, Irish cabhán, but the element seems to be more common in Ireland than in Scotland.

---

[25]AU, "Scandinavian influence on the toponymy of Ireland" p.20. See Speed's map.

Another important Gaelic element found in Man is *ros*, "wood" or "promontory", found as the diminutive *roiseán* in the name of the parish of Rushen. Names like this, a single element qualified by no other, are usually early (*PNIM* Intro §7.1). *Ros* appears in Ulster in the names Roslea, Rostrevor, Portrush (McKay 1999), while *roiseán* is found alone as a townland name in Fermanagh, at either end of the parish of Cleenish. I have given *ros* its meaning as in Ó Donaill's modern Irish dictionary, but in fact the earlier Dinneen defines it more loosely: "a wood or copse, often the site of an old cemetery, ...a promontory ...; a level tract of arable land ...*common in place-names*". Broderick translates Glen Rushen QL (TR *Glenrushen*) as "glen of the level tract of land" (*PNIM* i 111).

Man is a windswept island which lost its tree-cover early. Norse names like Gob Ago "headland of oak" from Gaelic *gob* + ON *eik*, and Eschedala "ash tree valley" ON *eski-dalr* (*PNIM* iv 114, 105) are evidence for trees in early times. However on Man the word *bile*, which in Irish signified a noteworthy or sacred tree (Joyce 1869, 409-500), became the ordinary word: *billey*. Some of its earlier significance may survive in place-names, as in Ballamiljyn QL meaning "farm of/by the ancient trees", and Ballavilley QL "farm of the [single] tree" which refers to Glion ny Billey Gorrym "glen of the blue tree" "believed to have referred to a venerated tree" (*PNIM* iv 243; iii 301, 397-8). *Cronk y Villey*, "hill of the single tree" was the name of a tumulus on Ballacree, now demolished and the hill levelled. Given the location, the tree may have held some religious significance (*PNIM* iii 228). Crowcreen "withered bush" QL must have been named from a significant landmark (*PNIM* iv 93).

The element derry (*doire* "oakgrove"), which in Ulster may signify "a dry spot in a bog (suitable for trees)" in Man has connotations of steepness, as in FN Drumdeary "ridge of the oakgrove/ wood/ thicket on a steep incline - the latter is the case here" (PNIM iii 298). Glen Darragh, "oaken glen" is described as "a narrow bushy ravine", while The Darragh "oakwood area" is "a little copse of stunted trees on the steep seabrow to the north of Laxey head" "believed to be some of the few oakwood relics in Man" (*PNIM* iv 304, 295).

Like Ireland, places are named from plant and tree species: Baldrine QL "blackthorn farm", Ballure QL "yew-tree farm" (*PNIM* iv 25, 59). Rhencullen QL "holly division" (*PNIM* iv 150) was known in 1286, the only Gaelic name in a set of monastic bounds (iv 426 also ii 94). These three names do not contain the article, a feature which becomes more prevalent in later names. A few names have adjectival or locative endings, familiar in Ireland, although Broderick wonders if initial *balla* has been lost in Leaghyrney QL "rushy area" and the Guilcagh, QL (TR *Gilcagh*) "place of broom" (*PNIM* iv 125; iii 124) which preserves the older form of the word, Irish *giolcach*, Manx *giucklagh*. Other quarterland names are Glentramman QL "glen of the elder trees" (PNIM iii 296); Ballajucklee QL "broom farm", Ballarhennie QL "bracken farm" (ii 28, 39); Ballasalla QL "willow farm" (ii 218), Shoughlaig QL "little willow grove" (ii 96); Ballashaughlaig QL "farm of the willow grove" (iv 49); Ballaskeig QL "hawthorn farm" (iv 50). Not all the trees named in Irish place-names (alder, birch) are mentioned in the Manx names.

Some names commemorate animals and birds that are now extinct. Kneen (p 44) noted of the place-name Leim y Chynnee "fox's leap" that foxes no longer existed on Man while place-names showed they were once common. Cronk y Chayt (*PNIM* iv 91) is translated "hill of the (wild) cat" but Kneen was puzzled that "our historians do not mention wild cats" (Kneen 44; 438, 530). Labbee yn Turk is 'lair of the wild boar" (*PNIM* iv 321), although Broderick notes that torc is otherwise unattested in Manx. One name commemorates the eagle FN: *Cronk Urleigh* (*PNIM* i 118).

References to horses are often not what they seem. Broderick's list of common elements (*PNIM* Introduction §6), includes *cabbyl*, Irish *capall* "horse" and *sharragh*, Irish *searrach* "foal", but these denote a coastal or inland rock respectively. Cabbyl ny Lord, Cabbyl Vedn, Cabbyl Veg, Cabbyl Vooar "Lord's horse, white horse, little horse, big horse" (*PNIM* i 63) are all rock features and the last is a reef. Sharragh Bane denotes a "white rock" (*PNIM* ii 199; iv 348.) An Irish parallel, the Co. Antrim subtownland name of Capplecarry in Ramoan parish, was explained last century as referring to a cliff, "from the fanciful comparison of some of the projecting rocks to a mangy horse" (*Ordnance Survey Revision Name-book* in *PNI* vii 266 (Mac Gabhann sh.4), and a 17th-century Strabane example is a stone marking the barony boundary called *gerane bane* "white horse".[26] In Man, the Gownies "heifers" are two rocks by Dhoon bay (*PNIM* iv 116). The same metaphor is attested in the Old Irish story *Fingal Rónáin*, (Greene 1955 5, 11, 84 - 5) where the uselessness of a tryst at which the loved one never appeared is likened to herding two white stones on the hillside known as *Ba Aoife* "Aoife's cows": "That is the vain herding, without cows, without the one you love".

The words for early Irish secular buildings *dún, ráth, lios*, common in townland names, are not present in Manx, although there are 617 names in *dún*, 53 in *ráth* and 13 including *lios* in Scotland.[27] Sacred sites fare better. Appyn, translated "abbeyland", not exactly located, and two places called Nappin, one a quarterland, contain an old (pre-Scandinavian) Gaelic ecclesiastical element seen in Scottish Appin, which "would refer to the Early Christian period" (Watson 1926, 124; *PNIM* i 19; ii 257; iv 339). It is possible that the site and quarterland in Kirk Andreas called *Knock y Doonee* preserves the word *domhnach* "early church", not found in Scotland or elsewhere in Manx, and means "hill of the church", because of the ruined *keeill* with a bilingual Latin/Ogam cross-slab of c.500 AD (*PNIM* iii 136).

Keeill, Gaelic *cill* is the normal word for a church site, and some of these have given name to quarterlands: Ballakilmartin QL with a ruined *keeill*, "farm of Martin's church"; Ballakilmurray QL "farm of Mary's church"; Ballakillingan QL "farm by St Finghein's church" (*PNIM* iv 369; i 190; iii 290). There are many celebrated or holy wells, with names beginning *chibber*, Irish *tiobra*: Chibber Feeyney "well of wine", Chibber y Vashtee "well of baptising", Chibber Vaghal "Maughold's well" on Maughold Head, Chibber Me Leah which both Kneen and Broderick attribute to an unknown saint, but could it be a variant spelling of *Mo Lua*, as in Kirk Malew? (*PNIM* iv 264, 75, 73). There are also typical Gaelic occupation names: Ballaseyr QL "farm of the craftsmen", Glencrutchery QL "harper's glen", and a recurring Ballalheih which may mean "doctor's farm" (*PNIM* iii 54; iv 394; ii 31).

In the combined preliminary study of the element *baile* in place names organised by Deirdre Flanagan in 1978, she made the following comments: the first examples appear

---

[26]Simington Civil Survey iii 389, c.1655.
[27]MacDonald, A. 1987. *"Caiseal, cathair, dún, lios* and *ráth* in Scotland": part 1 *dún* BUPNS 2.3, 30- 39; part 2 *ráth* BUPNS 2.4, 32-57; part 3 *Lios, Ainm* i 37-54.

in a charter relating the monastery of Kells c. 1150 and consist of *baile* plus surname "homestead of X" (Price 1963). Other earlier examples of the word in Irish texts confirm the meaning homestead or settlement. It is now "by far the commonest settlement term in Irish townland names" with the highest incidence in areas of extensive Anglo-Norman settlement, influenced by their use of Latin *villa* or English *tun* (town) with the name of the feudal tenant. Although ownership names remained common, many of the present examples are descriptive, and clearly refer to the townland area as much as to a focal farm within it (Flanagan 1978).

Ian Fiaser said that in Scotland "*baile* is one of the most common Gaelic place name elements ... perhaps farms ... established from the 10th century onwards". The spread of Gaelic into Pictland resulted in *baile* replacing *pit* "share, portion" in many place names. East Central Scotland north of the Forth is where *baile* became commonest, since the Hebrides were still in the control of Norse-speakers. Most of the names are descriptive, but a good number of the *baile*-names in the Hebrides and Galloway, 12th century and later, contain personal names (Fraser 1978).

George Broderick documented the earliest example of Manx *baile* names in the survey of the lands owned by Rushen Abbey c. 1280. *Balla-* seems to occur as an equivalent to *villa,* which is recorded with the names of holders in the mid 12th century. He goes on to say that *Balla-* appears in 20 of the 93 treen names, but 217 of the 362 quarterland names (Broderick 1978, 17). This is a very high proportion, considering that the names of many of the treens and quarterlands are not Gaelic at all but Scandinavian. In the Anglo-Norman settled Ards peninsula in Ireland, where almost all of the townlands appear in Gaelic dress, 103 out of 210 townland names begin with *baile.* The Ulster percentage is 49% the Manx percentage 59%.

Some of these quarterlands are called quarter: Kerroodhoo QL "black quarter"; Kerrooglass QL "green quarterland"; Lheahkerroo QL "half-quarterland" (*PNIM* iii 246, iv 402; ii 78; iii 144). Others, like the tree and church names quoted above, are descriptive, and this is the case with many *baile/balla* names. Place names can be very basic, but these are both simple and recurrent: Ballachrink QL "hill farm" (*PNIM* ii 208, iii 181,278, iv 31,364); Ballachurry QL "marsh farm" (iii 29, iv 366); Baldromma QL "ridge farm" (iii 274, iv 26 - on the TR called *Rigg,* iv 347); Ballalheaney QL "farm of the meadow" (iv 240); Ballalhergey QL "farm of the slope" (iii 196, 293, iv 373); Ballig QL "farm of the hollow" (i 202, ii 44, 221, iv 252, 374) of which Broderick says "this name is common in Man". There is far more linguistic variety in the names of non-quarterland features, to which some of these names seem to refer. The general impression is that administrative officialdom has influenced the creation of Manx *baile* names.

In many cases *baile/balla* is followed by personal and family names, as in the earliest and many current Irish examples. Some include Scandinavian personal names, but a sure indication of lateness is that some include English surnames: Ballacleator QL, Ballaoates, Ballaradcliffe QL (iii 31, i 194, iii 53). Most of the Gaelic surnames are formed with *mac* "son" and show the reduced form *'ic* rather than *mhic,* so that the anglicised form begins with C or K. The anglicised form is spelled as the surname would be in Man today, so that these names must have been transparent in either language: Ballacain QL originally from *Baile 'ic Catháin,* (*PNIM* iv 363); Ballacannall QL from *'ic Dhomhnaill;* (iv 228); Ballacojean QL from *'ic Phaidin,* (iv 230);

Ballacollister QL from *'ic Alasdair,* (iv 231); Ballacorteen QL from *'ic Mháirtín* (iv 33); Ballacowin QL from *'ic Comhghain,* (iv 232); Ballacowle QL from *'ic Comhgaill* (iv 232); Ballakaighin QL from *'ic Eachainn* (iv 368); Ballakelly QL from *'ic Ceallaigh* (iii 43); Ballakey QL from *'ic Aodha,* (iv 239). Balyfayle, "Paul's farm" or "farm of the hedge", a treen name, is divided up like a post-Plantation Ulster townland into holdings by three families, whose surname follows Ballafayle: Ballafayle Y Callow from *'ic Amblaibh,* Ballafayle Y Cannell from *'ic Dhomhnaill,* Ballafayle Y Kerruish from *'ic Fhearghuis* (*PNIM* iv 35-37). Similarly-formed surnames, but preserving Mac or Mc, exist in Ulster and Scotland.

A reminder of continuing contact between Ulster and Man is provided by names apparently imported from the north-east of Ireland: Belfast QL, Cooleraine, probably named by "settlers from Coleraine in Ireland"; Cushington which according to tradition must have been named after Cushendun; Dundalk; the Irish Cottages/Houses: built for Irish slate labourers and 19th-century seasonal workers; and the Strongford (*PNIM* iii 73, 92; iv 295; ii 174; iii 406,170).

Bibliography

Abbreviations

AU	*Annals of Ulster,* Mac Airt S, 1983, ed., (Dublin).
BUPNS	*Bulletin of the Ulster Place-name Society.*
PNI	*Place-Names of Northern Ireland,* Stockman G, ed., 1992 - 7, 7 vols.
PNIM	*Place-Names of the Isle of Man,* Broderick G, 1994- 2000, 5 vols.
QL	Quarterland (Manx place-name types as used in *PNIM*)
TR	Treen
FN	Field name

References

Best R I & Lawlor H J, (eds) 1931, *The Martyrology of Tallaght* (London).
Bieler L, (ed.), 1979, *The Patrician Texts in the Book of Armagh.*
Bhreathnach E, 1995, *Tara: a select bibliography,* Discovery Progamme, (Dublin).
Bowen G, 1977, *Saints, Seaways and Settlement.*
Broderick G, 1978, "*Baile* in Manx nomenclature", *BUPNS* 2.1 16-18.
Broderick G, 1980-1, "*Arddae hUimnonn* - a Manx place name?" *BUPNS* 2.3 13-15.
Broderick G, 1994-2000, *Place-Names of the Isle of Man,* 5 vols (*PNIM,* in progress).
Colgan J, 1647, Jocelin of Furness *Vita Sancti Patricii, Triadis Thaumaturgae* (Louvain).
Cubbon A M, 1974, *Early Maps of the Isle of Man* (4th edn) 24-5, 35.
Flanagan D, 1969, 'Lann', *An t-Ultach, Iúil* p 8.
Flanagan D, 1978, "Common elements in Irish place-names: *baile*", *BUPNS* 2.1 8-13.
Forbes A P, 1872, Calendars of Scottish Saints, (Edinburgh).
Fraser I, 1978, "*Baile* in Scots Gaelic" *BUPNS* 2.1 14-15.

Gill W W, 1963, *A Third Manx Scrapbook* p.327, part reprint ed. S. Miller, Chiollagh Books (1993) p.19.

Greene D, (ed.), 1955, *Fingal Rónáin*, Medieval and Modern Irish Series, (Dublin).

Hughes A J & Hannan R H, 1992, *PNI* ii *The Ards Peninsula.*

Joyce P W, 1869 - 1913, *The origin and history of Irish names of places*, 3 vols, (Dublin).

Kermode P M C, 1907, *Manx Crosses*. (Reprint 1999).

Kneen J J, 1925-8, *Place-Names of the Isle of Man*. 6 vols, (Douglas).

Latham R E, 1965, *Revised Medieval Latin Word List* (London).

Mac Airt S, (ed.), 1983, *Annals of Ulster*, (Dublin).

Mac Gabhann F, 1997, *PNI* vii, *North-east Co. Antrim.*

McKay P, 1995, *PNI* iv, *The Baronies of Toome.*

McKay P, 1999, *A Dictionary of Ulster Place-Names*, (Belfast).

MacQueen J, 1956, "Kirk- and Kil- in Galloway place-names", *Archivium Linguisticum* 8, 135-49;

Marstrander C, 1937, "Treen og Keeill", *Norsk Tidsshrift for Sprogvidenskap* vol. 8, 287 - 442, (Oslo).

Mawer A, (ed.), 1930, *The chief elements used in English place-names, EPNS* (Cambridge).

Megaw B R S, 1962-3, "Who was St Conchan? A consideration of Manx Christian origins" *Journal of the Manx Museum* vi no.79: 187-92.

Meyer K, (ed.), 1895, London. *Immram Brain. The voyage of Bran son of Febal to the Land of the Living*. 8thc. (London).

Muhr K, 1996a, "Place-Names in the Ulster Cycle pt ii. The East Ulster perspective on the Ulster Cycle tales", *Emania* 14, 51-63.

Muhr K. 1996b, *PNI* vi, *North-west Co. Down/Iveagh.*

Muhr K, 1999a, "Water Imagery in Early Irish", *Celtica* xxiii 193-210.

Muhr K, 1999b, *Celebrating Ulster's Townlands*, (Belfast).

Muhr K, 2001,"Territories, people and place-names of County Armagh" *Armagh History and Society*, at press.

Nicolaisen W H F, 1976, *Scottish Place-Names*, (London).

Price L, 1963, "A note on the use of the word *Baile* in place-names", *Celtica* vi 119-26.

O Mainnin M, 1993, *PNI* iii, *The Mournes.*

O'Rahilly T F, 1946, *Early Irish Mythology*, (Dublin).

O Riain P, (ed.), 1995, *Corpus Genealogiarum Sanctorum Hiberniae (CSH)*, (Dublin).

Simington R C, 1931 - 61, *The Civil Survey* 10 vols, Irish MSS commission, Dublin, vol iii, *Donegal, Derry, Tyrone* 1937.

Stokes W, (ed), 1895, *The Martyrology of Gorman*, (London).

Thomson R L, 1961, "The Manx Traditional Ballad", *Études Celtiques*, 9 pt 2, 521 - 548, 10 pt 1, (1962) 60 - 87.

Todd J H & Reeves W, (eds), 1864 *The Martyrology of Donegal*, (trans. J O'Donovan, Dublin).

Todd J H & Reeves W, (eds), 1864 *The Martyrology of Donegal,* (trans. J O'Donovan, Dublin).

Toner G, 1988, *Emania* iv 32 - 5 "Emain Macha in the literature".

Toner G & O Mainnín M, 1992, *PNI* i, *Newry and South-west Down.*

Wagner H, 1977, "The Archaic *Dind Ríg* poem and related problems", *Ériu* 28 1 - 17

Wagner H, 1981, "Origins of Pagan Irish Religion", *Zeitschrift fur Celtische Philologie,* 38, 1- 28.

Wagner H, 1981, "Origins of Pagan Irish Religion", *Zeitschrift fur Celtische Philologie,* 38, 1- 28.

Watson W J, 1926, *The history of the Celtic place-names of Scotland,* (Edinburgh, reprinted Irish Academic Press 1986).

Emerging from the Mist: Ireland and Man in the Eleventh Century

Seán Duffy

The famous king of Leinster, Diarmait mac Máel na mBó, on his death in 1072, was acclaimed by an Irish annalist as *rí Innsi Gall* (king of the isles of the foreigners). These were the islands between Britain and Ireland which had been settled by or made subject to the Vikings, who were the original *Gaill* of the title. At a later period the term may have been limited to the outer Hebrides, but in the period under discussion here, it clearly refers to any of the Irish Sea islands north of and including Man, periodically subjected to the control of Gaelic or Scandinavian rulers. As such, it is synonymous with the *Sudreyiar* of Norse usage. Such an all-embracing term, however, applied to so many islands in such a fractious region, is likely to have been an exaggeration if used to describe the sphere of direct authority of any one man; frequently, it may have meant no more than that an individual ruled one of the larger islands, Man or Islay or Lewis or Skye, and *sought* to rule the others. In the eleventh century, because of the Isle of Man's close connexion with the affairs of the Viking town of Dublin in particular, the title *rí Innsi Gall* seems in most instances to refer to the ruler of Man and would-be ruler of the other islands.[1]

There is a near total silence by Irish writers about the affairs of Man and the Isles for the first two-thirds of the eleventh century. This makes it very difficult to chart the progress of Irish involvement in the region or, for that matter, to say with any degree of certainty whether the ruling Viking (or Ostman) dynasty of Dublin held sway there. It is interesting, though, that we have a good deal of information about the contacts of the Dublin Ostmen with the east-Ulster kingdom of Ulaid (modern Counties Antrim and Down). This is the Irish territory that lies closest to the Isle of Man and the intrusion of Dubliners into its affairs is probably due to the latters' Manx links (s.aa. 1000 (AI); 1001 (AFM); 1022 (AFM; ATig); 1038 (AFM; ATig); 1045 (AFM; ATig; AI; AClon). The first hard evidence, though, only comes in 1052 when Diarmait mac Máel na mBó expelled the reigning king of Dublin, an Ostman with the rather Irish-looking name of Echmarcach mac Ragnaill, who thereupon went *'tar muir* (over the sea)' (AU; CS; AFM s.a.1052). Even then we cannot be sure that he fled to Man because when Echmarcach died in 1065 the Irish chronicler Marianus Scotus called

---

[1] I have discussed the relationship at length in *Ériu*, (1992), and what follows is a summary of the evidence.

him king of '*na Renn* (the Rhinns [of Galloway])' (Anderson 1922, I, 592; Byrne 1982).[2] Nevertheless, it does look as though he took initial refuge in Man. After Diarmait mac Máel na mBó seized Dublin he appointed his own son Murchad (ancestor of the famous MacMurrough family) to rule the city.[3] But in 1061 the Irish annals record that Murchad invaded the Isle of Man, took tribute (*cáin*) from it, and defeated mac Ragnaill, presumably Echmarcach (AFM; ATig s.a.1061). The taking of *cáin* was 'a definitive right of kingship' (Simms 1985). Although it could be exercised by an overking without displacing an existing subject ruler, the fact that Echmarcach shortly turns up as king only in the Rhinns of Galloway suggests that he fled there after 1061. The events of 1061 are a most revealing glimpse, the first clear insight we get into the way in which Irishmen were enveloped in the politics of the Irish Sea as a result of their assertion of authority over the Ostmen.

In a way that no previous Irish king had attempted, Diarmait mac Mael na mBó's son Murchad was able to maintain his rule over Dublin for many years, and presumably over Man for the best part of a decade until his death in 1070 (Ó Corrain 1972). At his death, his father resumed control over Dublin (and, one assumes, Man). When Diarmait himself was killed in battle in 1072, it was at the head of an army made up not just of Leinstermen but of Ostmen, many hundreds of whom were slain (AFM s.a.1072). This assumption of his son's place is the justification for one annalist's application to him of the title *rí Laigen & Gall* (AU s.a.1072). But, as we have seen, another set, the annals of 'Tigernach', includes among his subjects not only the Gaill of Dublin but also those of *Innsi Gall*; if we accept that the jewel in the crown of the latter is the Isle of Man, overlordship of which his son Murchad had established in 1061, the obituarist cannot be said to be taking too great a liberty.

After Diarmait's death his former ally, the Munster king Toirrdelbach ua Briain (O'Brien), intent upon enforcing his claim to the high-kingship of Ireland, led an expedition to Dublin. There, the Ostmen granted to him what Diarmait mac Mael na mBó had forcibly snatched exactly twenty years earlier, the kingship of Dublin (AI s.a.1072).[4] This was an extraordinary development, the start of a half-century of intrusion by the Uí Briain royal house of Munster into the affairs of Dublin. Hand in hand with that went a thirst for adventure in the Isles. The Leinstermen had been kings of Dublin for nearly a decade before we hear of any involvement in the Irish Sea islands; but, remarkably, the Munstermen turn up in Man within a year of their annexation of Dublin. In 1073 two members of the Ui Briain - either brothers or first-cousins of Toirrdelbach were killed in the Isle of Man along with a certain Sitriuc son of Olaf (AU; cf.ALCé s.a.1073). The circumstances of their deaths are unclear. Who Sitriuc was, who exactly the two Uí Briain were, whether or not they had the backing of Toirrdelbach ua Briain, is all open to conjecture. But it can hardly be doubted that their presence in Man a year after Toirrdelbach seized Dublin was part and parcel of Munster's attempt to control the city and its insular possessions.

---

[2]Marianus knew what he was talking about because he entered the monastery of Mag Bile (Moville) in the Ards peninsula directly across the channel from the Rhinns of Galloway in the very year of Echmarcach's expulsion (Kenney 1929).

[3]AFM s.a. 1059 calls him '*tigherna Gall* (lord of the foreigners)'. See Ó Corráin (1971)

[4]'*co tucsat Gaill ríge Átha Cliath dó'.*

The early stages of that struggle are largely hidden from us, but we know that in 1075 Toirrdelbach decided to do as Diarmait mac Mael na mBó had, and he installed his own son Muirchertach as king of Dublin; it seems too that another of Toirrdelbach's sons, Diarmait, had begun to act as governor of the other main Ostman city of Waterford, from where he led a raid on Wales in 1080 (AI s.aa.1075, 1080).[5] But the advances the Munstermen had made in dominating Dublin's affairs suffered considerably when a succession dispute broke out after the death of Toirrdelbach ua Briain in 1086. Muirchertach attempted to seize the kingship of all Munster and had Diarmait banished. The latter then seems to have gained control of the entire Ostman fleet.[6] The sons of another brother, Tadc, also played a part in undermining their uncle (AFM s.a.1091). According to the contemporary text on the famous women of Ireland known as the *Banshenchas*, Tadc was married to a daughter of the former Ostman king of Dublin, Echmarcach mac Ragnaill.[7] A year after Toirrdelbach ua Briain's death, the Annals of Ulster report that there was 'a sea expedition by the sons of mac Ragnaill and by the son of the king of Ulaid into Man, and in it fell the sons of mac Ragnaill'. Clearly, in the confusion of the Munster succession race, the Meic Ragnaill had re-emerged to threaten Man. They were probably backed by the sons of Tadc Ua Briain, one of whom was killed in Man in 1096 (AFM s.a.1096), another of whom, as we shall see, was later to make himself king of the Isles. Since Muirchertach was at this point still hoping to make good his claim to be king of Dublin - and with that went an effort to wield authority in Man - this alliance of his enemies appears to have been an attempt to undermine it.

The instability produced by the Munster squabbles meant that Dublin came within the sights of others. It is important to bear in mind that we are not dealing merely with Irishmen who were brought to contemplate expansion into the Isles by virtue of their success in annexing Dublin. The reverse also happens; men come to power in the Isles for whom it is a natural next step to seek to add Dublin to their domain: the pretensions of the ruling Ostman élite within the city's walls, and the claims of Irish kings to overlordship of its citizens, were cast aside, so that the Dubliners embraced the overtures of a sea-lord from Man, or the Scottish isles, or Scandinavia. The first of these was Godred Crovan.

In spite of his success in implanting a dynasty that ruled over the kingdom of Man and the Isles, whole and in part, for nearly two hundred years, very little is known about the origins of Godred Crovan or about the way in which he managed to do so.[8] One set of Irish annals calls him Gofraidh mac mic Arailt (ATig s.a.1091), which most probably means that he was a son or nephew of the Ivar Haraldsson (Ímar mac Arailt,

[5] AI s.aa. 1075, 1080; we still have a letter from the people of Waterford to Archbishop Anselm of Canterbury, circa 1095-6, which is co-signed by 'Dermeth Dux':(Ussher 1632).

[6] AI s.a 1087 reports that Diarmait led a naval force 'on a circuit' and plundered Cloyne in County Cork. But the other Irish annals report the following encounter for the same year: 'Great slaughter of the foreigners of Dublin, Waterford, and Wexford by the Uí Echach Muman on the day they intended to plunder Cork' (AU; AFM). They may both be describing different episodes on the same naval expedition along the Cork coast led by Diarmait Ua Briain.

[7] He had by her three sons, Donnchad, Domnall and Amlaíb, and a daughter, Bé Binn (*Revue Celtique*, 48 (1931), 196).

[8] The Manx chronicle claims that he was *'filius Haraldi nigri de ysland'* (CrMi fol. 32v.). This presumably refers to Iceland (if it is not a misreading for the contemporary English spelling for Ireland, a suggestion I owe to Dr Alex Woolf), but if so we know nothing of this part of his life.

d. 1054) who ruled as king in Dublin from 1038 to 1046, and who in turn was probably a nephew of the famous King Sitrinc Silkenbeard.[9] He therefore had good credentials. He seems to have made a career for himself as a mercenary and allegedly fought at Stamford Bridge (CrMi fol 32v).[10] From there he fled to Man, but nothing further is heard of him for some thirteen years or so until he eventually conquered the island for himself, about 1079, with the help of men from the other islands in the region. It is only in 1091 that Godred (or Gofraid) makes his first appearance in Dublin. The annals of 'Tigernach' have simply, in an entry recounting the events of this year, *'Gofraid mac mic Arailt rí Átha Cliath* (Gofraid son of the son of Harald king of Dublin)', which seems to mean that he assumed the kingship of the city at that date. If the Manx chronicle is to be believed, Gofraid 'subdued Dublin and a great part of Leinster *(subiugauit sibi dubliniam & magnam partem laynestir)'* (CrMi fol. 33r.), patently an exaggeration, but it may record a tradition that he had gained control not merely over the city of Dublin but over the full extent of its hinterland, *Fine Gall* (north County Dublin), with, possibly, suzerainty over some neighbouring territories.

Gofraid Méránach lasted only a few years in Dublin. The Annals of Inisfallen say of 1094 that there was 'Great warfare in [this] year between Ua Briain and the northern half of Ireland, and Gofraid, king of Dublin'. This seems to be a significant statement: it marks Gofraid out as a man apart. He was not simply one of the small fry making up the host of Muirchertach Ua Briain's enemies: the partisan Munster chronicle reveals the perception of those in the latter province that its king faced a war on two fronts, a land army made up of many of the kings of the north of Ireland (led by his chief opponent, the Ulster king Domnall Mac Lochlainn of Cenél nEógain) and a battle-hardened naval force from the Irish Sea region allied to them under (Gofraid). In the struggle, Muirchertach's forces expelled Gofraid from Dublin (AFM s.a. 1094; cf AU; AClon; AI.). He died in Islay in the following year (CrMi fol. 33v.), which may suggest that Ua Briain was able to oust him from Man as well. In his obit, Gofraid is called by the annals compiled by the Four Masters *'tighearna Gall Átha Cliath & na nInnsedh* (lord of the foreigners of Dublin and of the Isles)'. The Inisfallen annalist also calls him *rig Átha Cliath & Inse Gall* (king of Dublin and of the Isles). This is a title granted, as noted above, to Diarmait mac Máel na mBó in one set of annals, but, as far as I am aware, no other person ever bore it. That is not to say that no other person ever exercised kingship simultaneously in both Dublin and the Isles; many of those whom the Irish annals classify simply as *'rí Gall* (king of the foreigners)' clearly did. But its use in both these late eleventh-century cases may be by way of emphasis. In the case of Diarmait, the annalist appears to be stressing his achievement in extending his authority into the Isles. As for Gofraid, it was this Islesman's accession to power in Dublin that was the important point.

---

[9]Sitriuc had a brother Harald (d. 999): AU. Godred's Irish background probably accounts also for his soubriquet (in the Manx chronicle) 'Crovan', which appears Gaelic, though in Irish sources he is referred to as Méránach'. The late Brian Ó Cuív is the only scholar to attempt to explain the connexion, if any, between the two (*méaránach* from *méar,* 'a finger', *crovan* from *crobh-bhán,* 'of the white hand'): 'A poem in praise of Raghnall, king of Man', *Éigse,* 8 (1957), 283-301. See also Broderick (1980).

[10]It is just possible that he formed part of an Irish contingent there, if Adam of Bremen is right (which may be doubted) in saying that a *rex Hiberniae* was killed in the battle: M.G.H. Scriptores, VII, 356; (Anderson 1922, II, 16, n. 4.)

Dramatic developments followed Gofraid's death. It was apparently at this point that all the noblemen of the Isles sent an embassy to Muirchertach Ua Briain, 'requesting that he send some worthy man of royal stock to act as regent until Olaf, son of Gofraid, came of age'; he willingly agreed, and sent a certain Domnall son of Tadc (CrMi fol.33v).[11] This is a development of some importance. That the king of Munster or any other Irish king should have a role in the provision of a king of the Isles is all but unique. It may be partly the consequence of Muirchertach's stature abroad; it is more likely to have arisen from a position of authority in the region which he had lately attained.[12] Domnall son of Tadc was Muirchertach's nephew and his decision to send him to the Isles sits ill with what we know of the earlier opposition which the sons of Tadc had shown to Muirchertach. Furthermore, the Irish annals have no mention of these developments.[13] But the claim has one important piece of corroboration: an Amlaíb (Olaf) son of Tadc was killed in Man in the following year (AFM s.a. 1096). This is Domnall's brother,[14] and his death in conflict on the Isle of Man surely reflects the brothers' efforts to gain control of the island. In any case, whatever the circumstances of Domnall's elevation to kingship in the Isles, what matters is not so much *when* he ruled there (and whether he had Muirchertach's approval) as that he did so at all. It was a remarkable episode - the culmination of a period of rapid intensification of Irish dominance in the region - and boded ill for those for whom such a development would be unwelcome. That was a surprisingly large body of opinion which included the kings of England and Scotland, the Uí Briain's opponents within Ireland, and the would-be suzerain of the Isles, the king of Norway.

It was possibly this Irish intrusion into the region that brought King Magnus Barelegs of Norway west in 1098. Several sources of Irish, Scandinavian, Welsh, Manx and Anglo-Norman origin are in agreement in citing his activities as an act of aggression against Ireland.[15] His first western expedition was in 1098 during which he took into his hands the Orkneys and that part of the northern Scottish mainland which the earls of Orkney were used to controlling, the Western Isles (which the new Scots king, Edgar, happily ceded to him, having little or no authority there in any case), and Man. If forcing its inhabitants to provide timber for his encastellation process is any guide, he may also have exercised suzerainty over Galloway. He may too have received the submission of Gwynedd.[16] It was, on paper, a sizeable achievement, but there is no hard evidence of contact with Ireland on this occasion. In fact, if we were dependent on Irish sources alone we would not know that Magnus's first expedition ever took place. The only whiff of involvement is preserved in a record of conflict in 1098

---

[11]*'Dompnaldum filium Tadc'.*

[12]When the bishop of Dublin, Donngus Ua hAingliu, died towards the end of 1095, his successor, Samuel, was chosen by 'Murierdach, king of Ireland', along with the clergy and people (Rule 1884).

[13]AI, in fact, has Domnall son of Tadc seizing the kingship of the Isles in 1111.

[14]See note 7 above.

[15]There is an authoritative analysis of the subject in Power 1986.

[16]The Manx chronicle says that 'he sailed to Anglesey ... and subjected the island to his rule'; Norse sources relate that after defeating the Normans in Anglesey he went on to possess the whole island, 'the most southerly place where former kings of Norway had owned dominion' (The *Heimshringla* Magnus Barelegs's Saga, quoted in Anderson, 1922, II, 112). On his second expedition, Welsh sources have it, Gruffudd ap Cynan, prince of Gwynedd, provided timber for his castles (Jones 1952); for the possible practice of rendering timber as tribute, see Flanagan (1989).

between the Ulaid and 'three of the ships of the foreigners of the Isles',[17] in which the entire crews, a little over 120 men, were killed.[18]

Only on the second expedition in 1102 do Irish sources have a good deal to report of his actions. This time he seems to have come to deal specifically with the Irish. His arrival certainly frightened them. It is noticeable that the annalists see Magnus as a threat to every side in Ireland.[19] The Welsh *Brut* histories have Magnus 'hoisting his sails against the men of Scotland' obviously mistranslating the *Scottos* (= Irish) of the Latin original (Jones 1952, 25).[20] Orderic Vitalis says that Magnus 'planned an attack on the Irish (*Irenses*) and prepared a fleet of sixty ships to sail against them'.[21] His envoys, the Manx chronicle reports, told him of Ireland's beauty and fertility, and 'when Magnus heard this he thought of nothing other than to subjugate the whole of Ireland to his sway' (CrMi fol.36r). The Annals of Ulster bluntly state that in 1102 Magnus came to the Isle of Man with a great fleet and made 'a year's peace' with the Irish. This in itself is indicative of enmity, as these peaces were diplomatic devices developed to provide a breathing-space for a country where warfare was sometimes close to endemic. But implicit in the annalist's remark that he came to Man and thereupon made peace with the Irish is that arriving in Man put Magnus into an Irish context. The Four Masters add that this truce was agreed after 'the men of Ireland made a hosting to Dublin to oppose Magnus *(Sloighedh fer Éreand co hÁth Cliath i naghaidh Maghnusa)*' which is a strong hint that he had actually taken the city.[22] That the Irish compromised with him in reaching peaceful terms suggests an acknowledgement of his position there. This is precisely what Magnus Barelegs's Saga claims for him: 'King Magnus proceeded with his host to Ireland, and plundered there. Then King Muirchertach *(Myrjartak)* came to join him, and they won much of the land - Dublin and Dublinshire' (Anderson 1922, II, 127).

It is probably incorrect to see Magnus and Muirchertach as allied from the start. The effect, and presumably the original intention, of Magnus's assertion of overlordship in the Irish Sea was to circumscribe Munster's sphere of influence. From Ua Briain's point of view, the threat to Dublin was more worrying still. Furthermore, the collision course with Ua Briain upon which Magnus had entered made him the natural bedfellow of the northern king Domnall Mac Lochlainn, Muirchertach's rival for the high-kingship, with whom he was at war. But the 'year's peace' negotiated at Dublin in 1102 probably

---

[17]*'tri longa do longaibh Gall na nInnsi'*: AU; AFM s.a. 1098.

[18]This may have been in response to what Norse sources describe as having happened during Magnus's voyage south in that year: in sailing southwards by Kintyre, he 'plundered on both boards - up in Scotland, and out in Ireland. He accomplished there many great deeds in both kingdoms'. So says the *Fagrskinna*, a version of the kings' sagas, compiled in Norway in the 1220s (Clover 1982); I have again used the translation by Anderson 1922, II, 109, n. 2.

[19]Magnus and the Gaill of Lochlainn came, they tell us, to invade Ireland (*'tangattar diondradh Éreann'*: AFM); he came to take Ireland (*'do thiachtain do ghabháil Éreann'*: CS; AFM); he intended to besiege Ireland (*'fer ro triall forbais for Érinn'*: ATig).

[20]*Brut y Tywysogyon*, 25 and note.

[21]Later he tells us that 'the noble-minded king prepared an expedition against the Irish and approached the Irish coast with his fleet' (Chibnall 1969 - 80)

[22]The author of the *Annales Cambriae* (p. 35) thought so, because he believed that Magnus was eventually killed in Dublin (ed. J. Williams (London, 1860). Verses are extant which are ascribed to Magnus, referring to his Irish lover (we know that he fathered at least one son by her, Harold Gilli, who eventually succeeded him) and which say that his heart is in Dublin (Power 1986, 117, n. 1).

changed the situation and removed the threat for Ua Briain. The Four Masters claim that Ua Briain then 'gave his daughter to Sichraidh, son of Magnus, and gave him many jewels and gifts'. It is a story confirmed by Magnus Barelegs's Saga (Anderson 1922, II, 116 - 7). This marriage-alliance copperfastened Munster's Irish Sea interests. Magnus was about to withdraw to Norway but left his infant son, now Muirchertach's son-in-law, as king of the Isles: there can be little doubt as to who the real power in the region would then be. Furthermore, Ua Briain now had an ally in Magnus rather than a rival. And the latter's saga has it that after Muirchertach agreed to Magnus's taking of Dublin and Fine Gall, the Norse king spent the winter of 1102-3 with the king of Munster: 'and when spring came, the two kings with their army went west to Ulster (*Uladstir*); and they had there many battles, and won the land' (Anderson, 1922, II, 128). However, the king of Norway was killed by the men of Ulaid near the east coast of Ulster in obscure circumstances in 1103 and was buried, the Manx chronicle has it, near the church of St Patrick at Down (Power 1986, 127 - 9). His son Sigurd on hearing the news cast aside his child-bride and returned to Norway. Thus ended the period of direct Norwegian rule over the Irish Sea islands. None of their kings visited the region again for over a hundred and fifty years, though their claim to overlordship remained intact and was acknowledged to a greater or lesser extent thereafter (Johnsen 1969).

With Magnus out of the way Dublin seems to have continued to play host to the still dominant Uí Briain, and we may suppose that his death resurrected hopes of securing the Munstermen's hegemony over the Irish Sea region. In this, the prime movers were the sons of Muirchertach's brother Tadc. We hear that Domnall mac Taidc was fettered or imprisoned (*do cuibhreach*) by his uncle Muirchertach in 1107, but immediately released: critically, the deed was done in Dublin, which confirms their continued interest and presence in the area (AFM s.a. 1107). When, therefore, in 1111 Domnall mac Taidc assumed (or re-assumed) the kingship of the Isles by force (*ar égein*), we may take it that he did so against his uncle's wishes (AI s.a. 1111). But perhaps the most interesting part of the annalist's brief account is the information that Domnall 'went into the north of Ireland (*do dul ... i tuascert Hérend*)' to seize the kingdom of the Isles. Why should his invasion be initiated from there? Dublin would be the natural launching pad for any attempt to take the Isles by an individual who controlled it. It looks as if Muirchertach in taking Domnall captive in the city in 1107 put an end to his authority there. He later launched an invasion of the Isles four years on with the backing, one assumes, of Muirchertach's northern opponents. It can hardly be a surprise, therefore, to find that Muirchertach went on an expedition to Dublin in 1111, remaining there from Michaelmas (29 September) to Christmas of that year. This is most assuredly connected with his nephew's annexation of the Isles. For Muirchertach to spend a three-month period in the city must mean that he took recent developments very seriously. It must also mean that Dublin was an effective base from which not merely to monitor events but to respond. We can envisage him trying to choke off any naval or victualling assistance the Dubliners may have contemplated giving Domnall, or overseeing armed expeditions to the Isles to counter his actions. It indicates the firmness of Ua Briain's grasp on Dublin's resources, and how much the Ostmen's own independence of action had declined since the days when it had a thriving dynasty of its own at the helm: with the king of Munster in residence there for a quarter of a year, it is almost beginning to look like a home from home for Irish princes.

If Domnall mac Taidc 'forcibly' seized the kingdom of the Isles, he must have faced internal opposition there too. Olaf, Gofraid Méránach's son, died as king of the Isles in 1152, after a reign of forty years, according to the Manx chronicle. If the latter is accurate, he became king almost immediately after Domnall made his bid for power. Quite possibly Olaf was foisted on the Islesmen by a patron anxious to put paid to Irish interference there. But by whom? The Manx chronicle may again supply the answer: it says that Olaf was conducted to the Isles, by its chief men, from the court of Henry I of England, where he had presumably been raised since infancy (CrMi fol.35r).[23] If this is true (and we have no confirmation of it from elsewhere), it may have important implications. At some stage a decision was made to send Gofraid Méránach's youngest son to the Anglo-Norman court. He was presumably not a ward of court in the sense that that carries of a feudal relationship existing between England and the Isles, but his presence there may represent moves to establish a closer bond. If so, if Olaf was Henry I's protégé, the English king must have been opposed to the attempt of the Uí Briain to exert dominance over the Irish Sea islands.

Muirchertach Ua Briain fell from power when stricken by severe illness in 1114 and Domnall mac Taidc was enticed home from the Isles by the prospects of bigger fish in Munster. The personal nature of Muirchertach's dominance over Dublin was such that with his demise Munster's authority there began to melt away almost immediately. I have argued elsewhere that Henry I was more than aware of Muirchertach's potential to put a spoke in his own wheel, at least as far as his plans for Wales were concerned (Duffy 1999, 98 - 113), and one imagines that the same was true with regard to the Irish Sea region as a whole: securing the succession of his protégé Olaf to Man was one way of keeping the Irish out. And so it transpired. From this point onwards, direct Irish influence on Man was clearly on the wane. The Norse, the Scots, and the English competed with each other for control, and ultimately the latter won out.

Bibliography

Abbreviations

AI   *The annals of Inisfallen,* ed. S. MacAirt (Dublin, 1951).
AFM   *The annals of the kingdom of Ireland by the Four Masters,* ed. J O'Donovan, 7 vols (Dublin 1851).
AlCé   *The annals of Loch Cé,* ed. W. M. Hennessy (London, 1871).
ATig   *The annals of Tigernach,* ed. W. Stokes, 2 vols (Felinfach,1993).
AClon   *The annals of Clonmacnoise,* ed. D. Murphy (Dublin, 1892).
CS   *Chronicon Scotorum,* ed. W. M. Hennessy, (London, 1866).
CrMi   *Cronica regum Mannie & insularum,* ed. G. Broderick (Belfast, 1979).

---

[23] '*miserunt principes insularum propter olauum filium godredi crouan ... qui tunc temporis degebat in curia henrici regis anglie filii willelmi, & adduxerunt eum*'.

References

Anderson A O, (ed.), 1922, *Early sources of Scottish history*, 500-1286 (Edinburgh).

Broderick G, 1980, 'Irish and Welsh strands in the genealogy of Godred Crovan', *The Journal of the Manx Museum*, 8, 32-8.

Byrne F J, 1982, 'Onomastica 2: Na Renna', *Peritia*, 1, 267

Chibnall M, (ed.), 1969 - 80, *Historia ecclesiastica*, 6 vols (Oxford), V, 218-g; VI, 48-9).

Clover C J, 1982, *The medieval saga* (Ithica N.Y. and London), 170-72.

Duffy S, 1999, 'The 1169 invasion as a turning-point in Irish-Welsh relations', in *Britain and Ireland 900-1300. Insular responses to medieval European change*, ed. B. Smith (Cambridge), 98-113.

Ériu, 1992, 'Irishmen and Islesmen in the kingdoms of Dublin and Man, 1052 - 1171', 43, 93-133.

Flanagan M T, 1989, *Irish society, Anglo-Norman settlers, Angevin kingship* (Oxford), 48, n. 130.

Johnsen A O, 1969, 'The payments from the Hebrides and the Isle of Man to the crown of Norway, 1153-1263', *Scot. Hist. Rev.* 48,18-34.

Jones T, (ed.), 1952, *Brut y Tywysogyon or the chronicle of the princes: Peniarth MS 20 version*, (Cardiff).

Kenney J, 1929, *Sources for the early history of Ireland: ecclesiastical* (New York) 615.

Ó Corráin D, 1971, 'The career of Diarmait mac Máel na mBó', *Old Wexford Society Journal* 3 pt 1 p 35.

Ó Corráin D, 1972, 'The career of Diarmait mac Máel na mBó', *Old Wexford Society Journal* 4 pt 2 18 - 21.

Power R, 1986, 'Magnus Bareleg's expeditions to the west', *Scottish Historical Review*, 65, 107-32.

Rule M, (ed.), 1884, Eadmar, *Historia Novorum*, (RS, London) 73.

Simms K, 1985, *From kings to warlords* (Woodbridge), 132.

Ussher J, 1632, *Veterum epistolarum Hibernicarum sylloge* (Dublin), no. XXXIIII.

Watch and Ward on the Isle of Man: The Medieval Re-occupation of Iron Age Promontory Forts

Andrew Johnson

Introduction

The Isle of Man boasts a rich selection of archaeological sites; a combination of circumstances – a varied topography and a relative lack of intensive farming techniques being most significant – has resulted in an historic landscape preserving up to 8000 years of human activity, from the Mesolithic down to the present day.

Amongst the most distinctive classes of site are the promontory forts which utilise the jagged and rocky character of much of the Island's periphery: around 20 sites are known (e.g., Bersu 1949, 77-9[1]). It is likely that additional sites once existed, but these may have been lost along the north-west and north-east coastlines where cliffs of glacially deposited sands and clays are vulnerable to erosion (Figure 1). A small number of these promontories have been investigated (Bersu *ibid;* Gelling 1952, 1957, 1959), leading to a view that several, apparently Iron Age in origin, were re-occupied in the Medieval period for domestic purposes. Although relatively few of these forts have been excavated, there is a general presumption that as a phenomenon they are Iron Age in date. This conjecture may be worthy of timely reconsideration.

A previous paper by the author (Johnson 2000), speculating on the possible antecedents of the Manx farmstead, inevitably referred to these sites, as they are amongst the only lowland examples of Medieval occupation to have been excavated on Man. It was, however, proposed that, far from being domestic structures, these sites were instead associated with the Medieval coastal defence of the Island known as the Watch and Ward.

---

[1]Bersu lists 21 sites. The Isle of Man National Monuments Record currently lists 22 forts, and a further 10 possible sites.

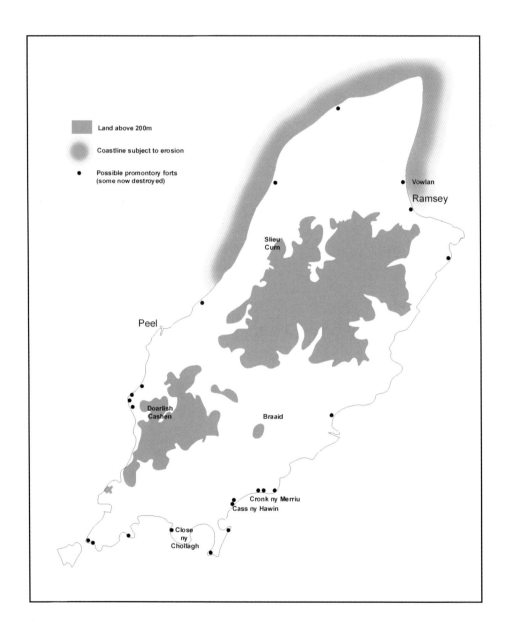

Figure 1: The Isle of Man: promontory forts and placements.

Vowlan

The first site to be archaeologically investigated was that of Vowlan near Ramsey in the north-east of the Island. The excavator successfully revealed the remains of six buildings (Bersu *ibid*), several of them overlying each other, constructed on a sandy promontory overlooking the much-altered estuary of the Sulby River (a seventh structure was much smaller and stratigraphically later than the others, which led its excavator to ignore it in his interpretation of the site).

The buildings survived as little more than shadows in the sandy soil; linear trenches suggested to the excavator that wattle walls were bedded in the ground, sometimes, according to the published plans, packed with stones. Overall, the structures were rectangular in form; a linear hearth lay along the long axis, and there was evidence that the interior was divided to form a central aisle (in which the hearth lay) with a further aisle to either side along both long walls. Subsequent excavations at the promontory forts described below would suggest that these were wide 'benches' for sitting and sleeping on. The largest building was 10.5 by 4.6m, the smallest 7.4 by 3.4m (all measurements are internal); due in part to the clear presence of a hearth in all six of the buildings, all were considered domestic structures rather than animal houses. An additional area of burnt material, 1m in diameter, was found towards the edge of the promontory, and interpreted as an open-air hearth. A very little burnt clay and some splinters of calcined bone were found in the hearths, which were noted to be quite deep, often containing up to 500mm of ash. No artefacts whatsoever were recovered. Bersu interpreted the site as temporary quarters, re-occupied on several occasions, belonging to guards left behind by Viking raiding parties whose longships were drawn up on the beach.

Until post-Medieval times, when riverine erosion, longshore coastal drift, and the need to develop a modern harbour for the settlement of Ramsey resulted in the abandonment of the old riverbed, the headland at Vowlan would have guarded the mouth of the Sulby River. In the light of this clear topographical relationship, and in view of the subsequent excavation of other defended promontories, Bersu's interpretation of the purpose of the site is worthy of re-examination.

In the following decade, Peter Gelling also uncovered rectangular buildings of Medieval date, this time within promontory forts at Cronk ny Merriu, Cass ny Hawin and Close ny Chollagh. Unlike Vowlan, all of these sites also provided clear evidence for earlier origins.

Cronk ny Merriu

Of the three sites, Cronk ny Merriu provided the best-preserved house structure (Gelling 1952). The house measured 11 by 4.3m internally, and had stone-faced walls. These were 1.2 to 1.5m thick, and were filled with an earth core. It appeared from the position and quantity of collapsed facing stone that the walls had been higher on the inside, and that the roof slope had continued across the thickness of the walls to within approximately 0.6m of ground-level on the outside. A reconstruction exercise at the time of the excavation, based on the available collapsed debris, suggested that the interior wall facing may have stood as high as 1.4m above floor level. Raised benches were set along the long walls and possibly across one end wall. These had been formed by leaving the natural soil undisturbed and excavating down to create a sunken floor level; the earth benches were revetted with stones set on edge. Two original doors were positioned towards the end of the long walls opposite each other (a third in one gable was believed to be later). There was slight and inconclusive evidence for a hearth, but the presence of a few fire-crazed stones in the floor implies that either cooking or heating may occasionally have occurred. Fired stones were also found towards the outer part of the promontory, together with a very few pieces of bone found within a posthole in the same area. Unfortunately, it is nowhere unequivocally stated that this intermittent occupation deposit was considered contemporary with the long house.

Although a dark brown earth (contrasting against the undisturbed reddish brown material from which the benches were formed) covered the floor area between the benches, and probably represents an occupation deposit, no artefacts were found except for a few fragments of broken quernstone built into the walls, and a quartzite cobble, which may have been used as a hammerstone. All of these may have related to the earlier occupation of the site, most obviously represented by the rampart and ditch on the landward side of the promontory; associated with this was a line of postholes, which appears to have supported a fighting platform. No structural evidence for actual domestic occupation predating the house was found. It was clear, however, that the rampart was in a dilapidated state when the rectangular house was built, and so predated it.

No clearly datable artefacts relating to the construction and occupation of the house were uncovered, forcing the excavator to suggest an occupation falling within a 10-12th century time frame. A few years later, when embarking upon excavation at Close ny Chollagh, the house at Cronk ny Merriu was described as 'a permanent house of Viking type ... built on a small promontory whose defensive rampart was already ruinous in Viking times' (Gelling 1957, 571). Almost two decades subsequent to excavation, however, a silver penny of Edward I was found by chance close to the rampart. Whilst this find has no archaeological context, its presence on the site must be considered in the light of the proposal put forward below that some at least of the forts were re-used for the purpose of coastal defence.

Close ny Chollagh

Cronk ny Merriu was investigated because of the obvious presence on the ground of a rectangular structure, which, it was hoped, would permit the investigation of remains more substantial than the shadows in the sand so painstakingly recovered by Bersu at Vowlan a few years earlier, and the chance to find better evidence by which to date this class of site. The lack of positive dating evidence led a year later to the investigation of another promontory within which there were again surface indications of a long house similar to that at Cronk ny Merriu; this was the site of Close ny Chollagh (Gelling *ibid*). It was hoped that the site would not only produce more precise evidence for the date of the Viking occupation of these promontories, but also demonstrate to what period the defences belonged, if once again they turned out to be earlier.

Close ny Chollagh is not a natural promontory, but was made defensible by excavating a ditch from the inland end of a deep, narrow sea-cut inlet on the south side of the site: the spoil from the ditch was used to create a substantial rampart, which was faced in stone. The defences were constructed to protect a group of four stone-built roundhouses occupied into the 1st century AD; the rampart was in a very collapsed condition by the time a Medieval rectangular building was constructed (Figure 2). The long south wall of this building, together with the east gable, were created by simply cutting back into the rear side of the rampart and revetting the exposed earth bank with stone. The walls survived in places to a height of three courses, perhaps 0.6m high.[2] The west gable took advantage of a natural rib in the bedrock; only the north wall was an entirely new structure. This survived to one or two courses in height, and was characterised by neat stone facings and a stone and earth core; it was 1.2m thick. A single doorway was positioned towards the west end.

Internally, the building measured 12.5 by 5m, and was the largest of the three coastal houses to be excavated by Gelling. Evidence for internal arrangements was scantier than at Cronk ny Merriu: a narrow bench only 400mm deep lay along the length of the south wall, and an irregular spread of four postholes led the excavator to suggest that the roof was supported as and when it showed signs of weakness or collapse, and even that it might have been single-pitch, sloping back into the rampart. There appear not to have been substantial quantities of collapsed wall material, and this is confirmed by photographs in the excavation archive. It is tempting to suggest that, unless systematic robbing subsequently took place (which would have had to be of this structure in favour of all others on the site, including the easily accessible rampart facing), the building may perhaps have never been particularly high or substantial. There was no sign of a hearth within the house, and at no point was such a feature, or even an area of burning, recorded anywhere else within the site at levels relating to the Medieval occupation.

Three other poorly built structures, interpreted as outbuildings, lay within the area enclosed by the rampart, all of them stratigraphically above the Iron Age roundhouses, and therefore not unreasonably judged to be broadly contemporary with the long house.

The most substantial of these structures comprised a 1m thick curved wall built into the angle of the rampart at the north-west corner of the site, enclosing an area approximately 7 by 3.6m. Between this structure and the long house, the incomplete remains of a circular stone building were recorded, whilst a single line of stones set on edge in the south-west corner of the enclosure suggested another, insubstantial building relying on the existing rampart for the remainder of its walls. The circular building was both stratigraphically higher, and far less substantially built, than most of the Iron Age roundhouses, and was therefore not ascribed to this earlier period; its close proximity to the single entrance to the long house is, however, somewhat uncomfortable and may therefore imply some unidentified subtlety in the site's chronology. Lastly, a set of stone steps, again well above Iron Age levels, led up onto the seaward rampart. There is certainly room to doubt that these structures were indeed contemporary with the house.

No datable finds could be ascribed to the Medieval occupation. It was considered that only the form of the long house and its vestigial bench (which was far narrower

---

[2]This estimate is derived from unpublished photographs included in the excavation archive.

Figure 2: Excavation photograph of Close ny Chollagh
(credit: Manx National Heritage).

and less pronounced that either Vowlan or Cronk ny Merriu) gave any clue of Scandinavian antecedents. As a result, a 12th, and more probably a 13th, century date was proposed for the occupation. The excavator was later even to consider the structural characteristics of the house so 'attenuated' as to opine that a 14th century date might be more appropriate (Gelling 1959, 38).[3]

Cass ny Hawin

Since excavation of Close ny Chollagh had not revealed a building of clearly Scandinavian style, a third promontory fort was investigated, this time at Cass ny Hawin (Gelling *ibid*). Here excavation revealed a single rectangular house orientated west-east: no other contemporary structures were met with. The floor of the house was created by digging down to the bedrock. This had been worked to achieve a fairly level surface, and was cut slightly lower in the centre to give the effect of benches along either side and across each end; the benches were between 0.8 and 1.5m wide. The interior of the house measured 9.5 by 4.5m. Beyond this cleared area of bedrock, the walls of the house were with difficulty identified in the trench sections: they were completely devoid of stonework, and appeared to have consisted entirely of turf. From the evidence of the trench sections, the walls of the house were approximately 2.4m thick; they survived to a height of no more than 0.25m, and must have been very much eroded.

Two entrances were identified, opening to the north and south close to the east end of the building. There must be some doubt as to the former, as it opens precipitously onto the northern edge of the promontory; upon investigation, the underlying rock in the cliff face does not appear unusually unstable, and there seems little reason to propose a major rockfall in the intervening centuries. The northerly entrance was not investigated further, but the southerly entrance was excavated completely, revealing a short passage through the thick turf side-wall which turned eastward through ninety degrees once outside. Two post holes marked the end of the passage, implying a doorway. Both doorway and passage are designed to avoid the prevailing wind.

Other than the nascent benches formed from the bedrock, evidence for internal arrangements was limited to six postholes and two concentrations of burnt material. Of the latter, one, positioned centrally, comprised a deep deposit of ash, under which the bedrock had been discoloured, indicating quite substantial use. The ash spread across an area of 2.4 by 0.4m, and although no kerbstones were found, was apparently clearly defined. On one of the benches, an area of burnt clay and ash, containing a potsherd, was found, and interpreted as the possible remains of a small, collapsed, oven.

---

[3]It is clear from the published report that the excavator was predisposed to consider the site as a farmstead, comprising a house and outbuildings. 'The people who lived in this farmstead were probably descendants of Viking settlers. They bred sheep, pigs and possibly goats, but there was nothing to suggest that they raised any kind of crop. The flesh of their domestic animals provided part, at least, of their diet, and bones were found scattered all over the floor of the house, with particular accumulations at the foot of both short walls. It may be conjectured that they fished, and they certainly ate shell-fish - periwinkle, limpet and dog-whelk - in considerable quantities. It is not clear where they did their cooking, as there was no trace of a hearth inside the house.' (Gelling 1957, 575). Very few bones and shells from the excavation were retained, and it is difficult to judge whether or not they represent a truly domestic midden.

The postholes were arranged in an orderly manner (in contrast to Close ny Chollagh), two close to the west end, and four near the east end not far from the doorways. It is possible that the posts in these positions supported and bolstered roof frames subjected to sideways pressures from a hipped roof, and that those towards the east end additionally had to support arrangements for a roof structure over the entrance (or entrances if the northerly doorway is accepted).

As well as the hearth, defined by a 'mound of ash' (Gelling *ibid*, 35), a thin deposit of ash and heated stones extended from the hearth to the doorways. In this was found the majority of the potsherds from the site. More than twenty sherds, separated into three broad types were found, including the locally-produced granite tempered ware (Barton 1999, 228). Other finds included an incomplete pair of iron shears and an iron missile head; both of these were recovered from the occupation deposit. Six other pieces of iron, two pieces of copper alloy, and some fragments of lead slag were also recovered, none of which were identifiable as artefacts. As was originally proposed, a date as early as the 13th century is still quite feasible for those finds which are datable, such as the pottery (Davey pers. comm.), and hence for the house as well, but equally both pottery and the long-lasting design of the shears allow for a slightly more recent date.

Discussion

Clearly, Gelling was predisposed to thinking that these sites were domestic, and, particularly where additional structures occurred as at Close ny Chollagh, that they represented farmsteads. The objections to such use are several.

Firstly, there is little midden material from any of the three sites, with the possible exception of Close ny Chollagh. Even here the bones and shellfish were apparently confined to the house - there is no record of any being found outside the house from Medieval levels. One might have expected at least a diffuse spread of material to have been found across the interior of the promontory fort if it were being used as a domestic site. At Cass ny Hawin there was no sign of an occupation deposit, nor of other features, outside the house. Here it was presumed that any remains of the former had been eroded, but one feels that there equally well need never have been any. The occupation deposit outside the long house at Cronk ny Merriu is not specifically ascribed to the same period as the house. In any case, its spread was discontinuous, and consisted almost entirely of fire-crazed stones; they were not particularly numerous. In short, the lack of clear midden deposits is problematic if the sites are to be interpreted as permanently occupied farmsteads. Whether or not one proposes that rubbish was usually deposited over the edge of each promontory, the general lack of at least some domestic finds spread across the ground at these sites is difficult to accept, unless the sites were in fact used in a different way.

Secondly, although it must be said that rural Medieval sites on the Island have been shown, from limited excavation, to be quite poor in total finds, the lack of a broad range of artefacts is also worrying. Pottery from Cass ny Hawin totals approximately 20 sherds, representing only a few vessels. Only this site produced metal objects during excavation, including the broken pair of shears and the missile head. Furthermore, the date of those few finds which have been made is significant. Those from Cass ny

Hawin are no earlier than the 13th century; meanwhile, Cronk ny Merriu has an apparent casual loss - a late 13th century silver penny - which whilst unstratified, is enough to emphasise that this site at least was visited at a time when Scandinavian influence was declining. In short, these sites were apparently being used at a time when Scandinavian influence was either at least well established, or perhaps actually waning.

Thirdly, hearths are not consistently present - only at Vowlan are they a feature of every house, and of the other three sites described, only Cass ny Hawin has clear evidence for repeated hearth use - and here there was no stone kerb. This most basic domestic feature should be consistently present if these sites are to be interpreted as homesteads or farmsteads.

Fourthly, the issue of location is also problematic. None of these sites can possibly be described as choice sites for farmsteads: exposed locations, poor access and lack of direct water supply all militate against their suitability. With the possible exception of Close ny Chollagh, where additional structures have been interpreted as outbuildings (although stratigraphic evidence is only that they postdate the Iron Age round houses), there is none of the infrastructure one would expect of a fully functional farmstead.[4]

Lastly, to a greater or lesser extent, all of the structures betray imperfections in build quality, care, design or features. The house at Close ny Chollagh takes advantage of the rampart for two of its walls (despite access to good building stone), has rather ad hoc arrangements for supporting the roof, no hearth, and only one narrow bench. At Cronk ny Merriu, there is no clear hearth, but the building is probably the best constructed example to have been investigated, and it has clearly defined benches; despite this, headroom appears to have been rather mean. Cass ny Hawin has an adequate hearth, rather basic benches, a sophisticated entrance, yet is built of rather temporary materials, despite easy access to excellent building stone. The timber houses at Vowlan are somewhat irregular in plan, though the provision of benches and hearths is consistently fulfilled.

Vowlan is unusual in that timber is an unlikely building material in a Manx context, although it should be noted that quarried stone is relatively in short supply in this part of the Island, due to its formation from glacial debris. There would, however, have been no shortage of turf and beach stones from which to build structures more typical of the local idiom. The presence here of postholes and foundation trenches 300-500mm across imply a post and timber sill-beam method of construction rather than Bersu's proposed wattle construction. One might infer that the buildings were more strongly and lastingly built than Bersu supposed, befitting the hearth pits filled to a depth of 500mm with charcoal and ash, which, it is contended, are too substantial for the fleetingly occupied guardhouses their excavator believed them to be. It is interesting that Bersu does not record any substantial humic deposits between any of the building levels, which suggests that the buildings could have been replaced immediately and consecutively, with little or no time elapse between. If anything, the site may have been occupied consistently and for a quite considerable length of time, if these buildings are to have had time to decay and be replaced.

---

[4]At Cass ny Hawin, a group of postholes was found beneath the east gable of the house, and another group were identified beneath the south-west corner of the house: all therefore securely predated the occupation associated with the long house.

It is important to note that at the time of Gelling's excavation campaign on the promontory forts, the opportunity of examining two inland farmsteads at the Braaid and Doarlish Cashen had not been taken.

In 1962 he re-investigated and re-interpreted the Braaid as a farmstead comprising a dwelling house and byre (Gelling 1964). The former was an enormous structure - by Manx standards - 20m long by 8m wide internally, with stone and earth side walls 2m thick, and gable walls of turf or turf and timber. A second structure stands just downslope from the house, 16.5m long and 6m wide, this time with straight long walls, and interpreted as a beast house with rudimentary stone stalls. A stone-built roundhouse is close by, and, whilst it is considered to be of the earlier indigenous building tradition, it is believed to have remained in use when the long houses were built. Unlike the promontory sites, the Braaid has the necessary attributes to be a substantial Viking period farmstead, provided with a house (so large it perhaps merits being called a hall) and a separate byre. Nevertheless, the site was abandoned, possibly for complicated reasons discussed elsewhere (Johnson *ibid,* 55-7).

Doarlish Cashen is the only Medieval upland farmstead yet to have been the subject of published archaeological investigation (Gelling 1970). The site comprised a group of perhaps ten structures associated with a field system. Three of the structures were excavated, and interpreted as a small rectangular house (measuring 7 by 3m internally), a corn-drying kiln, and an animal shelter. The site has recently been reconsidered at some length (Johnson *ibid,* 57-60). It is by no means certain that all of the ten structures originally identified need be contemporary; nevertheless, the arrangement of several of the buildings and their relationship to the nearby boundaries is a compelling illustration of how a Medieval farmstead might have been arranged - and is rather more complicated than allowed for within the restricted promontory sites.[5]

Although finds at Doarlish Cashen were severely restricted, a single sherd of very dark grey unglazed pottery, recovered from the floor deposit in the house, may still shed some additional light on the date of the farmstead through its similarity to material found on the slopes of Slieu Curn overlooking Glen Dhoo in the north-west of the Island. Here, a number of features have recently been surveyed; one of these features (Davey *et al.* 1997, 11, Site 15) has since been investigated, revealing a rectangular building with turf walls and containing three separate hearths. Samples from stratigraphically the earliest and latest of the hearths produced calibrated radiocarbon dates from the early and late thirteenth century.[6] As the latest hearth also produced fragments of burnt pottery reminiscent of the material from Doarlish Cashen, these dates are a welcome confirmation of the likely age of the latter site, despite dissimilarities in construction and internal arrangement. The house on Slieu Curn contained no signs of benches, nor revetting for such structures, and the hearths were well defined rather than spread across the floor.[7]

---

[5]Although not conclusive by itself, recent study by the writer of aerial photographs has revealed no crop-mark evidence to suggest either field systems or additional buildings formerly associated with these sites (1:7500 colour photographic survey by BKS, undertaken April - August, 2000, Manx National Heritage Library reference PG 7304).

[6]750 ± 40BP (laboratory reference AA-28386) and 830 ± 40BP (lab. ref. AA-28387). Both dates are quoted here in uncalibrated form.

[7]Excavation has proved this structure to be stratigraphically later than the field boundary next to it, but additional survey has since suggested that the field system in this area is more extensive and complex

An Alternative Interpretation

The re-use of earlier promontory forts for domestic purposes by Scandinavian settlers wary of unfriendly indigenous neighbours would be more acceptable if more of the sites showed evidence for this. Since so few of the forts apparently contain suitable remains that can be interpreted in this manner, however, there must be some doubt whether there actually existed a need for such precautions. Certainly, on the evidence of excavation, Cronk ny Merriu, Cass ny Hawin, and Close ny Chollagh all have rectangular buildings. Meanwhile, Boirane, a site north of Dalby Point on the west coast of the Island, has been noted for surface remains suggesting a building in the interior, though these are now difficult to interpret. This is, however, out of a score of promontory fortifications generally believed to be Iron Age in origin.

If the re-occupied promontories did not serve as domestic sites defensible to landward, there seems little justification for them to be put back into use again unless it were for more strategic reasons. If instead the sites excavated by Bersu and Gelling are considered from the perspective of providing coastal defence, a rather different picture emerges. Those forts investigated by Gelling provide an interesting illustration of the practicality of providing a coastal watch along the south-east and southern edge of the Island. Cronk ny Merriu (Figure 3) overlooks Port Grenaugh, the only possible landfall on a rocky stretch of coastline; Cass ny Hawin likewise guards the mouth of the Santon Burn, another suitable landing spot on a dangerous coast. In contrast, Close ny Chollagh instead provides a perfect view across the whole of Bay ny Carrickey, the shore of which would have been usable under most tidal conditions.

Cronk ny Merriu and Cass ny Hawin are both visible from Hango Brooch, a small fortification on the east coast of Langness which guards Derbyhaven, a sheltered tidal bay well suited to longships.[8] Recent excavation (Doonan et al 2001, 42-4) suggests that Hango Brooch may have been used as a beacon, and quantities of charred gorse, suitable as highly flammable kindling, have been recovered from a deliberately excavated fire pit. One wonders whether Bersu's open-air hearth at Vowlan might also have served a similar purpose.[9]

In applying these considerations to the west coast of the Island south of Peel, we find that Boirane, its surface remains not proved by excavation, combines a fine observation position with sufficient proximity to one of the few landing places along this stretch of coast. Two, perhaps three, more earthworks are recorded in the vicinity, between them providing very adequate coastal defence. Two of them, and one other a few miles away, are called Boirane (or its derivatives), a word used to refer to historical earthworks (Garrad 1990; Thomson 1992). The proximity and inter-visibility of these sites begs tantalising but as yet unanswerable questions about the existence of a system of coastal protection, and the time at which this may have existed, if indeed they are all of similar date.

---

than first thought (Johnson forthcoming). The complexity of remains associated with the Slieu Curn structure is in contrast to the promontory forts.

[8]The harbour features several times in the Chronicle of the Kings of Man and the Isles and was clearly both vulnerable and a favoured landing place for invaders and pirates.

[9]1070 ± 50BP (laboratory reference Beta-154618) and 1280 ± 50BP (lab. ref. Beta-154617). Both dates are quoted here in uncalibrated form. The dates are, however, very early in the context of this discussion, and may relate to an early example of a watch beacon, or indeed a structure of some completely different purpose.

Figure 3: Aerial photograph of Cronk ny Merriu
(credit: Manx National Heritage)

Another site, in the south-west of the Island, offers a further tantalising illustration of how a coastal system of watch and ward may have extended around this particularly difficult and secluded stretch of coastline. The site of Burroo Ned lies on a forbidding headland protected to landward by natural topography and a 150m long rampart. Within it lie the unexcavated and ephemeral remains of several sub-circular buildings, and one rectilinear structure. Sockets in exposed areas of bedrock are thought to represent the foundations for signalling posts. It is tempting to see Burroo Ned as a vantage point from which to observe not only the neighbouring coastline (itself almost impenetrable because of cliffs and tides) but also the nearby Calf of Man, an islet which for many years was the preserve of the Lords of Man and which was potentially more vulnerable.[10] At the first sign of danger, any such signal post would have been visible from the intervening high ground to the north-east, and a warning could thence be relayed on to the remainder of the Island's defenders.

Coastal defence - the watch and ward phenomenon - on the Isle of Man has been discussed by Cubbon (1930) and Megaw (1941), their work given impetus by the rediscovery of a document of 1627 listing the wardens for the day- and night-watches, and the locations where those on duty were to muster.[11] They were able to suggest locations for the majority of the sites from which a coastal watch was kept, day and night (Figure 4). The list is reproduced (Figure 5).[12] Of particular interest is that, whilst the daytime watchers were positioned on 'hills for day watch' giving elevated views out to sea, the night watch was kept at 'hills and ports for night watch' - sometimes from hills, but more often from, or close to, ports or, more precisely, potential landing places.

It must not be forgotten that the 1627 document records a system based on the sixteen coastal parishes, at that time in existence for about five hundred years, operating at a period long after the apparent time at which the various promontory forts were being re-used. Not unreasonably, however, both authors infer that the principle of watch and ward had been in existence from very much earlier times. Only Cubbon (1983, 18-19) and Bersu (1968, 88) have since tentatively suggested that the re-occupied promontory forts might be part of a coastal defence system. Quite reasonably, Cubbon *(ibid)* included the unusual structure initially interpreted by its excavator as a

---

[10]The Calf of Man was off limits to the Manx, and used by the Lords of Man for hunting. Its defence continued to prove a headache, resulting in the creation of at least two batteries of cannon there during the 1600s (Curphey 1967, 56).

[11]Castle Rushen Papers, Manx National Heritage Library reference CA1 Box 6 1600-1627.

[12]Notes relating to Fig. 5.

The text has been left unmodernised. Names in italics are not otherwise known. Some modern alternatives have been added ([ ]) to allow easier location.

Cronk Mooar and Knock y Dooney are prominent pagan Viking burial mounds.

Cronk ny Arrey Laa ('hill of the day watch') occurs in the parishes of Jurby, Bride and Rushen (twice). The name is not mentioned in the 1627 document, and may postdate it.

Cubbon (1930) identifies certain of the sites by looking at contemporary landownership evidence for the wardens. This is reflected in the locations marked on Fig. 4.

No relevant 17th century archaeological remains are known to relate to these sites, but Cass ny Hawin and Hango Broogh are convenient for Ronaldsway; Close ny Chollagh for Scarlett and Pooilvaaish; and Cronk ny Merriu for Port Grenaugh.

Although provision is made for more than one night port in the parishes of Maughold, Lonan and Malew, this is far from adequate on the ground.

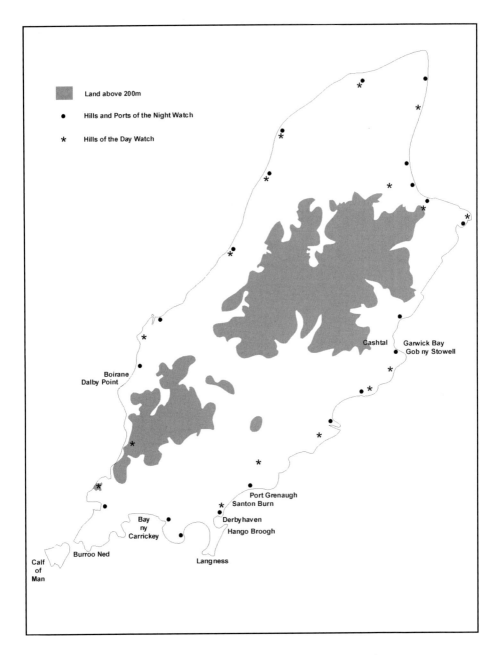

Figure 4: The Isle of Man: watch and ward stations and placenames.

A pfect Remembrance conteyning all the names of
the wardens both of the day and night watches throghout
the Isle of Man together with the names of evry
pishe and place where the watches are kept.
Ao dni 1627

Pishes	wardens for day watch	hills for day watch	wardens for night watch	hills and ports for night watch
Patr [Patrick}	Jo: Crosse	Knockaloe	Henry Ratclif	*Orestill*
Germa [German]	Wm Bridson	Knockaloe	Wm Bridson	Peeletowne [Peel] Trybane (crossed out) [Whitestrand]
Michaell [Michael]	Jo: Cayne	Borodaill [Glen Mooar]	Jo: Cannon	Borodaill [Glen Mooar]
Ballal [Ballaugh]	Sr Nich: Thompson	*Whetston hill*	Phill Corleod	*Whetston hill*
Jureby [Jurby]	Wm Clarke	Knockmore [Cronk Mooar]	Wm Clarke	Knockmore [Cronk Mooar]
Andreas	ffinlo Mrtin	Sonday hill [Knock e Dooney]	ffinlo Mrtin	Sonday hill [Knock e Dooney]
Bryde [Bride]	Wm Cowle	*Blew hill*	David Xpin	Cranstall port [Cranstal] *Dease hill* (crossed out)
Kk: Christ Ayre [Lezayre]	Jo: Curghie	Scayhold [Sky Hill]	Demster Xpin	Hangmans hill [Vowlan]
Magald [Maughold]	Ro: Xpin Jn Ro: Christian	Slewlage [Slieau Lewaigue] St Maghalds head [Maughold Head]	Ro: Xpin Jn Ro: Xpin Sen Tho: Xpi	*Ronaige* Port Donan [Dhyrnane] Ramsey
Lonan	Phil Moore	*Sr Wms hill*	James Kermod Phill Moore	Laxsey [Laxey] Gob Stoell [Gob Stowell]
Conchan [Onchan]	Tho: Bancks Ric Scarisbreck	Howe [Howstrake] Carnane	Tho: Bancks Ric Scarisbreck	port Conchan [Onchan Harbour] Duglas towne [Douglas]
Sanctan [Santon]	Xpher Brew	Knockloghan [Knock y Laughan]	Jo: Moore	Gren Vicke [Port Grenaugh]
Mallow [Malew]	nil	Barrow (crossed out) [The Broogh]	Demstr Xpin Wm. Pickard	Reynoldsway [Ronaldsway] Scarlett
Arbery [Arbory]	Jo: Cubon	*Echewle*	Geo.Symen	Polbash [Pooillvaaish]
Kk Christ Russhen [Rushen]	Danold Duke	Bradoe [Bradda]	Gilbt Nelson	port Yrne [Port Erin]

Figure 5: Watch and ward stations in 1627 (Castle Rushen Papers, MNHL ref CA1 Box 6 1600-1627).

period grain store (Bersu 1967) but later reassessed as a house of the same period[13] at the Cashtal, Ballagawne, despite its location some distance from the shore. This site, and its purpose, would benefit from reassessment.

Given the location of these promontories overlooking, or close to, sheltered inlets and river mouths, it is reasonable to view them as part of a system based more on a pragmatic need to watch those points on the coast where a raider might land than on a rigid requirement to muster a group of guards from each parish. Certainly Cronk ny Merriu is a clear candidate for the 1627 Santon port for the night watch located at 'Gren Vicke' (today's Port Grenaugh), whilst Vowlan could meet the same criterion for Lezayre's 'Hangman's hill'. Under a pre-parochial system, if one is to be postulated, Cass ny Hawin would also have provided a very necessary guard at a river mouth, whilst Close ny Chollagh would have secured a wide and vulnerable bay - until the delineation of Arbory and Malew left it in the 'wrong' parish.[14] Whether the Cashtal, Ballagawne, situated 750m from a landing spot at the mouth of the Garwick stream, can be regarded as sufficiently close to the coast to fit the pattern is questionable; what is not in doubt is the perceived need as late as 1627 to mount a night guard at Gob ny Stowell on the south side of Garwick Bay, close to a small beach which continued in use with crofting fishermen until the nineteenth century despite a complete lack of harbour works.

A strategic approach to watch and ward, when applied to the intricate and varied coastline of the Isle of Man, would surely result in a response which sought to protect those parts of the coast that were vulnerable to seaborne attack. As is implied by the foregoing, sandy beaches, sheltered havens and secluded inlets and river mouths all fall into this category, particularly whilst the easily beached longship and galley were the principal means of travel. By the 17th century, ships were of rather different character, requiring more often than not a specially constructed quayside; let it not be forgotten, however, that land attacks using ships' boats meant that those less accessible coastlines were still as vulnerable as before.

Perhaps the document of 1627 has unduly influenced consideration of Medieval and post-Medieval coastal defence on the Island, and has led to an expectation that the watch would be kept at one specific location per parish (or more in a few exceptional circumstances as it indeed acknowledges). What should now be clear is that this would have been inadequate for the practical protection of the coastline, and that instead the watch would have been maintained from those locations where it was necessary. It is also salutary to consider the extent to which the Island's north-west and north-east coastlines have altered since the 1627 document was written, for whilst Cubbon's (1930) identification of hills and ports for the day and night watches can point us towards the general location of the most significant mustering points, we should not be too confident of being able to identify every location where Manxmen once shivered through the night keeping a watch for unwelcome visitors. Certainly where the rockier coastlines of the Island have withstood the sea better, we can be more confident of

---

[13]See notes by Cubbon (Bersu 1967, 88-89, 114-119).
[14]The Arbory night port was at Polbash (now Pooilvaaish), complete with a miserably insignificant limestone rock outcrop known as Cronk y Watch ('Watch Hill' / 'Hill of the Watch'). Clearly the need for a watch at this point on the coastline was still felt, but the parochial basis for recruiting the manpower meant that a less suitable muster point was identified.

unlocking the full extent of the system. Previous consideration of watch and ward has concentrated on written evidence and the early Manx statutes, perhaps at the expense of the actual locations at which watch was kept: combining the insights these sources provide of the intent of watch and ward with a re-assessment of the archaeological finds made by Bersu and Gelling, and with continuing fieldwork, provides the exciting prospect of understanding the way in which the system actually developed, functioned and was eventually abandoned.

References

Barton R, 1999, 'Manx Granite Tempered Ware', in Davey P J, (ed.), 1999, *Recent Archaelogical Research on the Isle of Man, 221-240.*

Bersu G, 1949, 'A promontory fort on the shore of Ramsey Bay, Isle of Man', *Antiquaries Journal* XXIX, 62-79.

Bersu G, 1967, 'Excavation of the Cashtal, Ballagawne, Garwick, 1941', *Proceedings of the Isle of Man Natural History and Antiquarian Society VII, 88-119, with notes by A M Cubbon.*

Bersu G, 1968, 'The Vikings in the Isle of Man', *Journal of the Manx Museum VII, 83-88.*

Cubbon A M, 1983, 'The Archaeology of the Vikings in the Isle of Man', in Fell C E, Foote P, Graham-Campbell J and Thomson R, (eds.) *The Viking Age in the Isle of Man, 8-26.*

Cubbon W, 1930, 'Watch and Ward in AD 1627', *Proceedings of the Isle of Man Natural History and Antiquarian Society III, 258-265.*

Curphey R A, 1967, 'The Coastal Batteries', *Journal of the Manx Museum VII, 50-57.*

Darvill T, 2001, *Billown Neolithic Landscape Project, Malew, Isle of Man: Sixth Report 2000, Bournemouth University School of Conservation Sciences Research Report 9.*

Davey P J, Johnson N C, & Woodcock J J, 1997, *Upper Glendhoo, Ballaugh, Isle of Man: Field Survey, September 1996, Centre for Manx Studies Research Report 6.*

Davey P J, (ed.) 1999, *Recent Archaeological Research on the Isle of Man, British Archaeological Reports 278.*

Davey P J, (ed.) (forthcoming) *Recent Archaeological Research on the Isle of Man, 1998-2000, British Archaeological Reports.*

Doonan R C P, Cheetham P, O'Connor B, Eley T, Welham K, 2001, 'Investigations at Langness: the 2000 field-season', in Darvill T, 2001, 40-47.

Fell C E, Foote P, Graham-Campbell J & Thomson R, (eds.) 1983, *The Viking Age in the Isle of Man, The Viking Society for Northern Research, University College, London.*

Garrad L S 1990, 'Borrane' as a name for ancient sites in Man', *Proceedings of the Isle of Man Natural History and Antiquarian Society IX, 607.*

Gelling P S, 1952, 'Excavation of a promontory fort at Port Grenaugh, Santon', *Proceedings of the Isle of Man Natural History and Antiquarian Society V, 307-315.*

80 *Andrew Johnson*

Gelling P S, 1957, 'Excavation of a promontory fort at Scarlett, Castletown, Isle of Man', *Proceedings of the Isle of Man Natural History and Antiquarian Society V, 571-5.*

Gelling P S, 1959 'Excavation of a promontory fort at Cass ny Hawin, Malew, Isle of Man', *Proceedings of the Isle of Man Natural History and Antiquarian Society VI, 28-38.*

Gelling P S, 1964, 'The Braaid site', *Journal of the Manx Museum VI, 201-205.*

Gelling P S, 1970, 'A Norse Homestead near Doarlish Cashen, Kirk Patrick, Isle of Man', *Medieval Archaeology XI V, 74-82.*

Johnson A C C, 2000, 'A View From the Hills: Some thoughts on the re-occupation of promontory forts and the possible origins of the Manx farmstead.' *Proceedings of the Isle of Man Natural History and Antiquarian Society XI, 51-66.*

Johnson A C C, (forthcoming), 'Upper Glendhoo: Field Survey' in Davey P J (forthcoming)

Megaw B R S, 1941, 'A Thousand Years of Watch and Ward: From Viking Beacon to Home Guard', *Journal of the Manx Museum V, 8-13.*

Thomson R L, 1992, 'Borrane Again', *Proceedings of the Isle of Man Natural History and Antiquarian Society X, 161-2.*

At the crossroads of power and cultural influence: Manx archaeology in the high Middle Ages

Peter Davey

Introduction

It is in the nature of archaeological evidence that only rarely at a given site will the events which constitute political or dynastic history be verifiable. The quality of the dating evidence available to archaeologists, often expressed in terms of plus or minus 50 years for pottery for example, means that even if a great fire deposit is located, or the foundations of a prominent building are investigated, the archaeologist will often be unable to support or deny the evidence of documentary sources which apply to the case. Indeed, it is much more common for excavators of medieval structures to rely entirely on documentary sources for dating, not only the sites, but also the association of artifacts which go with them. Thus, for Manx medieval history the story told by The Chronicles of the Kings of Man and the Isles - from the foundation of a local Norwegian dynasty by Godred Crovan through to its demise at the Treaty of Perth in 1266 - cannot be verified by archaeological evidence, despite the considerable amount of new research which has been carried out during the last 15 years. Even such a major monument as Castle Rushen, which figures prominently in 13th and 14th century accounts of the Island, cannot be dated archaeologically even to the nearest one hundred years. Events such as the attack by Robert the Bruce in 1313 (Broderick 1979, f.50r; McNamee 1997, 58) and later Scottish efforts to control the Island, for example in 1456 (Megaw 1957), are invisible to archaeology.

The aim of this chapter is to suggest ways in which the new evidence from excavations at Peel, Castletown and Rushen Abbey in particular can, despite its chronological inadequacy, contribute to a better understanding of Man in the medieval period. A number of subject areas will be discussed: evidence for economic activity, for urbanisation, for external trade or political relations and for the internal dynamics of Island life. The questions which underlie the discussion include the degree to which the Island was isolated from contemporary developments, the backwardness or otherwise of Manx social and economic life, the coherence of insular political and social institutions and the evolution of a distinctively Manx identity during the medieval period.

Economic activity

The archaeological evidence for economic activity on Man during the high medieval period is largely confined to three sites which can hardly be described as representative of the wider state of affairs in the Island as a whole - Peel Castle (Freke 2002), Castle Rushen (Davey *et al.* 1996) and Rushen Abbey (Butler 1988; Butler in press; Davey (ed) 1999a). With the notable exception of the metal-working sites at Braddan Vicarage (Cubbon 1982-84), and Ronaldsway smelt (Stenning 1935-37), there has been no serious attempt by archaeologists to investigate the nature of settlement or the quality of life beyond. In particular, none of the 700 or so quarterland farms - the backbone of Manx social and economic life from the Norse period - has been excavated.

The level and quality of medieval economic activity on Man, as evidenced by the Castles and Abbey, can be partially assessed by looking at the evidence of artifacts such as pottery, metalwork, glass and coins which have been recovered from recent archaeological excavations. Questions of diet and food supply and, therefore, resource management, can also be addressed.

The ceramic evidence has been discussed at length elsewhere (Davey & Johnson 1996; Davey 1999b; Davey 2000; Davey 2001; Davey 2002).

In brief, with the exception of a handful of early medieval imports and the use of pottery crucibles in the later Iron Age and Early Christian periods, the Island was a-ceramic from the middle of the Bronze Age (*c*1000 BC) until the 11th or 12th century With the establishment of Norse rule the production of local hand-made cooking ware, characterized by being grogged with freshly crushed Foxdale granite, was initiated. This "granite-tempered ware" continued in production until late in the 16th century. For the first two or three centuries of local production a "granite-free" ware was also in use for the production of jugs and other table wares. Associated with these insular wares, the Island was in receipt of considerable quantities of imports from Britain and the continent. The very limited evidence from other, lower status sites - such as the metalworking complex at Braddan or the small farm at Kerrowdhoo (Davey 1995) suggests that, although imports were in general circulation on the Island, they were present in only very small quantities outside the major centres.

Metalwork, whether of iron or copper alloy, does not survive well in Manx soils. Even at Peel Castle, outside the Norse grave groups, only small numbers of metal artifacts survived. The copper alloy finds consist for the most of wire pins and needles, lace chapes and dress accessories such as strap ends and belt fittings (Freke & Graham-Campbell 2002). Castle Rushen produced a similar though much smaller range of items which included metalworking evidence in the form of several cut fragments of sheeting and folded rivets for repairing bronze vessels (Egan 1996). At Rushen Abbey, whilst a majority of recent finds are from Dissolution demolition deposits, small numbers of medieval copper alloy lace tags, studs, needles, dress fittings and repaired bronze vessel fragments have been found (Davey 1999a).

Iron artifacts occur even less frequently. At Peel, apart from some 754 nails and rivets, and with the extensive use of X-ray photography, only seven items were recovered - a knife, a spur, a flesh hook, a fish hook, a projectile point and two chapes (Freke 2002) - which must represent a very small proportion of the iron objects actually in use at any time in the medieval period. At Castle Rushen no medieval iron objects were recovered (Johnson 1996).

These assemblages of metal artifacts, although extremely vestigial, do establish that at the main sites, metal was in widespread use for a range of purposes. The Manx finds exhibit no particularly insular features. They lie within the mainstream of the available technologies within the British Isles.

In addition, the presence of a smelt for lead and possibly silver, owned by Furness Abbey and located on the coast at Ronaldsway together with a number of ironworking sites such as the one excavated by Cubbon at Braddan Vicarage and that located by Larch Garrad (1984) at Ballavarry, Andreas, show that the mineral resources of the Island were certainly being widely exploited.

Medieval glass is even more rarely found. Four sherds from a crumbling potash glass vessel were found at Peel (Hurst-Vose 2002), together with some 220 sherds of extremely weathered window glass, including ten with traces of grisaille decoration. Many fragments of window glass, fragments of a urinal and a lamp were recovered from Rushen Abbey, the latter within a burial (Butler 1988, 99, Fig 17, No 4). There was no medieval glass from Castle Rushen.

To date five coin hoards, one of the late 12th and the others of the early 14th century have been found on Man, together with 36 single coin finds. In her recent study Bornholdt (in press), has commented:

"The total number of single finds from Man is suspiciously low for a population apparently familiar with coinage, but Man's excavated site totals are not out of keeping in a British Isles context".

The paucity of rural finds, compared with England, has led her to conclude " ... that currency was not used regularly by the majority of folk in Man during the middle ages." A number of factors suggest that this statement is rather too extreme. First, unlike England, medieval Man had no villages and therefore no deserted medieval villages. There has been no local tradition of field-walking for medieval finds; indeed the numbers of sherds of pottery found outside formal excavations is also very small - a handful of sherds from 11 sites (eg Garrad 1977). In addition, the 13th and 14th-century synodal statutes (Cheney 1984) show that tithes, payable by the majority of the 700 or so quarterland farms, were valued in monetary terms. Although payments in kind were also acceptable, it is clear from the records of episcopal payments of Papal taxation, via Nidaros, that commodities such as sheep, honey or grain must have been cash convertible, as Sodor and Man's valuation, at 660 Florins for an incoming bishop, was a significant one in regional terms. The money was generally paid late, and in instalments, but it was paid (Storm 1897).

The few surviving medieval buildings on the Island also give some indication of economic activity. With the exception of the residence of the bishop at Bishopscourt, no domestic buildings survive. Of the ecclesiastical buildings, the Cathedral of St German at Peel is pre-eminent. The construction of the crossing arch, vaults and chancel exhibit very good quality workmanship using varieties of Peel Sandstone. Similarly, fine sculptured capitals are in evidence at St Trinians and decorated jams at St Runus Church, Marown with local granite being exploited (Kermode 1910). Although at Rushen Abbey most of the architectural fragments recovered from the excavations appear to be using imported sandstones, the principal walls of the cloistral buildings were constructed using large blocks of finely dressed local limestone (Coppack & Johnson in prep.). In all of these cases it is possible that masons were brought in specially, from Furness or Whithorn (in the case of St Trinians). Even so, both Rushen Abbey and St German's Cathedral show a number of phases of workmanship and alterations in windows and doors which imply resident skills in the Manx population. The wide timespan over which major phases of work were carried out at Castle Rushen and at Peel tend to confirm this. All of these buildings have produced evidence for competent lead working, slating, carpentry and glazing of a quality equivalent to their architecture and status. Given the lack of fieldwork, how far these skills were available or appropriate to the wider population of the Island remains unclear.

Recent archaeological excavations, especially those at Peel Castle have provided a wide range of information about the exploitation of natural resources, especially animals, birds and fish (Tomlinson 2002; Crellin 2002; Fisher 2002; Hutchinson & Jones 2002; McMillan 2002). Over 50,000 fragments of large mammal bone were recovered from the excavations. In the medieval period cattle form by far the largest group, followed by sheep and pig. A few horse, deer and dog bones were also recovered. Apart from rabbit which occurred in a number of genuinely medieval contexts, most of the small mammal bone was found in bulk sampling and represents elements of the contemporary fauna of St Patrick's Isle rather than human food. In contrast, of the 45 species of bird recovered, only five were of domesticated varieties (chicken, greylag goose, mallard, rock dove and peafowl), yet there was evidence of at least 38 of them forming part of human diet. Many of these latter were seabirds such as shag, shearwater, kittiwake, cormorant, goldeneye, long-tailed duck and tufted duck, some of which may also have been obtained for oil. Fish also formed an important element in the assemblage from Peel. Of the 28 species confidently identified in the 6,373 bones collected, some implied the organization of deep sea fleets, others inshore fishing, possibly with hand lines. There was very little evidence of fresh-water fish. Limpets, dogwhelks and winkles were also consumed in quantity, as were oysters which also formed part of a small medieval assemblage at Castle Rushen (Davey 1996). These results from Peel show that Manx medieval society not only relied on domesticated animals and birds, but exploited local populations of wild birds, fish and shellfish to a much greater degree than previously thought.

Because of lack of organic preservation within the sieved deposits, no medieval plant remains were recovered from either Peel or Castle Rushen. At Rushen Abbey two of the trial trenches produced charred grains of wheat, barley and oats (Tomlinson 1999). Documentary sources suggest that cereal production, especially of wheat, was an important element in Manx medieval agriculture.[1] It remains for the right deposits to be examined to confirm this.[2]

Urbanisation

Papal decrees, for example on the election of a new Bishop of the Isles, often contained a phrase in greeting or direction to the people of the diocese such as: *In eundem modo populum civitatis et diocecesis Sodorensis.*[3] This formula, used in many papal promulgations, presupposes that a diocese would have an urban centre at its core. Recent archaeological research has failed to find any settlement evidence on the Island which could be construed as urban until the end of the 15th century, at the earliest.

In Peel itself extensive sampling excavations retrieved medieval evidence only from a very small area on the harbour edge, immediately opposite the castle (Philpott & Davey 1992). Recent excavations just to the south of the promenade have located urban-type deposits of 16th-century date, with a few possible 15th century residual artifacts (Johnson forthcoming).

These finds echo those recovered in 1992 from the silting up harbour. In the historic core of Castletown much larger groups of 16th-century artifacts have been found, in association with what appeared to be an organised phase of town planning, only some 35m from the outworks of the castle (Higgins 1996). In 1506 there were 86 'cottages' in Castletown (Roscow 1996). There is no sign of typical urban structures or organisational features such as defensive walls, gates, markets, burgage plots, or town officials. The same is true at Peel. The papal instructions were directed at a rural population who happened to have the seat of a bishop located in their midst.

External trade and political relations

Although not easily susceptible to close dating, the archaeological evidence may, with caution, be used to suggest something of the nature of external links and trade. In the case of the Isle of Man, how was the Island seen by its neighbours?

There are two elements in its natural position which together need to be given due weight in any assessment of the Island and its role in regional political, economic and social history (Figure 1). First, the Island proved a serious hazard to navigation through the North Channel. Its long axis lies almost perpendicular to the channel and, with a huge tidal range (more than 10 metres) and ferocious tidal streams its presence could not be ignored. It lies on a direct southerly route from the Western and Northern Isles

---

[1] eg *De granis decimalibus* in Bishop Simon's Synodal Ordinances, Manx Society, xviii, 51. The implication of this is that each rector had his own store in which to receive the grain tithes, 'for the greater convenience of the bailiffs'.

[2] Grain production on the Island began early in the Neolithic; a recent C[14] date for cereal pollen at Ballachrink, Jurby is one of the oldest in northwest Europe. At Peel Castle a huge Iron Age grain store which had been destroyed by fire was uncovered (cf Tomlinson P R 'The charred cereal deposit' in: Tomlinson P R, Allison E P, Innes J B and Kenward H K, 'Environmental evidence from the prehistoric period' in: Freke 2002, 231-247.

[3] In the same way to the people of the Sodor city and diocese.

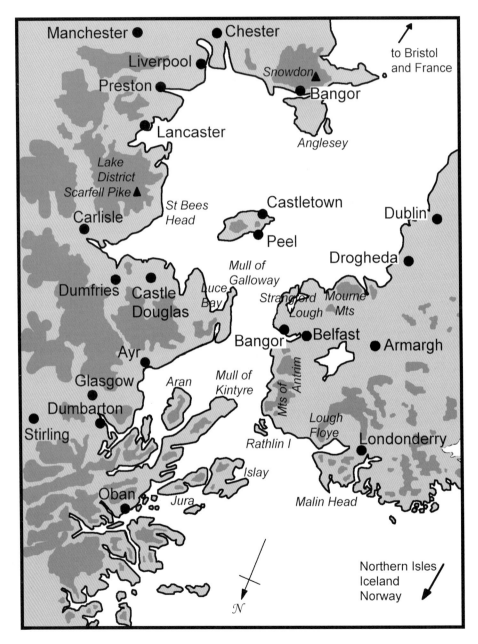

Figure 1: Position of the Isle of Man from a "northern" perpective.

and Scandinavia to south-west Scotland, Cumbria, north-west England, north Wales, Ireland and France. It also lies across the more "internal" routes from the Solway and Cumbrian ports to Dublin and southern Ireland. Its strategic significance in the fluctuating power struggles in the neighbouring lands is self-evident.

Secondly, compared with other small islands in the west it is extremely fertile. Is has an equable climate for its latitude with relatively low rainfall, good sunshine records and very little frost. In 1500 some 50% of the land surface was under the plough. The most recent soil map shows a range of productive agricultural soils, particularly those based on limestone in the south-east and glacial deposits in the north (Figure 2) (Harris *et al.* 2001). The Island boasts a proportion of Grade 1/11 and Grade 11 soils which is unparalleled in an equivalent area in the west of Britain and Ireland. Even today, with a population of over 70,000, Man is self-sufficient in grain - surplus barley being exported to Bushmills in Ulster - and a serious exporter of beef and lamb to Britain, Ireland and France. In addition, there is a good range of minerals such as lead, copper, silver and zinc, some of which have been exploited from earliest times. As an economic, as well as a strategic prize, the Island had real value.

The trade and external relations

At Peel some 60% of all medieval ceramic finds were British in origin. It has proved difficult to establish the actual centre of production for almost half of this material. The main sources are Cumbria and Cheshire, with sizable groups from the Bristol region and Somerset. No certain Scottish or Irish pottery has yet been identified (Davey 2002, 365).

The continental wares derive mainly from France, with smaller groups from Iberia, the Low Countries, Germany and Italy (Davey 1999b). The source of the French material, in common with the pattern from southern England, appears to be focused on the north in the 11th and 12th centuries, whilst during the 13th century exports from the Saintonge area becomes paramount. The reasons for this change are complex. The marriage of Henry II and Eleanor of Aquitaine in 1152 which united England and Gascony, the loss of Normandy in 1204 and the apparent decline of English vineyards, probably due to climatic deterioration, all played their part (Clarke 1983). The main interest in the Manx finds is their quantity. At Peel Castle, for example, medieval continental imports formed some 12% of the total assemblage (Davey 1999b, 246) - a much higher proportion than in English ports such as Carlisle, Chester, Bristol, Newcastle or Boston (Davey 2002). There are also a number of ware types, for example Beauvais Red Painted and Normandy Gritty which are not normally found so far north. The latter has been found on Man at four sites and in some quantity (Davey 1999b, 243-5).

There are a number of possible explanations for the apparent dominance of British and southern wares in the Manx assemblages. The Norse kings of Man may have retained closer contacts with equivalent settlements in Northern France, than did their English counterparts which might explain the quantities of Normandy products, some of which may be as early as 10th century.[4] The high proportion of imports generally is

---

[4]Davey P J 2002, cf Ailsa Mainman's identification of the red-painted ware as 10th century Beauvais.

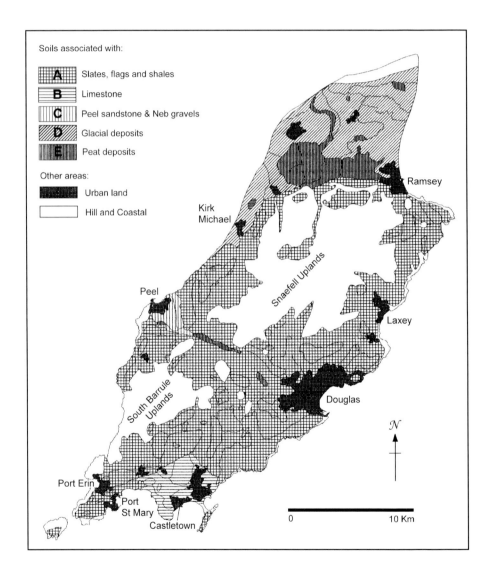

Figure 2: Simplified agricultural soil classification of the Isle of Man.

is probably due to the relatively primitive nature of the native hand-made pottery. At sites such as Peel, Castle Rushen and Rushen Abbey British and continental products provided much higher quality wares, appropriate to the status of those sites.

The larger southern component in the Manx medieval ceramic assemblages may also be due to some common factor which is not directly related to the pottery itself. For example, ceramic products might be used as ballast by vessels coming to the northern Irish Sea to collect their principle trading commodity such as butter, grain or leather, a pattern well established for north Devon wares in the post-medieval period (Grant 1983). Further detailed study of production centres throughout the Irish Sea area will be required before the ceramic evidence can be used more precisely to define the chronology and geography of external trade.

From the evidence of hoards and stray finds the medieval coinage in circulation on Man is dominated by English issues. Although the earliest hoard of c1174, discovered in 1769, included one English and four Scottish coins, of the remaining four hoards containing a total of 876 coins, only 38 were Scottish. All of the 36 single finds are English. Bornhold (in press) comments: 'The hoards and the significant peak in English finds in the first decades of the fourteenth century reflect a dramatic shift in Man's political orientation and economic connections'.

With so few surviving medieval buildings it is difficult to generalize about their sources of inspiration, especially as, with the exception of the Lord's domestic quarters at Peel Castle, no recent architectural studies have been carried out. The suite of buildings to the north of the Cathedral at Peel contain no geographically diagnostic styles and, in any case, were constructed by the Stanleys (Slade 2002). Bishopscourt and the tower-houses around the perimeter of Peel Castle appear similar to contemporary buildings in northern England and Scotland; the extensive, unfocussed, nature of Peel is difficult to parallel in England, unlike Castle Rushen whose concentric, concentrated plan seems to follow English proto-types.

Religious buildings fare a little better. St German's Cathedral boasts good examples of Early Gothic (in the crossing) and Early English (chancel). The carved capitals at St Trinians are classic Romanesque. At Rushen Abbey the surviving Romanesque arch in the North Transept is, as might be expected of a reforming order, extremely simple in design. Equally, most of the architectural fragments from the recent excavations although exhibiting good quality workmanship have little decorative detail. The surviving east window of the Chapel at Ballabeg is similarly uninformative, even though the Friary was founded from Dublin. Although these examples show that the island was not remote from the stylistic developments of the time, they do not give any clear idea of the specific sources of influence.

Thus, the ceramic finds, the coins and the surviving and excavated architecture show that the Isle of Man was not isolated from trends in the rest of the British Isles. Its major economic orientation appears to have been towards England. At the time of Godred Croven, the Island looked to Norway for its political and economic direction. But as the Norse kings became more thoroughly assimilated into an Irish Sea world, so the importance of the native peoples and the power of the English came to the fore. One outcome of this was possibly the fusion of granite tempering technology brought from Scandinavia with the everted-rim wares encountered in Ulster, resulting in the

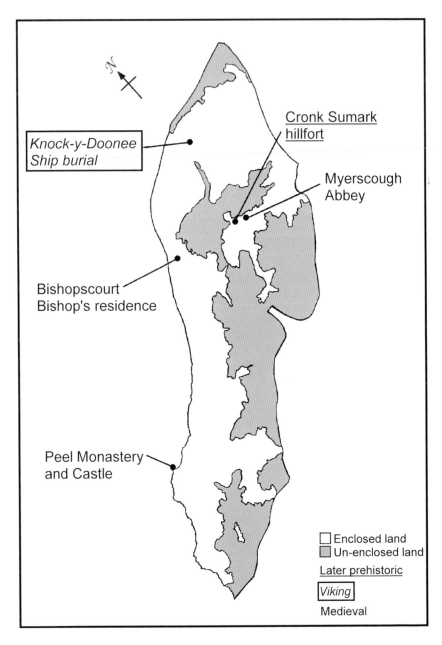

Figure 3: North Mann

distinctive Manx Granite Tempered Ware (Davey 2000, 109). Although the creation of a north-facing bishopric maintained Scandinavian and Scottish links long after the Treaty of Perth in 1266, the transfer of real influence to England seems to have begun with the reforms of Olaf I. He invited two English Abbeys (Furness and Rievaulx) to found daughter houses, established the modern parochial system and maintained close contact with the English court where he had been brought up. Under his successors a dependent relationship was further developed when, in 1212, Reginald became a liegeman of King John and was paid a knight's fee for the protection of the English coastline (Oliver 1861, 25-37). The construction of Castle Rushen – the Manx equivalent of the Anglo-Norman stronghold of Trim – and the reversion of Peel to an ecclesiastical function began an Anglo-Manx journey which was later formalized in the placing of the kingship into the hands of an English family. The archaeological evidence, particularly that of the pottery and the coins suggest that this transfer of influence was well in place by the 13th century.

Internal dynamics: two islands?

In considering the relationships between medieval Mann and its neighbours, especially with respect to such questions as autonomy and identity, recent trends in the perceptions of the peoples of the adjacent islands are not without relevance. In Ireland, over the past two centuries, the dominant psychological and physical pressures have been to establish that island as a single political and cultural entity. In contrast, in Britain, recent constitutional changes have given Wales, and especially Scotland a considerable degree of self rule. In Man an independence movement has continued to grow despite the rapid emergence of a high degree of self-determination during the 20th century. As a relatively small island, there has always been an assumption in recent times that the Isle of Man and its people were to be considered as a singularity. The thesis of the final part of this paper is that, in the medieval period at least, much of Manx archaeology and history is best seen as reflecting a dual historic identity, - North Mann and South Mann - which the documentary sources refer to as Northside and Southside.

The duality of Manx medieval identity is a product both of its location and environment, and of its previous history. The central spine of upland running from North Barrule to Cronk ny Eerie Laa divides two very different landscapes. To the north and west, in North Mann, low-lying glacial deposits predominate with extensive Holocene wetlands; a small down-faulted area of Old Red Sandstone forms the Peel Embayment (Figure 3). To the south and east, in South Mann, glaciated landforms are covered with mainly clay-based diamicts with an important cluster of drumlins around Ballasalla and a few later wetlands. In the south-east a significant area around Castletown is underlain by down-faulted Carboniferous limestones which create a distinctive topography and ecology (Figure 4).

In North Mann, the extensive outwash gravels have developed light soils, easy to clear and plough, with evidence from recent pollen analysis for cereal production as early as 4,000 BC. The Northern Plain was densely settled throughout earlier prehistory, from the mesolithic to the Bronze Age. It still provides the principal cereal producing area on the Island. In South Mann the heavier soils are more difficult to clear and work.

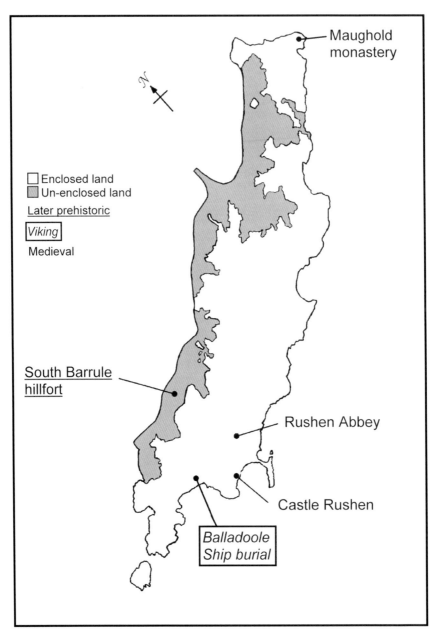

Figure 4: South Mann

On the limestone, however, mineral retention is good and prehistoric peoples thrived, especially in the area around Billown which has been the subject of major research and rescue excavations by the University of Bournemouth over the last six years. The same area still boasts the highest soil productivity in the whole Island. Despite these physical and environmental differences there is no convincing indication in earlier prehistory of any major differences between the human cultures which developed in the two parts of the Island. All but one of the megalithic tombs are located in the South and are mostly standard Court/Clyde cairns. The site at the Kew, Liaght ny Foawr, which is just in the North (above the eastern edge of the Peel Embayment), although damaged, was clearly some form of passage grave. But for the rest of the Neolithic and Bronze Age the same pottery and lithic types, some of them uniquely Manx, occur throughout the Island.

In many ways the Iron Age has proved the most enigmatic and elusive of periods in Manx prehistory. Peter Gelling, in a lifetime of work, examined many sites which belonged typologically to the period, such as round houses, hill- and promontory forts, upland mounds, only to find that at least half them belonged to other times. Many of the promontory forts, for example, only produced Norse finds and structures. Despite the elusiveness of Iron Age sites, there are two classic hillforts; one in the North at Cronk Sumark, the other in the South on South Barrule (Figure 5). The contrast between these two forts is very marked. Cronk Sumark consists of a very small enclosure on top of an isolated rocky boss situated just to the north of the main line of hills in Lezayre. At a lower level two larger earthworks, in part vitrified, surround the hill. Until drainage in the 17th century it dominated a large wetland - the Curragh - to the north. It is reminiscent of many Scottish vitrified forts; in particular its siting, size and levels are similar to the site at Dunadd, in Argyle. South Barrule, on the other hand, is set on the summit of the southern uplands of the Island, encloses a large area and contains at least 80 round-houses within two, wide-spaced ramparts. In this case comparisons are most easily made with forts in southern Britain, especially Wales - for example the groups of large forts on the Lleyn Peninsular.

Do the stark differences between the principal forts in North and South Mann represent changed political or cultural allegiances over time or do they imply two contemporary separate entities? Whichever is the case, it seems unlikely to be accidental that the site in the North is Scottish in character, whilst that in the South is Welsh.

A similar line of argument can be applied to the two main sites in the early medieval period - the monasteries at Maughold lying at one end of South Mann and Peel at the opposite end of the North. Maughold with its tradition of links with the British church lies in sight of Cumbria, whilst Peel with its dedication to St Patrick and its Round Tower lying opposite to County Down has distinctly Irish associations. Did these monasteries exist in separate political and cultural environments? Is it a coincidence that when Viking incomers first buried their dead, the two ship burials - at Knock y Doonee in the North and Balladoole in the South should be at opposite ends of the Island? Although both sites are located quite close to the sea, their common feature is to have been placed on the highest point within the fertile lowlands from where the whole of the arable lands of North and South Mann respectively could be seen - from Knock y Doonee the whole sweep of land from Bride to Cronk ny Arrey Laa and from Balladoole the vista from Mull Hill to North Barrule. The sites seem to be territorially

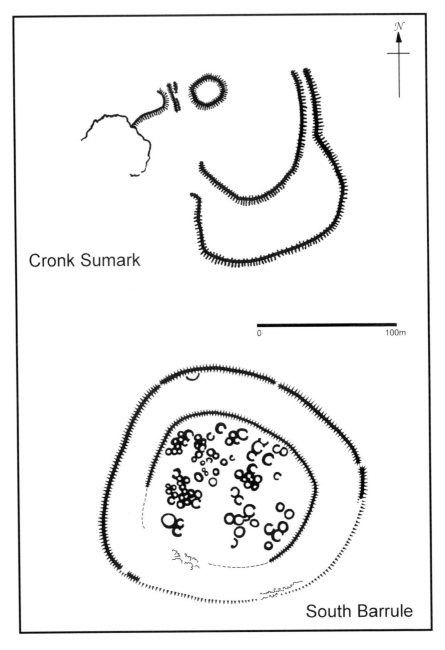

Figure 5: Comparative plans of Cronk Sumark and South Barrule hillforts.

placed. Did the early Viking settlers rule Man as two kingdoms? Did they respect existing divisions? The existence of a multiple estate land tenure system has recently been proposed by Moore on the basis of field evidence and the detail contained in Rent Rolls which, by the early 1500s, give a complete account of the agricultural land surface of the Island (Moore 1999). He has argued persuasively that Man was thought of and administered as two such estates, the internal organization of which bears a close resemblance to that known in early medieval Wales. The parish and sheading system also adhere to a dual division.

There is some medieval documentary evidence which supports the idea of the two estates of Mann. According to the Chronicles, after the Battle of Sky Hill in 1079, Godred Croven:

'... granted the southern part of the island to the few islanders who stayed with him and the northern part to the remainder of the Manxmen, on such terms that none of them should at any time dare usurp any part of the land for himself by right of inheritance.' (Broderick 1979, f.33r.)

The persistence of serious political division in the island, possibly as a result of this attempt to separate the rival contenders is apparent from the subsequent description of the visit of Magnus king of Norway to Man in 1098:

'When he landed at St Patrick's Isle he came to view the place of battle which the Manxmen had fought a short while before between themselves, because many bodies of the slain were still unburied.' (Broderick 1979, f.34v.)

Although under the 40-year rule of Godred's son Olaf these factional divisions seemed to have been kept under firm control, the Chronicles account of the aftermath of his assassination in 1152 raises further issues about the geography and ethnicity of the medieval settlement of Man:

'After the perpetration of so grave a crime they (the sons of Harold, Olaf's brother) immediately divided the island between themselves. A few days later a fleet was assembled and they sailed over to Galloway wishing to subject it to their rule. However the people of Galloway massed together and after a great onslaught joined battle with them. They straightway turned tale and fled amid great confusion back to Man. All the Galloway men living in Man they either slaughtered or expelled' (Broderick 1979, f.36v.).

It is clear, for example, from the first written law code of 1422 that there remained some differences of customary law between the two estates each of which had its own designated deemster. Many aspects of Manx administration, for example, the collection of rents and the operation of the legal system remained separate until quite recently. Fleure and Davies' physical anthropological studies also appeared to show that distinctively northern and southern types survived into the 20th century (Davies & Fleure 1936, Fleure & Davies 1937).

Castles

The Castles too are remarkably different from one another, as contrasting as the Manx hillforts (Figure 6). At Peel a series of super-imposed structures, some religious, some

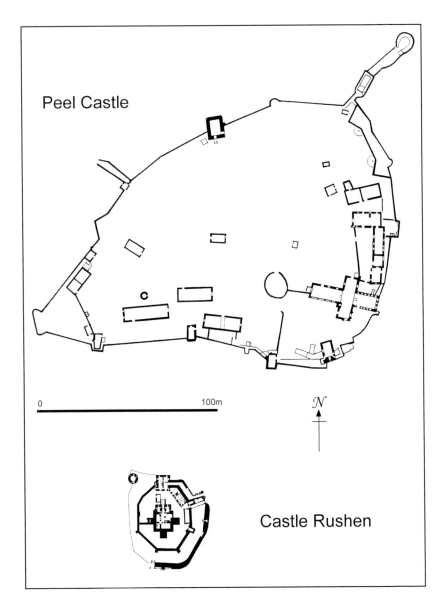

Figure 6: Comparative plans of Peel Castle and Castle Rushen.

military, can still be discerned. Their orientation and style is definitely to the north, reflecting interests and power base of the earliest Norse kings and the bishop. Castle Rushen is very much a single concept structure. Whether its origins are in the late 12th century or in the 13th, and whether the visible breaks in building lines represent a shorter or longer constructional history, the Castle represents a singular statement of royal power.

Monasteries and baronies

When Olaf and his successors began a programme of modernisation in the early part of the 12th century, it is noteworthy that two monasteries were founded on the Island, one in the south at Rushen, in 1134, and the other in the north at Myroscough in 1176. The former was a daughter of the Savignac house of Furness and the latter of the Cistercian Abbey of Riveaulx (Davey in press). The provision of land for these new orders was one aspect of Olaf's reformation of religion on the Island. The choice of site was probably also intended to keep the influence and activities of the two abbeys separate from one another. Given the relatively small area of land provided for Myroscough in Lezayre it seems possible that Rushen Abbey's later property in German (in the North) might have formed part of the original endowment for Myroscough. There are no extant charters which explain how this land was acquired by Rushen. A larger original land holding for Myroscough would make sense in economic terms; it would also maintain the territorial division between Rushen in the South and Myroscough in the North.

The location of the remaining monastic holdings on the Island is largely geographically determined (Figure 7), though there is less apparent concern with any north-south division. The land belonging to the Irish Augustinian houses at Bangor and Sabal lie together on the west coast of the Island, south of Peel, within sight of Downpatrick. Similarly the dispersed properties of the Benedictine Cell of St Bees in Cumbria are situated on the east coast, south of Maughold, immediately opposite the mother house. Whithorn, in addition to holding the vicarage of Lezayre owned a small barony centred on the medieval hospital of St Leonard in Marown, where it also had the vicarage. The form of wording of its earliest charter refers to the hospital in such a way as to imply that the connection was of long standing. St Trinian's chapel, at the focus of the Whithorn holding, still retains a number of fine Romanesque features.

Both the Cistercian nunnery at Douglas and the Dublin Order of Friars Minor's house at Bymaken (Ballabeg) were also in South Mann, together with a small holding of Furness at Ronaldsway where, it is thought, Rushen's mother house had located a mineral smelt.

The assimilation of Myroscough by Rushen is one element in a growing dominance of the South over North Mann which began, perhaps with the rise of Castle Rushen and the growth of English, as opposed to Norwegian power in the northern Irish sea, the transfer of the Island's capital from Peel to Castletown. Under the Stanleys whose home base was in Lancashire the Island became more closely dependent on its relationship with the north-west of England. The power and influence of South Mann, over the North continued to grow. The transfer of administration to Douglas and the growth of the Douglas/Onchan conurbation, stimulated initially by the English oriented tourist

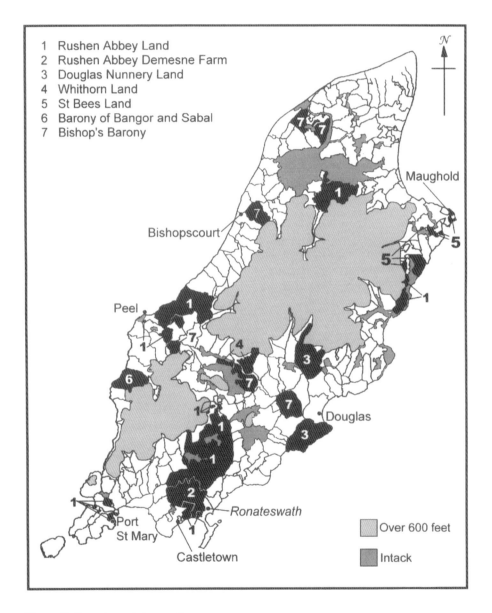

Figure 7: Location of the medieval baronies of the Isle of Man (colour version inside front cover).

trade and more recently exacerbated by the finance industry, has resulted in the almost complete dominance of the South. After the Second World War the decision to place the airport at Ronaldsway, as opposed to Jurby which has better weather and visibility records, was symptomatic. Since Olaf created the links with Furness in 1134 and his successors cemented financial and political ties with England in the decades which followed his death, South Mann has almost always been strategically, politically and socially dominant.

Summary

The archaeological evidence, strongly biased towards high status sites as it is, paints a picture of a well-organized society with a successful economy. There is little direct evidence for grain production, but animal husbandry was well advanced, as was the exploitation of a very wide range of birds, fish and shell-fish provided by the maritime environment. The inception of large-scale building projects such as Castle Rushen and Rushen Abbey involved the exploitation of the Island's mineral and rock sources to a high degree. A skills base in masonry, plumbing, glazing, carpentry and the organization needed to acquire the relevant raw materials must have developed among the wider population, though the absence of any surviving vernacular buildings of the period make it impossible to verify this.

Manx medieval society was essentially rural. Urban-like settlements around Castle Rushen and opposite Peel Castle only developed in the 16th century. The archaeological evidence for the nature of social and economic life beyond the castles and abbeys must reside in, under or around the 700 or so quarterland farms, none of which have been excavated.

In terms of external relations and trade the Island appears to have looked much more towards England and the continent than to Scandinavia and Scotland for its inspiration and trade, from at least the 12th century.

Within Man itself, the ancient division between North and South, which probably has its origins in prehistory, remains a significant element in social, economic legal and political life throughout the Middle Ages. The increasing dominance of the English connection emphasized and stimulated the growing dominance of South Mann over North Mann, a process which has continued to this day.

Bibliography

Bornholdt K, in press, 'Coinage' in: Duffy S (ed), in press.

Broderick G, 1979, *Cronica regum mannie & insularum*, Manx Museum and National Trust, Douglas.

Butler L A S, 1988, 'The Cistercian Abbey of St Mary of Rushen: Excavations 1978-79', *Journal of the British Archaeological Association*, 141, 60 - 104.

Butler L A S, in press, 'Report on Excavations at Rushen Abbey: the East Range, 1988-89', *Journal of the British Archaeological Association*.

Cheney C R, 1984, 'Manx synodal statutes AD 1230(?) to 1351. Part 1: Introduction and Latin text', Cambridge Medieval Celtic Studies, 7, 63-89.

Clarke H, 1983, 'The historical background to North Sea trade, c1200-1500' in: Davey and Hodges (eds), 1983, 17- 25.

Coppack G & Johnson N C, in preparation, 'The architectural fragments' in: Davey (ed), in prep.

Crellin C, 2002, 'The Small Mammal Bones', in: Freke 2002, 250-251.

Cubbon A M, 1982-84, 'Excavation of a medieval metal-working site, Braddan Vicarage 1966', *Proceedings of the Isle of Man Natural History and Antiquarian Society,* 9:2, 197-237.

Davey P J, 1977, *Medieval Pottery from Excavations in the north-west,* (University of Liverpool).

Davey P J, 1995, 'The cultural affinities and dating of the ceramic finds' in: Davey *et al.,* 1995, 61 - 62.

Davey P J, 1996, 'Molluscs' in: Davey *et al.,* 1996, 151 - 154.

Davey P J, 1999a, 'The metalwork from the 1998 excavation' in: Davey (ed) 1999a, 62-3.

Davey P J, 1999b, 'Medieval and post-medieval continental ceramics from the Isle of Man' in: Davey (ed) 1999b, 241-272.

Davey P J, 2000, 'Medieval and later pottery from the Isle of Man', *Proceedings of the Isle of Man Natural History and Antiquarian Society,* 11, No.1, 91 - 114.

Davey P J, 2001, 'Medieval pottery studies in the Isle of Man', *Medieval Ceramics,* 24.

Davey P J, 2002, 'Pottery' in: Freke, 2002, 363-427.

Davey P J, in press, 'Medieval monasticism and the Isle of Man c1130-1540' in: Duffy, in press.

Davey P J (ed) 1999a, *Rushen Abbey, Ballasalla, Isle of Man: First Archaeological Report,* Centre for Manx Studies Research Report 7.

Davey P J, (ed) 1999b, *Recent archaeological research on the Isle of Man,* BAR British Series 278, Oxford, 241-260.

Davey P J, (ed) forthcoming, *Archaeological Research in the Isle of Man 1998-2000,* British Archaeological reports, British Series.

Davey P J (ed), in prep. Rushen Abbey, Ballasalla, Isle of Man: Second Archaeological Report, Centre for Manx Studies.

Davey P J, Freke D J & Higgins D A, 1996, *Excavations in Castletown, Isle of Man, 1989-92,* (Liverpool University Press).

Davey P J, Higgins D A, Johnson N C, McCartan S B & Woodcock J J, 1995, *Kerrowdhoo, Bride, Isle of Man: fieldwork and excavations 1992-1994,* Centre for Manx Studies Research Report 4, Douglas.

Davey P J & Hodges R (eds), 1983, *Ceramic and Trade: the production and distribution of later medieval pottery in north-west Europe,* (Department of Prehistory and Archaeology, University of Sheffield).

Davey P J & Johnson A, 1996, 'Pottery' in: Davey *et al.*, 1996, 16- 22, 65 - 88.

Davies E & Fleure H J, 1936, 'The Manx people and their origins', *Journal of the Royal Anthropological Institute*, 66, 129-188.

Duffy S (ed), in press, *A New History of the Isle of Man, Volume 3: The medieval Period*, (Liverpool University Press).

Egan G, 1996, 'Non-Ferrous Metal' in: Davey *et al*, 1996, 29-34.

Fisher C, 2002, 'The Bird Bones', in: Freke 2002, 252-257.

Fleure H J & Davies E, 1937, 'The Manx people and their origins', *Journal of the Manx Museum*, 3 (50 and 51), 172-177, 187-189.

Freke D J, 2002, *Excavations on St Patrick's Isle, Isle of Man, Prehistoric, Viking, Medieval and Later*, 1982-88 (Liverpool University Press).

Freke D J & Graham-Campbell, 2002, 'Metal artifacts' in: Freke 2002, 308-319.

Garrad L S, 1977, 'Was pottery made in the Isle of Man in medieval times?, in: Davey 1977, 109-112.

Garrad L S, 1984, 'Andreas, Ballavarry (SC 405983)', Medieval Archaeology, 28, 251 2.

Grant A, 1983, *North Devon Pottery: the Seventeenth Century*, (University of Exeter), 85-99.

Harris J, Fullen M A & Hallett M D, 2001, *Agricultural Soils of the Isle of Man*, Centre for Manx Studies Research Report 9, Douglas, 2-9, Fig 4.

Higgins D A, 1996, 'Excavations at Castle Rushen Stores, 1991-1992, in: Davey *et al.*, 1996, 49- 125.

Hurst-Vose R, 2002, 'Vessel and Window Glass' in: Freke, 2002, 331-338.

Hutchinson A R & Jones A K G, 2002, 'The Fish Remains' in: Freke 2002, 258-261.

Johnson N C, 1996, 'Ironwork' in Davey *et al*, 1996, 29.

Johnson N C forthcoming, 'Rescue excavations at the IRIS site, Peel, 2000' in: Davey (ed) forthcoming.

Kermode P M C,1910, 'S.Trinians', *Proceedings of the Isle of Man Natural History and Antiquarian Society*, New Series 1, 328-332.

Lewis J M, (ed), Peel Town: an archaeological and architectural assessment, (Isle of Man Government and University of Liverpool, Douglas), 55-74.

McMillan N, 2002, 'The Molluscs' in: Freke 2002, 262-263.

McNamee C, 1997, *The Wars of the Bruces: Scotland, England and Ireland, 1806-1328*, Tuckwell Press, East Linton, 58.

Megaw B R S, 1957, 'The Scottish invasion of Man in 1456', *Journal of the Manx Museum*, VI (74), 23-4.

Moore R A, 1999, 'The Manx Multiple Estate: evidence for undertones in the Manx land-system?' in: Davey (ed), 1999b, 171-182.

Oliver J R, 1861, *Monumenta de Insula Manniae*, 2, Manx Society vol. 7, Douglas.

Philpott R A & Davey P J, 1992, 'Peel Town sampling project 1985' in: Lewis (ed), 1992, 55-74.

Roscow J, 1996, 'Castletown Cottages', in: Davey *et al.*, 1996, 157-160.

Slade H G, 2002, 'Architectural Interpretation' in: Freke 2002, 209-220.

Stenning E H, 1935-37, 'Ancient structures uncovered at Derbyhaven May 1935', *Proceedings of the Isle of Man Natural History and Antiquarian Society*, 4, 145-51.

Storm G, 1897, *Exactions from the Norwegian Church Province to the Apostolic Chamber and College of Cardinals 1311-1523 from entries in the Papal Archives, Special publication to His Majesty King Oscar 11 on the occasion of the Government Jubilee, 1897,* Christiana. [Part translation from Norwegian (by J Farrington) and Latin (by W R Serjeant), 1956-57; Manx Museum Library F22/26]

Tomlinson P R, 1999, 'Biological Evidence from the 1998 excavations at Rushen Abbey' in: Davey (ed), 1999a, 72-76.

Tomlinson P R, 2002, 'Interim Report on the Larger Mammal Bones' in: Freke 2002, 248-249.

Painting of James Murray, the 2nd Duke of Atholl (1690-1764) (colour version inside back cover).

A Brief Encounter:
The Duke of Atholl
and the Isle of Man 1736 - 1764

Ros Stott

In 1736 James Murray, 2nd Duke of Atholl (1690-1764) inherited the Isle of Man. He was not the first Scottish lord of the Island.[1] Nor would he be the last.[2] He was, however, the only Scottish lord who held the Island as a feudal dependency of the English crown. In 1406 the Isle of Man had been granted in perpetuity to Sir John Stanley and his heirs (later Earls of Derby) and in 1610 to the heirs of James, 7th Earl of Derby. In 1736 the 10th Earl died without issue, leaving James Murray the closest male heir.[3] When he died in 1764, his heir sold the sovereign rights to the Island in the following year to the crown and the contract was confirmed by an act of Parliament known as the Revestment Act. In effect, therefore, James Murray was the Island's last feudal lord.

Every feudal lordship is unique and the distinguishing feature of the Duke of Atholl's lordship of the Isle of Man was the fact that it was only a temporary expedient. When he inherited the Island in 1736 questions of loyalty swirled around both the Duke and his inheritance. The Duke had been compromised by the actions of his brothers, and the Island was discredited by the row over trade which coloured all its relations with England in the eighteenth century. He therefore took possession of his property with great circumspection. His first Governor was sent to the Island with only his wit to ensure "quiet possession" of the Island and the continued observance of traditional symbols of feudal power. In sum then, the Duke's political sovereignty of the Island seems to have been compromised from the start. His economic sovereignty, however, was not. Indeed the extent to which the 2nd Duke treated the Isle of Man as an item of negotiable real estate seems excessive even by the standards of the "new civilian

---

[1]In 1266 Magnus of Norway ceded the Island to Alexander III of Scotland. It came under the protection of Edward II in 1290, but fell again to the Scots in 1313 when Robert the Bruce successfully invaded it. It fell permanently to the English crown in 1334 when Edward Balliol returned it to Edward III.

[2]His nephew John Murray (1729-1774) succeeded him as 3rd Duke of Atholl and was in turn succeeded by his son John (1755-1830) as 4th Duke of Atholl.

[3]He was the grandson of Lady Amelia Sophia, daughter of the 7th Earl of Derby.

feudalism" of the eighteenth century (Namier 1961, 18 - 26). Feudal law concerned the disposal of a grant of land, a feudum, or fee, the definitive characteristics of which were that it was perpetual and hereditary. The Duke felt bound by neither. Even before inheriting the Island he had committed himself to selling it to the crown. Immediately after inheriting it he began settling it in trust on members of his family. These trusts observed the language and form of feudal law—tenants were required to attorn to the new owners, etc.—but their purpose was not to reinforce but to circumvent that law, by ignoring the natural course of inheritance and treating with interested parties with a view to the sale of the Island.

When, in 1405, Henry IV conveyed the Island, the two Castles of Rushen and Peel, 23 rights, liberties and franchises and 11 items of land in perpetuity to his servant Sir John Stanley, he did so in the language of "prevailing English feudal law and custom" (Hytner 1981). Through a combination of myth, this feudal grant, and accumulated feudal ordinances, more than ten generations of the Stanley family enjoyed popular legitimacy and virtual independence as Lords of Man (Dickinson 1996).[4] On such foundations were early western states raised and like its more powerful neighbours, the lordship of Man was hostage to the fortunes of birth (Pocock 1957, 1987). However, inheritance can fail and it did so for the Derbys in 1736.[5] It had been clear for several years that there would be no Stanley heir to the lordship but the 10th Earl seems never to have contemplated the idea that the title of almost 350 years could leave his family. He thought he could bequeath the Island in his will, but when he died on February 1 1736 the Island fell to James Murray, 2nd Duke of Atholl. The Stanleys would contest this in court, but in 1751 Chancellor Lord Hardwicke ruled that the inheritance of the Island was inalienably vested in the heirs of the 7th Earl of Derby. Thus through a strict application of feudal law, the Isle of Man fell to the Murrays.

It would not remain there long. When the 2nd Duke assumed the lordship his family was already under considerable obligation to the crown. His elder brother William, along with two of his younger brothers, Charles and George, had been amongst the first to join the Earl of Mar in 1715. They fled when the uprising failed and they were all attainted for treason. William forfeited his inheritance. The following year the crown agreed to allow James to inherit the Atholl estates and he did so on the death of his father in 1724. At the time of his death the 1st Duke was seeking a pardon for his son George (Charles had died in 1720) and this was granted just after the 2nd Duke came into his inheritance.

By the early 1730s the 2nd Duke knew that he stood to inherit the Isle of Man (Manx Museum (MM) 1). He must also have known, given his family's political vulnerability, that there would be conditions. The most drastic came from the Treasury. It had been trying for many years to protect English, Irish and—after 1707—Scottish trading interests, by discouraging "dependencies" such as the Isle of Man from allowing their

---

[4]A quasi-mythological "constitution of old time," also known as "The Supposed True Chronicle of the Isle of Man," described the Island as a kingship. It is printed in An Abstract of the Laws, Customs, and Ordinances of the Isle of Man; compiled by John Parr, ed. by James Gell, Manx Society vol. xii (Douglas 1866).

[5]An earlier failure, in the 1590s, had led to the act of 1610, which settled the inheritance on the 7th Earl of Derby.

bays and harbours to be used as entrepôt centres.[6] Their lordships had tried persuasion. When that had failed there had been a brief period of accommodation following the 1707 Act of Union, when the Manx people tried to negotiate a similar trade agreement. This also failed and in the early 1720s the Treasury turned to legislation, with two very clumsy attempts to restrict Manx trade. In 1720 parliament passed an act containing a clause specifically prohibiting the Isle of Man from importing East Indian products.[7] In 1726 another act directly interfered, for the first time, in Manx trade by prohibiting the entry of all goods from the Isle of Man except local produce, and prohibiting the drawback on tobacco and other goods exported to the island (MM 2).

The legislation was badly crafted, either in ignorance or with mischievous intent and when, in 1726, an English customs officer tried to seize a cargo of "East India Goods" brought into a Manx harbour by Richard Green in his ship 'Dove', the customs officer had been challenged, "... it being doubtfull ... whether the officers of the Customs placed there who have Deputations from the Commissioners of the Customs in England can make a Seizure in that Island and Prosecute in the Courts there" (MM 3). The Attorney General thought not; the commissions of English Customs Officers "doth not extend to that Isle to impower their officers to make Seizures."

The decision should not have surprised anyone. It had long been established that no English legal authority below the crown exercised jurisdiction in the Isle of Man. However, it may have come as a shock to the legislators to realize that instead of making life more difficult for Manx traders, the act made life difficult for the English customs officers. After the Attorney General ruled that they could not make seizures in their official capacity, he went on to say that they could do so as private citizens. Therefore, after 1726, when investigating cargoes arriving in Manx ports, English customs officers were dependent on the good will and support of the Manx officials for any seizure they might wish to make.

Perhaps anticipating all this, another clause in the 1726 act authorised the Treasury to negotiate with the lord for the purchase of the Island. The origins of this radical proposal are unknown. Again, it was a very blunt instrument to use against Manx trading delinquents, and was probably equally illegal. It was certainly unenforceable, and the 10th Earl of Derby never contemplated entering into any negotiations with the Treasury. That changed, however, with the likelihood that the Duke of Atholl would become lord. On May 17 1733 the Duke accepted that the clause in the 1726 act was indeed a valid authorization for the Treasury to proceed, and it was agreed that the Duke should inherit the Isle of Man on condition that he and his heirs agreed "to sell the Isle to the crown within 7 years of taking possession" (NRA (S)).

This promise was probably not the only limit placed on the power of the new lord of Man. Immediately the 10th Earl died, and over Stanley objections, the Duke of Atholl had despatched James Murray to the Island as his Governor (Mathieson 1959). He was the Duke's man, promising to do "what to my understanding is best for

---

[6]The basic protection came from the 1660s Navigation Acts.

[7]After June 24 1721 no East India goods to enter the Isle of Man but those "Shipt in ... Ships Navigated according to the several Laws now in being upon Penalty of forfeiting Ship and Goods and such Ship and Goods ... may be seized and the same ... prosecuted in any of his Majestys Courts of Record at Westminister or Dublin ...".

securing your interest and the Affections of the people ...". However, he was not totally bound to the Duke and others had probably had a role in his selection, because he was a retired military officer currently on leave from the Treasury, where he was the Receiver General of Scotland.

The Governor had instructions to secure the Island for the Duke and investigate the state of the revenues and, but for him, Atholl might not have assumed possession so effortlessly. By the time his Governorship was over in 1743, his successor was able to report that he was "universalie beloved and esteemed here to this day" (MM 4). Even a critic called him a man of "Most natural strong good Parts" with liberal inclinations, while adding "unfortunately most strongly influenced by Principles which are so peculiar to people of that nation ... [and] confirmed by a French Education ..." (MM 5).[8] Governor Murray's long letters to the Duke were not the equal of Boswell, but they were written in the same usefully observational style and shed a little more light on the character of this much admired man.

He arrived with little identification. The crowd waiting on shore that watched him disembark at Derbyhaven one Thursday morning in late March had no idea who he was, were quite in the dark about the inheritance, and were still loyal to the Stanley family (MM 6).[9] He was told that a few weeks before his arrival the people had been "firing ... cannon [and] making very merry" on the strength of a letter from the former Governor of the Island "that Sir Edward Stanley was Earl of Derby and undoubtedly Lord of Mann." By the middle of April Murray was still unable to counter rumours that Sir Edward had taken his seat in the House of Lords "and would as certainly be Lord of this Island" (MM 7).

He had no troops but he did have a strategy. Describing himself as "naturally cautious and mistrustfull," his main aim was to keep things "as quiet as could be imagined," to act "for Your Graces Interest and the quiet of Your Island" and he was indeed soon able to report that he had secured the "quiet possession of this Island" (MM 8). However, it was "a ticklish time", he wrote later, needing "some truths and some Seasonable Lies" (MM 9).

The problem seems to have been that the Duke did not have overall military command of the Island. He should have been able to give his Governor his commission, but when Murray presented himself to the Island's principal military officer, Major General Christian, and was asked for the "proper Authority" from Atholl, he could only say that he had to see the Bishop first. Later, in conversation with some people who "suspected I came with powers from Your Grace," he had "thought it best by insinuations to confirm them in that Opinion." The papers he revealed to the Bishop the following day showed that he had a letter from Atholl and a commission sent separately, "with instructions." Unfortunately, we learn nothing more about these important documents, beyond the fact that the Bishop "seemed ... pleased" and they also satisfied the Major General to whom Murray presented them the following day as promised (MM 10).

His second objective was the compliance of the Island's leading inhabitants. All those prepared to acknowledge the Duke's claim to the title were to be "kept in the same

---

[8]The writer was one of those rabidly xenophobic Englishmen common in mid-eighteenth century England, for whom effeminate, Scots and Fiench were equally damning epithets.
[9]His name soon circulated and they took this "to be a hint enough" (MM 6).

temper untill you were put in full possession of the Island. It will be time enough to make what changes you think proper on or after your Arrival," he wrote (MM 11). He met the Duke's officers for the first time on the morning of his swearing-in ceremony. It was necessary for them, too, to take oaths and they were invited to do so.[10] "They all made a low bow and said your Grace was most Gracious." The comptroller hesitated, but later decided he had been "ill advised" and Murray excused him, having no desire to make a martyr of him amongst "the mob" and no power anyway, he wrote, to replace someone who controlled "all business in the Island" (MM 12).[11]

It was probably with some relief, then, that Murray found himself greeting them all at his lodgings at three o'clock that afternoon. They walked to the castle "in great procession", where they were sworn in and listened to the Governor read his commission and "Instructions." Then he was "led up to a particular Stone in the pavement a White rod put in my hand and I took the usual oath" as 5 guns were fired. Thirty soldiers marched "up to the cross"; Murray followed "with my White Stick, [and] we drank health and prosperity to the Duke of Atholl & Lord of Mann and the Isles and 7 guns [were] fired from the castle." Toasts followed "to the King Queen etc., beer and punch to the people." And "all this" he marvelled, "without the least disturbance."

His third objective was to appear judicious. As governor he was also Chancellor, and "without appearing over fond of power", he wrote, "I shall endeavour to keep a just mean" (MM 13). He had no great knowledge of Island law and complained that the people are "... certainly the most litigious of all the human race" (MM 14). However, he dutifully took his seat as a judge in the Islands courts, although he came close to panic when he learnt that the Island's previous comptroller, now a Lancashire Attorney, had arrived on the Island (MM 15).[12] "For god's Sake My Lord come over directly and in the meantime I shall do my utmost to keep things right and Open."

His fourth objective was to observe other established customs and give proper regard to all other symbols of power. He was anxious to visit the forts, because it is custom, he wrote, "on such occasions to fire some guns" and he urged Atholl to take possession of the Island personally. Nothing would please the people more, he wrote; "all the people [are] fond of seeing their Lord it is indeed the only thing they agree in" (MM 16).[13] The Duke must come to the annual Tynwald Court on June 24th. There was more chance of having "any Law [passed] you may think for Your advantage at the beginning of Your Reign than any other time."

The Governor promised "a magnificent cavalcade" and began to fuss over details, (all of which came to pass when the Duke did indeed visit the Island as requested). The Duke's arrival had to be carefully orchestrated; he must take care to signal his arrival; all the Officers must be there; addresses must be read; "everything shall be managed with as much Solemnity as possible." There was also the question of the regalia. "The

---

[10]The Comptroller and Attorney General kept the Island's legal and finance records. The receiver General and the Water Bailiff collected the rents, fines and customs. Two Deemsters and 24 Keys, the Island's assembly of tenants, made up the rest of the legislature.

[11]He was keeper of the records (MM 12).

[12]The Sheading, or Common Law, courts were conducted in Manx, and "the Governor has only the pleasure of Sitting eight hours a Cypher?" (MM 15).

[13] "Since their dear Lord William's dayes (pre 1702) they have never seen anything above a Governor ..." (MM 16).

Sword of State might have been a fine thing in the days of Yore but now rusty and very paultry Yr' Grace should order Another. Let it only be glaring it is no matter what metal it is made of."

Without force, then, but with military determination, Governor Murray achieved "quiet possession" of the Island. It was a provisional possession, because the 2nd Duke knew he wouldn't hold the Island in perpetuity. He was, however, determined to profit from it. There was a "constant cry for money" from the Dukes of Atholl throughout the eighteenth century and the 2nd Duke seemed particularly needy (Leneman 1986). He had houses and estates to beautify and an aristocratic family to support. Towards all this the Island had to contribute. Services and produce were welcome, but what the Duke really wanted from the Isle of Man was cash.

After securing the Island, Governor Murray had orders to review the Island's revenues. Rules and regulations concerning the collection of revenue were centuries old. Murray's job was to modernize procedures for the new regime. He soon found that he had a great many interests to accommodate. The Derbys for example, continued to hover around the Treasury. Murray found it locked and the Duke ordered it opened by force, but Murray refused. The previous Governor had already taken most of the money away, but what remained had not been collected by Atholl's Officers and it was felt a representative of the late Earl ought to be present (MM 17). Murray thought it "better they at present should be humour'd" and ordered another room set up for Atholl's money.

Merchants also had to be accommodated. "Locking up all the merchants Cellars in the Island" till he had Atholl's instructions wouldn't do because it "might have put a Stop to all trade" (MM 18). Insisting on the full amount of customs duty might equally "stop trade" and also "give a bad notion of the lenity of Yr Grace's government." The usual practice was to make a bargain with them "as it is none of your interest I hope [and] none of your inclination to totally ruin the merchant."[14] Finally the Duke's officers had to be remembered; the practice was to divide up the duty, with one quarter going to the comptroller, one quarter to the collector and a half to the Lord.

All this probably came as an unwelcome shock to the Duke, but Murray made one improvement which no doubt pleased him. Not long after he arrived the Governor noticed ships in Douglas bay whose cargoes were being broken up and transferred into wherries. Some merchants broke up cargoes to avoid paying Manx customs duties; others did so because they supplied merchants who couldn't afford to pay duty on a whole cargo (MM 19). Murray was concerned with neither. He insisted that the practice must stop because "by the Law of England breaking bulk at Sea forfeits Ship and Cargo" (MM 20).

Manxmen were not generally agreeable to the enforcement of English Law in their waters but in this case there was little complaint. By forcing merchants to land their cargoes first, and pay the full Manx, or more precisely ducal, customs, Murray probably put some small traders out of business. Merchants dealing in whole cargoes suffered less. Manx customs were not heavy and, as we have seen, were subject to negotiation.

---

[14]Bargaining with foreign merchants was a long established custom on the Island, although historically, to protect the inhabitants not the merchants.

While Murray was probably not intending to favour the Duke—he was scrupulously honest, writing that "if any dar'd to talk to me of anything had relation to corruption I wold lay him in Irons"—the cynical saw it as a "masterly stroke of Policey, for it not only increas'd ... Athol's Revenues but it gave the utmost Encouragement to the inhabitants to extend their trade and to invite others to come and settle in the Island" (MM 21).

That this was indeed the case is born out in the record of cash periodically taken to Liverpool. The Attorney General usually transferred it, on the ships of a few trusted captains, into the hands of "a merchant of good credit" (MM 22). Sums steadily rose as Governor Murray's revenue reforms were implemented and customs revenues improved. £4,600 was carried to London in 1751-the largest sum ever to leave the Island (MM 23). In 1754 John Sanforth, a trusted Island trader for over 30 years, put 2500 gns "into our iron chest where we keep our money" (MM 24).

The Island itself was, of course, the biggest item for sale. After showing the Earl of Derby that he could not dispose of the Island as he wished, the Duke of Atholl then proceeded to do just that. Almost immediately after inheriting the Island the Duke began to deed it in trust to family members through a series of legal instruments (Train 1850). By the "Indenture or Deed of Feoffment with Livery and seisin ... Nov 14 1737" the 2nd Duke "did Sell Alien Enfeoff and Confirm" the Island to his uncle John late Earl of Dunmore, the Hon Wm Murray Solicitor General, later Attorney General [later Lord Mansfield] and John Murray of the City of Edinburgh Esq" (MM 25). The Trustees would "Execute all ... Leases:" Atholl would "enjoy ... the Rents." After his death the Trustees would continue to pay Fees out of the Islands Revenues to all Persons holding Office within the Isle." They were also allowed "with the Consent ... of whoever after Atholl's death might be entitled to the Island's Revenues, to sell the Island to any person and for such Price as they could reasonably get."

Over the next twenty-five years the trusteeship was revoked and rewritten as trustees died, new financial circumstances emerged, and the prospect of selling the Island waxed and waned. The most important revision was made in 1756 when the Duke of Argyle and Lord Stormont replaced Dunmore, who had died (Train 1850, MM 25). Instead of authorizing the trustees to sell to anyone, this new contract only authorised them to sell to the King. It also specified that the proceeds from such a sale were to be used to buy lands in Scotland for the benefit of the Duke's heirs.

Writing in 1765 or 1766, George Moore, a prominent merchant, claimed these trusteeships were meaningless (MM 26). The 2nd Duke "could neither alienate the Isle of Man nor newly model the succession of it ... all the feoffments and conveyances of the Island in his time were nullities and waste-paper ... the trust he created for sale of the Island was void." This may have been true, but it was surely irrelevant. The Trusts had existed and trustees had administered the Island for the Duke. In 1747 Lord Mansfield had been made the judge of appeals brought before the Duke of Atholl (MM 27). The Duke of Argyle had been consulted regarding incidents involving customs officers, proposals for the sale of the Island and the appointment of at least two, and probably all three Governors who succeeded Murray (MM 28).

When the 2nd Duke died in January 1764 his heir duly inherited the Island, but just twelve months later the contract was concluded between the Treasury, the Duke and Duchess of Atholl and *their trustees,* for the sale of the Island to the crown (MM 29). Moore might well conclude, as he did, that "... the agreement made by the Treasury for purchase of the Island was made with persons who were not authorized to sell," but by then the Island was sold. The Revestment Act is generally considered the instrument through which the lord of the Island sold his sovereign rights to the English crown. But, what, by that time, did this mean? Did the Duke of Atholl ever have sovereign rights to the Island, and if not, who really led this lordship during its brief encounter with Scottish authority?

Acknowledgement

Painting of the 2nd Duke of Atholl by permission of Blair Castle, Perthshire.

References

Dickinson J R, 1996, *The Lordship of Man under the Stanleys* (Preston).

Hytner J, 1981-83, in R. Crookall et al., Isle of Man Harbour Board, *Manx Law Reports* p. 274.

Leneman L, 1986, *Living in Atholl. A Social History of the Estates 1685-1785* (Edinburgh University Press) p. 9.

Mathieson N, 1959-64, 'The Governors during the Atholl Lordship'. *Proceedings of the Isle of Man Natural History and Antiquarian Society* v 6 pp. 46-63.

Moore A W, 1900, *History of the Isle of Man* (Douglas), 2 vols. p. 435.

Namier L B, 1961, *England in the Age of the American revolution,* pp. 18-26. (London).

Pocock J G A, 1957, 1987, *The Ancient Constitution and the Feudal Law. A Study of English Historical Thought in the Seventeenth Century* (Camb UP) pp. 100, 101, 107.

Train J, 1850, *An Historical and Statistical Account of the Isle of Man from the Earliest Times to the Present date* (Douglas) pp. 117-119.

MM 1: 'An Act for the Assuring and Establishing the IoM' (1731) and decision of P Yorke, June 11 1733. Atholl Papers (AP) 60(2)-2,3,25,26,27.

MM 2: AP 60(2)-34.

MM 3: Aug 23 1727 "Opinion of Att Gen [Sir P Yorke]" AP 60(2)-9.

MM 4: AP X/9-6 Mar 26 1736; AP X/42-18 May 23 1748; AP X/9-15 Nov 28 1736.

MM 5: GR1/73.

MM 6: AP X/9-6 Mar 26 1736.

MM 7: AP X/9-8 Apr 18 1736.

MM 8: AP X/9-7,10,15.

MM 9: AP X/9-10 May 1 1736.

MM 10: AP X/9-6 Mar 26 1736

MM 11: AP X/9-10 May 1 1736.

MM 12: AP X/9-6 Mar 26 1736.

MM 13: AP X/9-7 Apr 5 1736.

MM 14: AP X/9-12 May 5 1736.

MM 15: AP XO9/13.

MM 16: AP X/9-7 Apr 5 1736.

MM 17: AP X/9-6 Mar 26 1736.

MM 18: AP X/9-12 May 5 1736.

MM 19: AP 58-2.

MM 20: AP X/9-12.

MM 21: AP X/9-10 May 1 1736; MM GR 1/73.

MM 22: AP X/11-1,13.

MM 23: AP X/13-6.

MM 24: AP X027(2).

MM 25: GR 1/74.

MM 26: Ms 590C.

MM 27: Lib Can (Chancery Books) 1747.

MM 28: AP X/42-31; AP X8-19; AP X/14-14-17; AP X/26-24; AP X/10-42.

MM 29: Ms 590C.

NRA (S) (National Register of Archives (Scotland)) 0234 Murray Family, Dukes of Atholl 46(7)3 DoA to Geo II.

Manx Farming Communities and Traditions. An examination of Manx farming between 1750 and 1900

C J Page

Introduction

Set in the middle of the Irish Sea, the Isle of Man was far from being an isolated community. Being over 33 miles long by 13 miles wide, with a central mountainous land mass, meant that most of the cultivated area was not that far from the shore and the influence of the sea. Until recent years the Irish Sea was an extremely busy stretch of water, and the island greatly benefited from the trade passing through it. Manxmen had long been involved with the sea and were found around the world as members of the British merchant fleet and also in the British navy. Such people as Fletcher Christian from HMAV Bounty, (even its captain, Lieutenant Bligh was married in Onchan, near Douglas), and also John Quilliam who was First Lieutenant on Nelson's Victory during the Battle of Trafalgar, are some of the more notable examples.

However, it was fishing that employed many Manxmen, and most of these fishermen were also farmers, dividing their time between the two occupations (Kinvig 1975, 144). Fishing generally proved very lucrative, especially when it was combined with the other aspect of the sea - smuggling. Smuggling involved both the larger merchant ships and also the smaller fishing vessels, including the inshore craft. Such was the extent of this activity that by the mid-18th century it was costing the British and Irish Governments £350,000 in lost revenue, plus a further loss to the Irish administration of £200,000 (Moore 1900, 438). Not being able to countenance these losses any further the British Government took over the island for the Crown under 'The Revestment Act' in 1765. This put a stop to the main smuggling routes and it threw the Manx economy into chaos. Traders and merchantmen moved on to more lucrative areas and the Manx were left to look towards farming and fishing for their income. This event had the effect of stimulating agricultural development and numbers of the larger land-owners (who had also mainly been merchantmen) began to invest in the land.[1]

---

[1]In an undated letter (c.1813) in the Atholl collection in the Library of Manx National Heritage, Douglas: Major Taubman (one of the largest landowners) is identified as 'the son of the Taubman whose extensive

The status of agriculture began to rise, especially after 1765, with more attention being paid to increasing returns. The Manx were not unaware of the changes taking place within the farming industry abroad. As seafarers they were much travelled, with even the smaller farmers coming into contact with farming men in England, Scotland and Ireland, wherever they put into port during trading or fishing expeditions (Radcliffe 1991, 9).

The land on the island was also a temptation to farmers from England and Scotland who moved to take advantage of cheap farms, whilst having expanding markets close at hand, especially in Liverpool and the growing cotton towns. Some of these 'strangers' as they were called were wealthy, others succeeded by borrowing. Manx laws at this time protected residents on the island against debts incurred elsewhere. This encouraged many debtors to settle on the island, most were in Douglas and the other towns but a few farmed. This changed after 1814 when the law was repealed. Retired military officers and their families soon replaced the debtors. They were on half pay and, with low prices for commodities on the island, their pensions would go a long way (Belchem 2000, 18-22).

Many of the immigrant farmers worked their land to the latest methods of the time, and in a highly commercial fashion. However the levels of investment these people were putting into their businesses sometimes proved their downfall, with more than one farmer ending up in the debtors prison at Castle Rushen, Castletown.[2]

By the mid-19th century agriculture had become the mainstay of the island's economy. Tourism was growing, but this growth, although slow, helped to provide a lucrative market for the farmers. Only the smaller farmers and crofters still worked the dual economy of fishing and farming, coupled now with the added incentive of mining. Mining flourished from the 1830s to the 1890s but, by the end of the century, tourism had become one of the main sources of wealth. This is shown by the annual returns for visitors to the island between 1830 and 1900: In 1830, 20,000 people came to the island annually; in 1866 this had reached 60,000 and in 1880, 93,000. By 1885 it had jumped to 183,000, in 1890 to 294,000 and by 1900 it had reached 384,000. All these people had to be fed and serviced and this provided seasonal employment.

Tradition played its part within the Manx farms, but these traditions were tempered with economic reality. To a subsistence farmer the level of capital input was small, the main income for the family coming largely from fishing and mining. Traditional farming also provided continuity for that society. Its pace was governed by the state of the seasons and the involvement of the local community, especially at high points such as the hay and corn harvests. These farming methods were often referred to in a disparaging manner by contemporary writers and agricultural propagandists, yet they

---

smuggling transactions were the principal means of my family (Duke of Atholl) being deprived of their rights in the Island.'

[2]Isle of Man Gazette, 9 June 1812, a letter from Mr S.Bullock, a well known farmer who had settled from England and was now writing to his creditors from the debtors gaol, Castletown, pleading to be let out to harvest his crops.

had an efficient and effective use of labour, giving a good return on the limited capital available, especially on marginal land. This point was discussed by Bell (1986, 24-41).

The returns from the land had to be viewed against what was required by the farmer from his farm. The primary wish was to feed his family, which left only a small surplus to sell at open market (and fairs). With limited capital and time the low outputs of the farm matched the low inputs. The farmers and crofters gave their time to fishing as it was seen to give an assured and regular income. By the mid-19th century fishing was being challenged as the other part of this dual occupation with farming, with the rise of mining and tourism. The Manx farmer pursued this dual economy to achieve a level of efficiency that was reflected in their quality of life.

The agricultural methods used on the small Manx farms in the 1750s were vastly different from those used on such farms in 1900. The types of crop, rotations and equipment all were different, yet to mainstream agriculturalists they were regarded as traditional. The use of the iron swing plough on the upland farm of 1900 had been at the cutting edge of technology in 1800, when the small farms were still using wooden ploughs. Indeed many such farms at this time were still using lazy beds to grow crops and the spade to cultivate, a method that gradually died out by the end of the 19th century (Figure 1).

Change reflected the age and attitude of the farmer and also the surrounding community along with the economic pressures faced by the families. In general the change from subsistence to commercial farming was made between 1820 and 1850 with only the marginal small farmers hanging on until the early years of the 20th century.

Many of these small farms were referred to as crofters. This was not the same as the Scottish crofter but covered small farms on marginal land, either occupying high ground or stony and wet soils. The Manx word for croft was croit and land holdings bearing that name could be found in 17th and 18th century documents such as Croit Casteena (Christian's Croft) from Bride Mortgages of 1725 (Radcliffe 1982, 68).

The land and its administration

The island is divided into six administrative and political areas known as Sheadings. These are Ayre, Garff and Michael in the north and Glenfaba, Middle and Rushen in the south. Each had its own courts and maintained officers, the most important being the Coroner, who served summonses, returned juries and levied any fines, as well as disposing of estates on behalf of creditors.

Within each Sheading there were three parishes, apart from Glenfaba with two. These each had 'Locksmen' who aided the coroner in his work. The Sheading took on increased importance after 1866 when the Island's government, 'the House of Keys' became an elected body. Each Sheading put forward three members, with Douglas also represented by three members and Peel, Ramsey and Castletown each having one member.

Within each parish the land was divided down further into Treens, which certainly date from the medieval period and may possibly be earlier. Each Treen was further subdivided into Quarterlands. There were generally four to each Treen and were about

Figure 1: Two swing ploughs made by T and J Lewin, blacksmiths, Marown.

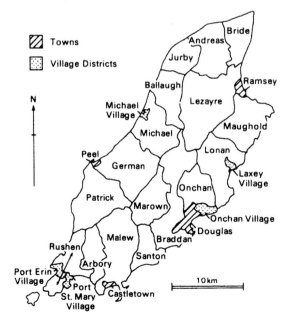

Figure 2: Parishes of the Isle of Man.

50 to 100 acres in size. They formed the land holding for the main farms, following similar subdivisions to those found on the West Coast of Scotland and within the Irish clachan (Page in preparation, 24) (Figure 2).

Some Quarterland farms were further subdivided as a result of marriage settlements or inter-family agreements. These small farms formed the crofts and their sizes could range from as little as 1 acre to around 30 acres (Radcliffe 1993, 6). Below these came a further group referred to under the English classification of cotter. The cotters generally were landless but grazed their livestock on common land and on the roadside, referred to as 'grazing the long acre'.

All land had originally belonged to the Lords of Man, who had been the Earls of Derby up until the 'Act of Settlement' in 1704, when ownership was confirmed to the existing tenants, and the rights of accession to the tenants' heirs was assured. From 1736 the lordship passed into the hands of the Dukes of Atholl (Kinvig 1975, 114). The common land, which included most of the upland above 600 feet, remained in the hands of the Lord of Man until the 'Act of Revestment' in 1765 when it was acquired for the British Crown. The common land became Crown property under the direction of a Forester, who was appointed to manage it including control of the livestock being grazed on the ground by neighbouring farmers and crofters. This common ground also provided domestic fuel in the form of turf, and it was these grazing and fuel rights that were so jealously guarded by the surrounding communities. Where this had been challenged it had often drawn a violent response.

Over the years, adjacent quarterland farms had gradually enclosed portions of these commons - sod-hedges or stonewalls being constructed to surround them. These grounds were known as 'intack land' and were bought from the Lord of Man. They provided secure rough grazing land, mainly for sheep, though some were cultivated for corn production. The grievances against enclosing such land came to a head in 1724 when a riot occurred over the granting of a licence for land on the mountain. Further disturbances occurred later in the century as more land became enclosed. In 1763 when John Llewellyn of Ramsey took over a large stretch of mountain land above the town, the Duke of Atholl was petitioned by 28 inhabitants of the parish of Maughold objecting to this enclosure. The dispute was settled relatively quietly but other occasions saw a more aggressive result. One of the more fierce was the 'Battle of Perk ny h' Earkan' which took place in 1854. Here a group of local men, known as the 'Sulby Cossacks', continuously destroyed the newly constructed walls surrounding a 300-acre stretch of land and threatened the new owner's life. This dispute eventually came to the House of Keys, resulting in the Disafforestation Act of 1860, which gave one third of the land to the Queen, a third to the people and made one third available for sale (Quayle 1979, 19).

This Act did not stop the animosity, however, as a new wall enclosing Park Llewellyn was thrown down in 1861 and tempers had to be cooled. Another volatile confrontation took place above Foxdale. Here the authorities used strong tactics through the use of the Militia. On throwing out the crofters from land soon to be sold, they then set fire to all their turf butts that had been drying ready for collection. This caused a riot that became more serious when the crofters were joined by the miners from Foxdale. It was only the intervention of the Mines' manager that stopped it escalating further. The soldiers that carried out this work were later reprimanded for

Figure 3: A stone-faced hedge being constructed at Manx National Heritage's farm at Cregneash in 1997. This was part of a competition designed to help preserve such skills.

their action. The people's third was vested in a board of trustees, which later became absorbed by the Manx Government under the Department of Forestry.

The distinctive hedges surrounding a patchwork quilt of numerous small fields shape the character of the Manx countryside. These hedges are formed from earth banks faced either with sod or stone and topped with gorse. There was no formal enclosure of the land but ground was temporarily enclosed in the summer, using turf banks, which were thrown down each winter. In 1656 these banks were ordered to be retained until later in the year due to the lateness of the harvest and in 1665 legislation was passed to retain these banks throughout the winter.

The sizes of these hedges were specified by law as 5' high, increasing to 5' 6" in 1691 or 6' if there was no trench by the side, the trench being set at 1'6" deep and 3' wide (Moore 1900, 918). Gorse was set in the top, with seeds being set into straw rope laid into a slot cut into the hedge. The rotting straw provided nutrition for the young gorse. The gorse protected the top of the hedge from livestock but it was common until the end of the 19th century to lanket both sheep and cattle to stop them jumping over the hedges and walls. These lankets, made from straw (suggane), tied one front foot to a back foot, so restricting the animal's ability to jump hedges. There are still lanket making competitions held on the island, although the act of using lankets has long since been banned due to animal welfare regulations and improved stock proof fencing. The sizes of fields range from 1 to 10 acres and are often of an irregular shape, the hedges being far from running a straight path. There are various reasons put forward as to why these hedges are not straight and of these the more credible include: that they were following secure ground for the foundations, or that they offer more protection to the livestock from strong winds.

Specific designs for spades have evolved to construct the Manx hedges and examples can be seen at the museum in Douglas. Reproductions have been used to good effect at Cregneash Village Folk Museum to enable the hedges to be restored using early construction techniques (Killip 1970, 60-66) (Figure 3).

In contrast, the stone walls of the upland farms and mountain intacks were built straight and bold, negotiating rock outcrops and often covering ground that looked impossible to traverse. These had been constructed since the 1860s, many by Cumberland wallers. Different styles can be found throughout the island and may reflect where the builders had originated. In Laxey some of the walls are tall and wide, capable of taking a cart on the top, similar to some northeastern Scottish dikes. A more consistent style is found in the large stone gate pillars, which reflect Irish practice more than English (Figure 4).

In an island such as this, one of the more constant problems other than wind is rain. There is a high average rainfall throughout but on the uplands this can very high indeed, 40 inches in Douglas and 57 inches in Druidale (Birch 1964).[3] Good for growing grass, it presented problems for producing crops, with cold soils, late germination and mildew being just part of the difficulties. To control this the lazy bed system of cultivation lasted until well into the 19th century. These were raised beds, formed with a spade, wide for corn, narrow for roots. This allowed excess water to safely drain away between the rows. The small fields enabled a system of surface

---

[3]These figures refer to information gained between 1918-1957.

Figure 4: Stone walling by students learning traditional skills at Manx National Heritage's farm at Cregneash in 1996.

drains to take water away quickly, these being supplied by slate lined box drains constructed 18 inches below the ground surface. This method of drainage seems to have begun in the late 18th century and was wide spread by the 1820s. Clay tile drains were introduced by Turnstall and Co at a brickworks near Ramsey, and attracted much attention when they exhibited examples at the Manx agricultural show of 1845 (Manx Sun 1845). As with hedge building, thatching and wall building, under draining was a recognised practice used by most farmers and farm workers.

The structure of the farm and cottage

Farms were generally found in isolated positions, set around the countryside to take advantage of shelter and fresh water. There were few villages and towns of size until the 19th century, the urban expansion really beginning after the 1820s.

Table: Population growth in the Isle of Man

Year	1792	1821	1841	1861	1881
Town	7237	11522	15167	20623	25816
Country	20676	28559	32819	31846	27742
Total	27913	40081	47986	52469	53558
Douglas	3625	6054	8647	12511	15719

Structures relied upon local material, and early buildings had their walls constructed of stone in the south and earth in the north. Stone buildings however were more common throughout the island with the style changing to accommodate the type of stone available. In the north they mainly used rounded stone collected from the shoreline. In central areas the walls were often found constructed of granite but slate was the main building material used. Sod houses could also be found throughout the island, especially used for temporary summer dwellings (sheilings) when cattle were taken out to the upland pastures. They were far more common in the north of the island where examples lasted until the 20th century (Figure 5).

Timber had always been a problem as the Isle of Man was devoid of significant woodland until recent years. Most timber had to be imported but there was a high level of re-use. Ships' timbers were common for roofing with masts, spars, even old oars being used in the cottages found at Cregneash. Discarded parts of agricultural equipment, especially old cart shafts found favour, as well as timber from earlier buildings. 'Waste not, want not' was a proverb well understood by all Manxmen.

The roofs were thatched, marram grass being preferred in the north, and wheat straw elsewhere, although oats, the prominent crop in most upland areas, would possibly be used (oats has a much shorter life span and would require thatching each year). Ling may also have been used especially for outbuildings.

The method of thatching was simple but effective with a base of turf strips, *skraa,* first being laid on the roof. The straw was then laid on this surface. It was not pegged as in the English style but was placed in layers then an old fishing net was laid over to be tied down tightly by a series of ropes running the length of the building and across, each rope *suggane* tied firmly to stone pegs *bwhid-suggane* set into the walls. The rope was originally made from straw but later, around 1850, it was replaced by coir. The hay

Figure 5: Mrs Mary Gilrea's sod cottage in the parish of Jurby, c1897; she was known as 'Gilrea of the Gorse'. The walls were built entirely of sod blocks and the roof was thatched with Marram grass.

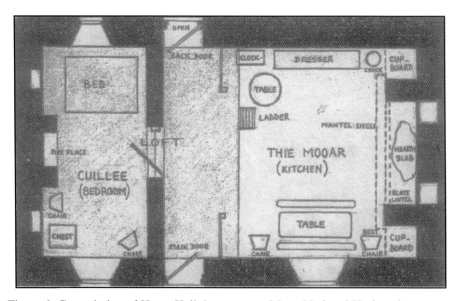

Figure 6: Ground plan of Harry Kelly's cottage at Manx National Heritage's museum and farm at Cregneash; it is typical of many Manx Cottages.

and corn stacks, often made in the round and called *thurrans,* were thatched in a similar way.

Inside a Manx cottage the dominant room was the kitchen/living room or *thie mooar.* This contained the open hearth *(chiollagh),* with its turf fire. At the other end of the building was a bedroom for the head of the family. Above was a half floor or cock loft, where the children slept. Below, between the two main rooms was the front door, which often had a second door in the opposite wall, so allowing for an airflow to aid the winnowing of the corn after threshing (Figure 6).

There were various ground plans to the farms in the island but two forms predominated. In one, the main farm buildings are placed at right angles to the farmhouse, and in the other they run parallel. The area between these farm buildings and the house was known as the street. A cow house (generally holding between 4 to 5 cattle), stable, pigsty or *mucklagh* and a calf house made up the early farms (Figure 7).

By the 1840s the designs were changing. The cottages on the small farms remained largely the same, but two storied barns were now being built, with space for cattle below and hay above. Stables were also built in a similar way. Pigsties now had runs rather than just letting the animal roam about the street. On some farms these sties were in two tiers, the pig occupying the bottom floor and hens above. This was more common on the large quarterland farms.

The quarterland farm houses were often two storied with two rooms on the ground floor plus a dairy and back kitchen. Above there were two to three main rooms with some smaller servants' rooms. The roof was usually covered with Welsh slates, a status symbol in itself; also a cast iron range had replaced the open *chiollagh,* especially when it was near the town where coal was readily available. During the Napoleonic period, between the 1830s and 40s, again in the 1860s and the last decades of the 19th century there were periods of extensive improvement to buildings and land. Indeed, the second half of the 19th century saw a much more steady economic growth with the development of the tourist industry.

A feature of the 1860s was the growth of threshing mills; many were light two horse machines with a distinctive circular horse walk set outside the barn, a characteristic symbol that appeared on the Ordnance Survey maps of the period. Many were powered by water and some by wind. Some of these machines were made on the island by firms such as Kelly and Corlett of Kirk Michael. Some were imported from Scotland. Drummonds of Cummnock constructed one at Cregneash in 1885.

A Scots farmer who had settled in the island first introduced threshing mills to the Isle of Man in 1798. This was only a few years after Andrew Meakle near Edinburgh had invented them in 1796. By 1812 there were 23 such mills in operation, both horse and water powered, and one driven by steam (Quayle 1812, 38). Two covered horse walks from this period still survive.[4] They were for the larger farms and were costly items to install. They replaced the flail that remained common until the end of the 19th century. Generally a jointed flail was used but in some areas of the island a crooked stick was used, with the operator having to kneel down to the work (Figure 8).

---

[4]One is at Balladoole, Castletown and the other is in Santon.

Figure 7: Karran's croft, 1947, a typical croft layout with the cottrage on the right and the farm buildings at right angles (to the left of the cottage) with the stable occupying the left end of this building and the cow house the right.

Figure 8: Threshing corn flails. These are fixed flails formed from angled branches; the operators have to kneel down to enable the flail to hit the crop flat on the ground.

By the 1860s portable threshing machines had appeared, with one of the earliest being owned by William Farrant at Ballamoore Castle, in the north. He owned a Clayton and Shuttleworth machine bought directly from Lincoln, but he hired an engineer from Scotland to attend it and train local people in its operation.[5] By the end of the 19th century there were a number of such machines run by farmers and contractors who travelled them around the country (Figure 9).

Investment by the bigger landowners resulted in large, well appointed farm buildings, often set around a central yard to give shelter. Staward Farm is a typical example; built in 1842 for Major Caesar Bacon it contained all that was modern and labour saving. Constructed in Manx slate with a Welsh slate roof, it was built by a Northumberland stone mason (the Bacon family had come from that county in 1724). It contained stables, cart sheds, loose boxes, a beef house, turnip and straw houses and stalls for milking cattle. The threshing mill added a year later had a Clayton and Shuttleworth machine driven by water. The Bacons had made their money as merchants, similar to many of the Manx gentry. Other native landowners had similar farms, which rivalled those operated by the immigrant Scottish and English farmers.

Farm Management

At the beginning of the 19th century reports on the state of Manx farming drew statements such as 'agriculture is here yet a recent art' (Quayle 1812, 20). This came from 1812, ten years later Hainings' guide to the island stated 'although agriculture is too much of the ancient kind, yet improvement has made good progress within these last thirty years' (Hainings 1822).

Those commentators were typical of their time being more concerned to promote the latest improved agricultural techniques as opposed to the older methods then popular. A primary subject for their disapproval was in crop management. Continuous cropping was practised by many 'native farmers' when they took successive crops until the yields fell away. At this stage the general practice was to let the land 'tumble down to grass'. Christian Curwen found that some of those employing 'more improved current practice' were only taking 2 to 3 white crops consecutively. Curwen also illustrated the work of one of the larger landowners from the south of the island, Edward Gawne. 'His rotation was: 1st - clover ley, 2nd - barley, 3rd - potatoes, 4th - undersown barley, 5th - hay; the land was limed every 5th or 6th year' (Curwen 1807, 66).

Rotation had become established practice by the 1840s, especially on the quarterland farms as recorded by the newly established Manx Agricultural Society. The formation of this organisation was in itself a mark of the rights of passage towards the dominance of commercial farming over the subsistence farming mentality. This was the first major, local, agricultural society, although a short-lived organisation had been formed between 1798 and 1801. After this the next attempt was made between 1806 and 1813, as a branch of the Workington Agricultural Society. John Christian Curwen, a remarkable, energetic character who was both a member of the House of Keys and the House of Commons, promoted it. Manx people are very suspicious of government interference and possible taxation and this caused the demise of both organisations

[5]An agreement was made on 27 August, 1861; in Farrant papers, MNHL.

Figure 9: Threshing by steam at Ballamona farm, October 1941, using a Clayton and
Shuttleworth 7 h.p. traction engine to drive a Clayton 54 inch threshing mill.

prior to 1840. This new society did not fare much better as most farmers did not like paying a subscription and so it died through lack of funds in 1847. A further reason for its demise was the age-old distrust of the inhabitants of the north of the island for those in the south and vice versa. A further agricultural society, founded in 1858, also suffered in a similar way but it managed to survive, mainly through skilful diplomacy by Richard Nickling, the secretary, who was also one of the main machinery dealers at that time.

The establishment of these organisations spread the knowledge of technological advances; their support of ploughing matches, trials of reapers and mowers provided a practical display. The more theoretical aspects were covered by the establishment of the Farmers Club in 1859; this held dinners and lectures in Douglas mainly attended by 'gentlemen farmers'.

One important area of agricultural development, encouraged by the societies, was livestock. Thomas Quayle had described the native cattle as being small, having poor conformation and yielding low levels of milk and meat. This also was said of the Manx sheep that were described as having a small carcass, producing only limited amounts of wool (Quayle 1812, 106 and 111). By the beginning of the 19th century such breeds were changing as natural developments of market forces were having an effect even on the remoter parts of the island. Irish cattle were regularly imported at this time and they were being crossed with the native breed. Quayle noted that although the quantities of meat and milk were small it was of a high quality. Also the local cattle thrived on the rough pasture and did not mind the sometimes-hostile weather. The Irish cattle however, required some time to acclimatise especially on the upland farms. This ensured the survival of the original breed in these more remote places although various crosses soon overtook them. Other breeds of cattle such as the Holderness, later to become the Shorthorn and the Dunlop, later to become the Ayrshire, were the province of the wealthy agriculturalist (Figure 10). Their importation during the early years of the 19th century provided a genetic base that eventually found its way to even the smallest farms. Again, the earliest examples of these animals found the Manx climate somewhat taxing and some like Joseph Foulder of Ronaldsway adopted the practice of 'soiling', that is keeping the cattle in shelter all year round and bringing the fodder to them (Curwen 1810, 148-9). As these cattle became hardier so their numbers grew with the local fairs being the main distribution points.

Sheep followed a similar pattern with the Leicester and Linton (later known as the Scottish Blackface) being preferred. The Cheviot soon followed but the use of the Marino, fashionable around 1810, was doomed to failure, despite crossing with the local breed. The Cotswold longwool found favour by the 1870s and soon after, the Shropshire dominated flocks through into the 20th century until the Suffolk gained popularity. The Manx breed survived for some time, being mentioned in sales of the 1850s but it became crossed out with the Blackface and Cheviot. This preserved its hardiness and wool but gave a far better carcass. An interesting survival of this early breed however was the Loughtan. This was a brown sheep variety and had gained a reputation with many Manx farmers and crofters especially with regard to the wool colour. The Loughtan still exists today as a rare breed, and there are thriving flocks on three of the museum sites managed by Manx National Heritage, one being on the small island at the extreme south of the country called the Calf of Man (Figure 11).

Figure 10: Shorthorn cow and calf at Manx National Heritage's farm at Cregneash in 1996.

Figure 11: Loaghtan ram from Manx National Heritage's flock at Druidale farm, Lezayre, in the summer of 1977.

Sheep were popular on the upland farms as they formed an easily manageable asset on the open hills. Folding was also practised, using single sod hedges that could be easily removed; some of these still survive on the outer fields at Cregneash. The sheep was an important commodity to the small farmer and crofter as the wool formed another area of income. Many wills refer to the spinning wheel in the main room, *thie mooar*. Weaving also formed another occupation to run with the farm work, other than fishing. Four of the cottages at Cregneash still have loom sheds *(thie coigee)*, and such buildings can be seen at other parts of the island. Mechanised weaving came in by the beginning of the 19th century with William Kelly's factory at Union Mills near Douglas. Now a distinct village, the site of the mill can still be seen. Woollen mills could be found in a number of places throughout the country but the largest was at St Johns, known as Tynwald Mills, which still exists, although now in use mainly as the focus of a retail complex. A smaller mill at Laxey continues to operate however, complete with hand as well as mechanised looms.

The People

The condition of the small farms and crofts at the end of the 18th century and the living conditions of their inhabitants within these 'mere hovels' drew comments of concern by visiting strangers (Killip 1971). The clothing and food likewise was looked on with distain, yet the families proved healthy. What was overlooked was that the buildings were ideal to cope with the weather, as was the clothing. It was mostly home produced, even to the shoes, if worn at all. These shoes were called *carranes*, and made like a moccasin out of cowhide, still with the coat intact (Radcliffe 1993, 14). The food was rather bland but wholesome, consisting of milk products, some meat and, most important, 'spuds and herring'. This dish remained dominant on the small and even medium farms until well into the 20th century. The reason for its popularity was not the taste, which had to be acquired, but rather economy. The potatoes were home grown and the salted herring were locally caught (Figure 12).

The income from such small farms is hard to identify. Thomas Quayle in 1812 estimated the annual outgoings of a cottager to be about £24 and the income left just 1/7d as clear profit. Wages also provide a guide but more as an indicator that they were static. In 1812 a single farm worker's wage was between £12 and £20. By 1857 it stood at £23 and by the end of the 19th century it was still between £18 and £20 (Killip 1971, 64). In 1812 Quayle thought that '... a croft is generally a losing concern ...'. The croft, however, thrived throughout the 19th century with its peak around 1890 and survived into the 20th century as a working unit (Birch 1964, 80).

The pace of work on the land was steady and continuous. However, there was always time for a talk, to collect the *skeet*, which brought the Manxmen into conflict with the commercially minded English and Scots farmers. This caused comments about laziness and lack of motivation. Yet with the use of traditional methods the work of the small farmer and crofter demanded both strength and stamina. The use of the creel on their backs to carry turf from the mountain, manure out to the potato ground and to harvest corn back to the farm needed a tenacity that denied laziness. These operations were not just confined to the men as the women had to manage the farm for the length of time the men were away at the fishing.

Figure 12: A posed photograph, c1890, of the Crennall family in front of their stone cottage at Ballacallow, Cranstal, Bride. Mr Crennall was a crofter/fisherman. This shows the suggane ropes holding down the thatch and achored to the building by the stone *bwhid-suggane*. Hanging from the wall is a *mollag*, which is a dog-skin fishing float.

Teamwork was also a feature of such communities, with the crofters and cottagers helping the larger neighbouring farmers. This may have been part of the rental arrangements if the croft formed part of the farm. Ploughing, potato planting and the hay and corn harvests were the most common shared arrangements but it also extended to carting. One of the hardest tasks on the farm was to collect wrack, seaweed, from the beach after the autumn storms. It took much strength to fill a cart full of wet wrack, then with a pair of horses cart it, often two to three miles, to the farm.

Harvest was often women's work whilst the sickle was in use, the men doing the binding and stooking, although the roles changed when the scythe began to dominate after 1860 (Figure 13). By this time mechanisation had started with the first horse-powered reaper being used on the island in 1852 (Manx Sun 21 August 1852). This had been made by a blacksmith, Thomas Teare from Ballaugh, who had been to the Great Exhibition, London in 1851. Men, women and children all became involved with the harvest and mechanisation served to speed the operation up so that more crops could be saved at an optimum time. The reaper binder further increased that efficiency, coming on to the larger farms by the 1890s. The small farms and crofts held to the scythe or the reaper until the coming of the tractor in the 1950s (Figure 14).

The crofters supported each other at certain crucial events. The local fair was more than a place of excitement and jollification, where the beer *(jough)* flowed freely. It was all of these things but also the place for selling the surplus young stock on to the lowland farmers. A man recalling to the Manx Folklife Survey, gave an account of his parents meeting up with other crofters at an arranged placed, then driving their livestock down to St Mark's Fair. They all helped to keep the animals safe on the road until they could be sold. Some of these fairs were also the hiring fairs for the larger farmers and so the major ones lasted until well into the 20th century.

Conclusion

What is traditional? To many it was perpetuating the methods of farming that had been perfected by their forefathers. Most of the crofts in the 1890s used techniques that had been at the cutting edge in 1800. For example, a crofter in 1800 was still using the lazy bed method of cultivation, but by 1890 he had the iron swing plough. This type of plough had been the latest item of equipment on an 1800 farm, whilst by 1890 the larger farmer had adopted the wheeled plough, with replaceable castings and bar point. The same can be seen with the livestock and the crops, even the management of the farm, as the crofter had by 1890 adopted liming and rotations to improve soil fertility.

The survival of the small farm and the croft was in many ways due to the prudence of the Manxmen and the ability to operate a dual economy. Fishing and mining were replaced by jobs in the tourist industry that dominated the island after 1890. With a low capital input the level of profit, often called the gross margin, was reasonable and sustainable, hence their survival. The upland crofts were the first to decline and did not last beyond the 1930s but it is only in recent years that the small farm has come under threat. However the role of a dual economy has started again with farmers running part of their income by working in the booming finance and building industries.

Figure 13: Harvesting corn with a sythe at Greeba.

Figure 14: Harvesting oats using a 'put-off' two horse reaper; the operator engaged in
raking the corn off the knife, is just seen behind the horses; the two women have
been tying bands to put around the crop to form a sheaf, c1890.

It is now left to a very small number of older Manx farmers to perpetuate the older methods. Whilst few of these traditions date beyond the turn of the 20th century, they do maintain the philosophy of life and belief that could be recognised by a farmer and crofter of 1800.

References

Belchem J, (ed.), 2000, *New history of the Isle of Man, Vol 5, The modern period* 1830-1999, (Liverpool University Press).

Birch J W, 1956, *The Isle of Man. A study in economic geography*, (Cambridge).

Bullock H A, 1816, *History of the Isle of Man with a comparative view of the past and present state of society and manners*, (London).

Burn R S, 1861, 'Brief notes of a visit to some of the agricultural districts of the Isle of Man', *Journal of the Highland and Agricultural Society of Scotland*, 57-71.

Curwen J C, 1808-1812, *Rules and proceedings of the Workington Agricultural Society, containing the presidential reports of the Isle of Man*, (Workington).

Emery N, 1985, 'Changing patterns of farming in an Isle of Man glen', *Post Medieval Archaeology*, 19.

Feltham, 1798, *Tour through the Isle of Man*, (London).

Gelling, Cannon J, 1998, *A history of the Manx church, 1698-1911*, (Douglas).

Haining S, 1822, *Haining's guide and historical sketch, etc., of the Isle of Man*, (Douglas).

Honeyman J, 1869, 'The Isle of Man - its agriculture, climate etc.', *Journal of the Highland and Agricultural Society of Scotland*, 359-368.

Kelly M I, 1989, *Twas thus and thus they lived*, (Douglas).

Killip I M, 1971, 'Crofting in the Isle of Man', *Folk life Journal*, 19, 61-78.

Killip I M, 1970, 'Spades in the Isle of Man', in: *The spade in Northern Europe, Ulster Folklife*, (Belfast).

Kinvig R H, 1975, *The Isle of Man, a social, cultural and political history*, (Liverpool).

Moore A W, 1992, *A history of the Isle of Man*, 2 Vols, (London, 1900, republished, Douglas).

Quayle, B, 1794, *General view of the agriculture of the Isle of Man*, (London).

Quayle G E, 1979, *Legends of a lifetime, aspects of Manx life*, (Wigan).

Quayle T, 1812, *General view of the agriculture of the Isle of Man*, (London).

Radcliffe F J, 1991, *Manx sea fishing*, (Douglas).

Radcliffe F J, 1993, *Manx farming and country life*, (Douglas).

Radcliffe W and C, 1979, *A history of Kirk Maughold*, (Douglas).

Radcliffe W and C, 1982, *Kirk Bride, a miscellany*, (Douglas).

Train J, 1845, *An historical and statistical account of the Isle of Man*, (London).

Wood G, 1811, *An account of the past and present state of the Isle of Man*, (Douglas).

Manx Folklore - a changing or continuous tradition?

Yvonne Cresswell

Introduction: Manx Folklore today...

To ask the question whether Manx folklore is subject to continuity or change and whether it is a changing or continuous tradition, presupposes one major factor, that Manx folklore still exists in any shape or form at the present day.

To many people on the Isle of Man, the answer to this question would be self-evident: that folklore does not exist and if it does, it is a very poor shadow of its former self. This view would be supported and vindicated by a wealth of literature written on the parlous state of Manx folklore over the past hundred years. Each generation of folklorists has bemoaned the fact that they are 50 years too late to collect anything of any real importance. For each successive group the opinion is voiced that only an earlier generation had access to an *authentic* and *genuine* corpus of Manx folklore (Moore 1891, ii; Killip 1975, 15-6; Paton 1942, v-vi).

This was, and in some cases still is, the complaint of most folklore collectors throughout the British Isles. This viewpoint is based on a particular concept and definition of folklore. It is perceived as a series of beliefs, customs and rituals that have survived, largely unaltered, over the centuries (potentially even millennia) until their rapid decline during the agrarian and industrial revolutions of the eighteenth to twentieth centuries (Baker 1974, 9-13).

The definition of folklore as a random collection of survivals and relics of an earlier and more complete body of customs and beliefs, usually of pagan if not pre-historic origin, implies that folklore and its subject matter is a dying field of enquiry (Simpson & Roud 2000, 134-5, 253-4; Georges & Owen Jones 1995, 59-67).

Therefore the definition of folklore and its subject matter needed to be radically revised if there is to be a body of evidence for future study. This has in part been achieved by revising the interpretation of the evidence for folklore. It is no longer perceived as a timeless and stable body of unchanging beliefs, rituals and customs.

Figure 1: Painting by Beatrice Fairless of the *chiollagh* (open hearth)
of Cooil Bane, Sulby, c.1910.

Figure 2: Manx spinning wheel.

Instead folklore is increasingly considered to be dynamic with change and evolution an essential part of its development over time. Therefore change and/or decline in the practice of specific customs does not indicate overall loss and disappearance of folklore but is indicative of and evidence of its dynamic nature (Toelken 1996, 19-54; Dundes 1980, 1-9; Simpson & Roud 2000, 131; Hutton 1996, 426-7).

The revised definition means that news of the death of Manx folklore has been exaggerated over the twentieth century. It can also be considered somewhat premature since folklore can still be found on the Island if one accepts it is not necessarily in the same form as it appeared in previous decades or centuries. Once one accepts that Manx folklore still exists in some form, to be discussed and considered later, the question can then be asked as to whether Manx folklore is developing in terms of change or continuity from past folklore traditions.

Overview of Manx Folklore

Hearth and Home

For the majority of the rural Manx population, whether one lived in a one roomed thatched cottage or a large quarterland farmhouse, the heart of the home was the large *chiollagh* (open hearth) in the *thie mooar* (kitchen/large room). The turf fire in the *chiollagh* provided all of life's necessities from heat for the main living room in the house, heat for all one's cooking and hot water, and it even provided a semblance of light on dark evenings to work by, so as not to waste valuable tallow candles or rush lights (Figure 1).

The *chiollagh* was a central feature of domestic folklore. When sweeping the floors one never swept the dust out of the doors but rather swept in towards the hearth. This meant that luck would be kept in a household rather than metaphorically (and literally) sweeping it away.[1]

The desire to keep luck within a family and within a house is also shown by the need to have all the jugs hanging on the dresser facing towards the *chiollagh* and not towards the door.[2]

Although recorded historically, these two customs are today observed on the Island by people still having jugs facing the fire and away from the door and by emptying the vacuum cleaner bag in the fire.

The importance of the *chiollagh* was traditionally reinforced by the nightly ritual before one went to bed of putting a small bowl of *pinjane* (milk rennet pudding), *cowree* (steeped oats) or some *bonna*g (soda bread) out for *themselves* (the fairies) at the side of the hearth (Roeder 1897, 148; Roeder 1904, 27-8).[3] One also took the band (strings) off the spinning wheel to make it inoperable. The reasoning behind these rituals was to placate *themselves* and to prevent them being mischievous, or worse, malevolent; therefore a small gift of supper would be made to them. The only problem

---

[1]Manx Folklife Survey, KJ-Bl9 (Mr J Kneen, Ballaugh Curraghs, 1950).
[2]Manx Folklife Survey, FCE-A4 (Mrs E Flanagan, Douglas, 1957).
[3]Manx Folklife Survey, K22-2 (Mrs Keig, Andreas, 1964).

was that if they wanted to be helpful, they might consider doing some spinning for you but 'though their meanins' well enough, the spinnin' they're doin' is nothin' to brag about' (Morrison 1911, 5). Therefore to remove temptation, one removed the band off the wheel (Figure 2).

One interpretation of this belief and associated ritual is that the hearth and chimney represents a liminal space between the physical house and external environment. Liminal areas in time and space, junctions between one world and another, are often considered dangerous unknowns (Narváez 1997, 337-8). It would appear that it was accepted that *Themselves* could gain entry to the home at night and that to render them harmless, a gift was made to ensure that no harm befell either the home or its occupants.

Another interpretation that one may make of the story of fairies inhabiting the *chiollagh* at night (it appears in Sophia Morrison's *Manx Fairy Tales* 1911 as the story *Themselves*) (Morrison 1911, 3-5) is that parents living in cottages with cock lofts (open lofts where the children slept) were telling moralistic warning stories to their children to ensure their safety. One might want to guarantee that one's children, if they awoke in the night, were never tempted either to wander around the open loft or down the step ladder into the *thie mooar* and near the unguarded open turf fire. In keeping with other aspects of fairy belief, this may be an example of an explicit belief in fairies and their malevolent potential or a form of the verbal control of children and of ensuring their safety at night, or it may be a combination of the two belief systems.

The hearth was also of great importance at New Year, both at *Hop tu naa* (31 October – traditionally considered the Celtic New Year) and New Year's Eve (31 December) when rites of divination were practised. Having spent all year carefully sweeping the household dust into the hearth, on New Year's Eve one would sweep the dust and ashes out from the hearth into the room. Once done the household would retire to bed and wait until morning to forecast the household's future for the forthcoming year. The signs looked for were small v-shaped footprints in the ashes. If the footprints went in towards the hearth, they heralded a new addition to the family, but if they were pointing in the direction towards the door, they foretold of a death in the family (Gill 1932, 112-9; Train 1845, 115-6). Interestingly it was noted by contemporary folklorists that no mention was made of either who or what were thought to have made these footprints (Rhys 1901, 318-9). This was a question left unasked and unanswered, as it was felt to be as well not to know or enquire too closely.

The rites of divination developed with the introduction of new domestic technology, since the folklorists also recorded people placing nuts on the fire grate. This was not to determine who would die during the year but rather to determine who would be 'sweethearts' and/or who would be compatible and faithful (Paton 1942, 77). To be noted is the fact that this is obviously associated with the introduction of cast iron fireplaces and ranges. This occurred later on the Isle of Man than the rest of mainland Britain, because the cost of importing coal had to become sufficiently low to outweigh the effort of digging one's own turf. On the Island this was between 1860 and 1890, if not later in certain places.

Agriculture

The highlight of the Manx agricultural year was the bringing in of the harvest. The climax of this was the cutting of the final sheaf, the *mheillea* (Killip 1975, 174 - 5; Moore 1891, 121; Gill 1963, 272 - 4; cf. Fenton 1978, 356; Fenton 1987, 124 - 5). This entailed much ceremony with the last sheaf being cut and then shaped into a *babban mheillea* (which may be translated as a harvest baby or even a corn dolly). Then it would be wrapped in a shawl and carried high, at arm's length, above the harvest gang as they made their way back to the farm for the harvest feast, to celebrate safely gathering in the harvest. A large spread would be laid out in the barn and there would be singing and dancing until the small hours of the morning. The *mheillea* would then be put up either in the barn or in the kitchen until the following harvest to ensure the success of the following year's harvest (Clague 1911, 79; Moore 1891, 122). The *mheillea* is a near universal custom found throughout Europe and beyond, and one that has caused considerable speculation on the part of generations of folklorists. Theories and speculations have been made that it involves the capture of the spirit of the Grain God and it was frequently cited as evidence of the pre-Christian/pagan and archaic origins of folklore, of which this was a relic survival, although this is now generally discredited (Baker 1974, 28- 33; Hole 1978, 135- 9; Hutton 1996, 335- 9).

The original Manx *mheillea,* based in the fields and on the farms, began to evolve and develop during the nineteenth century in response to the fears and concerns of the Methodist Church regarding the moral (and potentially immoral) tone of the festivities. The *mheilleas* have moved to the Chapels, becoming a Manx harvest festival with a concert and auction of produce to raise money for local charities. The transformation of the *mheillea* from a festival of active participation by the farmworkers to the predominantly passive involvement of the Chapel-goers cannot entirely be blamed on the temperant Methodist Church. The transition mirrors the wider social and technological changes taking place in agriculture as the men and women with scythes and sickles were increasingly replaced with mechanical reapers and binders.

The farm-based *mheillea* has evolved in other ways as well. Originally, before reapers and binders, the bulk of the harvest labour was expended in the cutting of a crop whilst the stooking (stacking sheaves) and drying of the crop, before it was brought into the barns, was the less labour intensive part of the process. Since the introduction of mechanised harvesting techniques, the cutting of the harvest is now less labour intensive and the physical gathering in of the harvest is relatively more labour intensive. Therefore on modern Manx farms, the *mheillea* will now be celebrated (if at all) as the last sheaf is gathered into the barn. The *mheillea* is therefore still an opportunity for a communal gathering, when the largest number of people are involved, to celebrate the safely gathering in of the harvest, whether in the field or as now in the barn.

The increasingly mechanised nature of the harvest means that most churches and chapels have problems now even acquiring a 'harvest' sheaf for the Harvest Festival service. As a result, Cregneash Open Air Village Folk Museum, where a horse drawn binder is still used for the harvest, is annually inundated with requests for sheaves.

The chapel *mheillea* has also undergone a period of transformation as the chapel ceases to be a focal point of community life. The *mheillea* concert is still celebrated in some chapels but is more likely to be a non-denominational concert held in the local

Figure 3: Group of Manx Fishermen.

Figure 4: Manx Pixie charm.

Figure 5: Herd of Shorthorn cattle at Cregneash.

village hall or, even more likely, an auction of produce for local charities held in the village public house. The auction will contain everything from bags of potatoes and vegetables from local farms through to novelty items, which have included a chocolate penis. The bidding can become extremely competitive, with success becoming a matter of honour and pride as witnessed by the prices achieved by certain people's home-made apple pies and fruit cakes.

Although the form of the *mheillea* has altered dramatically in terms of participants, location and apparent function, at another level it can be considered to have altered very little. The *mheillea* is still a communal festival, and it continues to contain elements of the 'feast of misrule'. In modern rural society where the majority of the community is not involved with work on the land, it provides an unique opportunity for the community to gather and celebrate together.

Fishing

The fishing industry underwent as significant a transformation as agriculture during the nineteenth century with the introduction of new technology and full-time employment for fishermen. Of all quarters of Manx life, economic and cultural, the fishing community has always been considered to be the most 'superstitious' and to hold the largest single body of folklore (Cashen 1912, 27 - 43) (Figure 3).

The most significant and obvious folklore associated with 'the fishing' is the prohibition of certain words which were not to be used in general conversation and definitely not whilst on board ship. The proscribed words for which *noa* (new) words had to be substituted were generally the names of creatures such as rats, rabbits, pigs and cats.[4] In the case of rats, these were known as 'longtails', 'ring tailed gentlemen' and 'ringies'. The use of proscribed words on board would be punished with the use of *could iron* (for example, the removal of a hot nut off the ship's boiler with one's teeth), a punishment that ensured that the misdemeanour would not be repeated.[5] The concern over the use of proscribed words on board fishing vessels is still prevalent in the modern Manx fishing fleet, although the punishment is less exacting. The use of *noa* words certainly develops and evolves since salmon are no longer known as *Red fish*[6] but as 'john westies' (after the well-known brand of tinned salmon).

The proscription of the use of the word 'rat' has changed from being a custom specifically observed by fishing communities (and certain rural communities) to an Island wide phenomenon. Since the major influx of immigrants to the Island in the 1960s, each successive wave is told during their first few months of residence that various terms cannot be used, for example: the Isle of Man Steam Packet vessel is the 'boat' not a ferry, the adjacent landmass to the east is referred to as 'across' not as 'the mainland' and most importantly there are no rats just 'longtails'. This informal Manx induction course means that the use of the word 'longtail' is now almost universal and is considered to be an *authentic* Manx tradition of long-standing. As a result older Manx-born residents who use the term 'rat' are not now considered by the wider Island community to be 'truly Manx'.

---

[4]Manx Folklife Survey, ME-A1 (Mr E Maddrell, Glen Chass, 1944).
[5]Manx Folklife Survey, KM-A4 (Mr J Callister, Laxey, 1950).
[6]Manx Folklife Survey, G22 (Mr L Greggor, Peel, 1958).

The preservation of a fishing boat's 'luck' was essential together with maintaining safety at sea. As a result great care was always taken to ensure that there were no white stones, in particular white quartz pebbles, in the stone ballast of a vessel (Gill 1963, 282-3; Rhys 1901, 344-5). Even though no specific reasons were given to Folklore collectors for quartz pebbles being unlucky, their inclusion in Early Christian and Medieval graves on the Island almost certainly meant that they were associated with death. Changes in boat design and ballast have made this particular belief generally obsolete, although it is interesting to note that when a traditional Manx fishing boat was recently restored and by mistake quartz pebbles were put in the ballast, no-one was surprised when her mast broke in a subsequent rough Irish Sea crossing.

There were several ways that fishermen could ensure that the luck of their vessel was maintained, but they also had ways in which it could be increased. This was done by 'stealing' the good luck of another fishing boat, an act that was particularly prevalent when in port and one could gauge the success of other vessels by the size of the catches they were landing. To 'steal' the good luck one needed to take an item of little worth or consequence from the other boat, a particularly effective item for transferring good luck was a dish cloth (the older and dirtier the better). Therefore if one's own vessel was doing well, one had to be particularly vigilant against other fishermen trying to steal things from the boat. Together with trying to avoid the use of prohibited words (and the associated penalties), the young cook, often a lad no more than 13 or 14 years old, also had to ensure that nothing was stolen from the vessel whilst in port.[7]

Supernatural Creatures

Folklore beliefs, customs and rituals surrounded and influenced one both at home and work but they were also an important part of the wider physical and mental landscape in which one lived. The Manx farmer and his family occupied an enlarged cosmos which was inhabited by a whole bestiary of supernatural creatures ranging from *themselves* (the fairies) (Evans Wentz 1911, 117-135), *phynodderrees* (similarto hobs and brownies), *bugganes* (similar to hobgoblins and trolls) through to the *moddey dhoo* (black dog), *glashtin* (water horse) and *tarroo ushtey* (the water bull) (Moore 1891, 33-62; Rhys 1901, 284-93).

Each of these creatures populated specific locations on the Island and were known for their particular personality traits and behaviour, malevolent or benevolent. Therefore the stories told about them could be viewed primarily as cautionary tales about how one should treat them (or not) for one's own personal safety and well-being. *Themselves* were seen as members of an alternative culture that occupied a different dimension and only occasionally came into direct contact with human society. As with the fairies themselves, to have contact with them was considered an ambivalent blessing. Although they could bestow gifts, both material (money) and non-material (music and powers of healing), they could also cause great mischief or even worse steal a baby and leave a changeling in its place (Moore 1891, 43-7).

But for all the ambivalence felt by the Manx towards their supernatural neighbours, the stories relating to their passing illuminate feelings of a greater loss. There are

---

[7]Manx Folklife Survey S16-B3 (Mr J Smith, Peel, 1950).

several stories relating to *themselves* leaving the Island. In some they were driven out by the Methodist Chapels that sprung up in every remote corner of the Island (Killip 1975, 30-2). In others it was by the noise and clamour of the new textile mills (specifically a tuck mill with its heavy fulling hammers) and the lead mines (Killip 1975, 39-40). The impression left is that in the new hustle and bustle of the nineteenth century with its Evangelical Christianity and Industrial Revolution, there was no space left for the 'old ways'. It may be speculated that the 'old ways' may have been defined in a variety of ways in the listener's or teller's mind. These could range from a simple straightforward belief in fairies, to a Christian faith that included fairies and other creatures within a cosmos learned from the Book of Genesis, from a Manx Gaelic speaking rural population who lived and worked closely with the land around them, to an English speaking population increasingly associated with towns, villages and industry. Whatever aspect of the 'old ways' the listener was thinking of when he heard these stories, it appears that the central theme was that a whole way of life had disappeared together with the fairies.

Interestingly although an apparently literal belief in fairies has disappeared, and it should be remembered that it is almost impossible to prove that people did literally believe in physical entities called fairies rather than hold other less literal forms of belief, themselves are still an important part of Manx life in the 21st century. The Fairy Bridge (on the main road between Douglas and Castletown) is still where every visitor to the Island is told by their taxi driver or coach driver and every child is told by their parent to say 'hello' to the fairies when crossing the bridge. The purists insist that this is not the actual Fairy Bridge, which is on an older Douglas to Castletown thoroughfare. Historians will tell you that the Fairy Bridge marks the boundary of the old Medieval Abbey estates and one is saying 'hello' as one enters and leaves the Abbeylands (Killip 1975, 99-100). The reality is that the Fairy Bridge has grown immensely in popularity with the growth of tourism on the Island with generations of charabanc and now coach drivers telling their passengers to say 'hello'. The ritual is also popular amongst the Manx population with many stories circulating about the ill fortune, in particular relating to vehicles breaking down, that befalls people who do not acknowledge *themselves*.

In the local souvenir shops one can buy postcards of the Fairy Bridge and even small pixie figures for charm bracelets (which have been dipped in the stream at the Fairy Bridge to make them more effectual) (Figure 4). The folklore surrounding the Bridge is evolving all the time and a recent development has been the hanging of small messages and plaques on the thorn tree adjacent to the Bridge. On closer inspection these are requests made to the fairies for good luck, in particular success with the Lottery. This is an interesting development of an older folkloric tradition of hanging rags on a thorn tree by a well or spring known for its healing properties. The logic behind the use of sympathetic magic is that having used the water on a particular ailment and left a rag on the thorn, as the rag rotted away so one's ailment would also disappear. In the case of the Fairy Bridge, several of the messages and requests are written on plastic plaques or sheets of headed notepaper put into plastic bags so they will not rot with the weather. The tradition seems to date from about 1997-8 with a dramatic increase being witnessed during the Tynwald period (the annual open-air sitting of the Manx Parliament on Old Midsummer's Day), and several of the messages were written on hotel notepaper and apparently by visiting overseas delegates of the Commonwealth Parliamentary Association. One assumes that it began with one specific group and is now becoming more universally practised, although many local residents disapprove of the custom and think the notes should be removed.

Although a general belief in entities called fairies has all but disappeared, both on the Island and elsewhere, it may be noted that a belief in small green creatures has not been entirely lost. These creatures have an ambivalent reputation, are associated with strange lights at night, are able to change and disorientate one's perception of both time and space and are even 'known' to abduct people. Our forefathers would have instantly recognised such behaviour as being that of fairies, although in the rational and scientific 21st century some may prefer to call them aliens from space (Rojcewicz 1997, 479-514). Interestingly, although a significant proportion of the population do believe in them, due to their prevalence and popularity in the mass media and perhaps therefore our consciousness, the majority of us accept them as part of a symbolic or cultural cosmos, if not as a physical and literal reality. This may explain the role and position held by the fairy in the perceptions of individuals and communities in the past. Paraphrasing the creed *I want to believe* from the popular Science Fiction series 'The X-Files', we may wish to believe but that does not necessarily mean we do believe.

Strangely for a culture that held fairy belief as a core element of its folklore, aliens and UFO sightings are absent on the Isle of Man, unlike some other parts of the British Isles. But although Manx fairies do not appear to have been resurrected as aliens, they may still survive in a modified form on the Island. General conversations about Manx folklore have brought, in passing, unsolicited comments about angels and personal beliefs in the existence of one's own guardian angel. So the old household fairy, the *phynodderree*, may still exist but be transformed into a guardian angel.

Calendar Customs

Manx calendar customs highlight the variety of ways in which the Manx perceived the world around them and responded to it; they also show the many ways in which the Island's folklore has developed and evolved over the past two centuries. From the many customs and festivals that could be considered, the one chosen for this paper is:

May Eve

For the pastoral farming regions of Britain, May Day was a pivotal point in the farming calendar. This was the official beginning of summer and was often the time when stock that had been housed throughout the winter months could be put out onto the pastures to graze (Hutton 1996, 218; Killip 1975, 172-3).

Its title as a Celtic quarter day was Beltane and there has been considerable discussion over the decades as to whether this is derived from Baal and thereby illustrates its pre-Christian origins and links to sacred fires (Hutton 1996, 218-25). What is known is that the rational concerns of the farmers concerning the well-being of their livestock are then expressed in a series of apparently irrational actions (rituals and customs) practised on May Eve, to provide some degree of protection against dangerous and malevolent forces.

The degree of importance bestowed upon the date is mirrored in the associated concerns and anxieties expressed regarding the cattle (Figure 5). As previously noted, liminal times and spaces were considered dangerous junctions between the known and the unknown, this world, its reality and the next. The time between the death of winter and the rebirth of summer was therefore particularly dangerous and midnight on May Eve was a time when witches and fairies were considered to be at their most potent and potentially most malicious (Moore 1891, 110-1; Clague 1911, 47; Baker 1974, 114-5). Therefore although seemingly a time of celebration, the coming of summer was perceived as a dangerous time when one sought protection from whatever was abroad. A distinct contrast may be drawn between arable lowland Britain, where May Day was celebrated with gusto as a time of fertility, with the peripheral pastoral regions of Britain where the emphasis was on May Eve/Beltane and the need for protection.

The paradox of the rebirth of summer and the need for protection can be considered further when one compares and contrasts May Eve with its opposite, but intrinsically linked, festival of Samhain/ All Hallows (31 October), known on the Isle of Man as *Hop tu naa*. This was a time when summer died and winter was triumphant, the cattle were brought in under cover for the winter and again witches and fairies were thought to be exceptionally powerful. Although perceived as a festival associated with death, the activities engaged in were ones of divination (looking into the future - often for a husband) and communal and familial enjoyment including making turnip lanterns and going from house to house singing songs (in hope of treats such as sweets or pennies). The good-natured enjoyment and fun that characterised descriptions of *Hop tu naa* festivities contrast with the apprehensions and concerns apparent in descriptions of May Eve with its desperate need for protection of one's home and livestock.

To allay fears on May Eve there were various forms of protection that one could employ. The principal one was the making of *crosh cuirns* (rowan/ mountain ash crosses) to be attached to the lintel above the doors to the house and the cow byre (to prevent 'anything' unwanted crossing the threshold) and to the tails of the cows. The *croshs*, to be effective, had to be made in a particular way, with no iron being used to cut the twigs and handtwisted/ spun wool being used to tie the two twigs together in the shape of the cross. The combination of the use of the cross and of rowan (traditionally considered the 'witch tree' that gives protection against witches) was felt to be particularly effectual. As an added layer of protection, yellow flowers (usually primroses but sometimes buttercups) would be gathered and strewn across the threshold as a further deterrent to anything 'unwanted' entering the house (Moore 1891, 110; Roeder 1891, 292; Roeder 1904, 13-4). Older people will tell you that the more 'authentic' and 'traditional' way is to gather *blutan* (yellow Kingcups) to strew on the threshold (Killip 1975, 173). Those who know where to find this increasingly rare flower keep that knowledge well hidden, so that only a 'privileged' few are able to maintain this ritual in its 'authentic' form.

The final part of the May Eve rites to ensure protection and safety for one's household and livestock, involved the younger members of the community setting light to the gorse bushes to drive out the fairies and/ or the witches (Rhys 1901, 308). Of note is the fact that whilst the majority of the activities engaged in on May Eve were domestic or family orientated and predominantly involved parents and young children, this last aspect was communal and involved adolescents. Traditionally this would be seen as the last relics of an age-old rite of sacred fire. In contrast a modern interpretation might be that it was an opportunity for the community's young people 'to let off steam' and enjoy themselves in a manner that was both sanctioned and approved of by the wider community, not as an everyday occurrence but an annually accepted one. A more pragmatic view might be that the burning of the gorse served a highly practical function by burning off the old woody growth and the carpet of gorse needles that build-up over time and smother any potential new growth. The promotion of new tender gorse shoots would provide a better harvest that could then be used as valuable animal fodder during the subsequent winter months. The burning of gorse was originally associated with the ritual of cattle being driven through the dying embers of the fire, this has been interpreted as being part of a symbolic purification ritual of the livestock before they are put out into the summer pastures (Killip 1975, 173). It may be speculated that the 'purification' was not necessarily purely symbolic and may have served a practical purpose. The potash in the gorse ashes will have had an antiseptic effect on the hooves of the cattle and may have been part of a cleaning process to prevent, or even help cure, foot rot in livestock that had been housed inside over the winter and were about to be put out to pasture. The smoke and heat from the dying fire may also have been important in ridding animals of parasites, such as warble fly, and in 'cleaning' their coats. To be noted is the fact that when folklorists witnessed these practices, they recorded them and subsequently defined them in terms of archaic and Pagan rituals, whose origins were lost in the mists of time, but whose primary *raison d'être* was symbolic. The general assumption that the practices were purely, or even merely, symbolic means that no consideration is given to discovering the practical and more pragmatic reasoning that may underlie the practices and why they might be effective. In the past there was a tendency not to ask participants why they performed certain rituals and even now the question is rarely asked, *Why did* or *Why should a ritual be effective?*

Interestingly only specific aspects of the May Eve rituals have survived and been maintained. The burning of gorse is no longer performed by young people on May Eve (but rather is done as a controlled exercise on a sporadic basis by farmers) and paradoxically in our apparently more liberal society, it would be viewed as vandalism and considered symptomatic of an 'out of control' youth culture. Therefore the youthful high jinx of the past, condoned and legitimised as being traditional and of long standing, would now result in court cases for criminal damage.

The putting up of *crosh cuirns* and the strewing of yellow flowers (primroses and Kingcups) is still done in a large number of households on the Island on May Eve. But although the action and the ritual have continued with almost no change, the belief underlying it and the context in which it is performed have changed dramatically. The initial belief was one of protection and the context one of dairy farming, the protection of one's home and one's house cow (or small herd of cattle). The degree to which this was a literal belief is now difficult to ascertain, as is the time-scale for its transformation. The custom today may be considered as appertaining to an expression of Manx national and cultural identity. Its prominent display in some households is significant as it would be viewed as an explicit declaration by the occupants of their perceived cultural identity. Therefore the custom is frequently found practised in households where members are involved in other explicit assertions of a Manx identity such as participation in the ongoing revival and maintenance of the Manx Gaelic language, dance and music and also Manx Nationalist politics, although not exclusively so in regard to the latter. Another significant group who practice the custom are older Manx-born Island residents, who would consider themselves to be 'truly Manx born and bred'. They frequently express a proactive desire to maintain 'traditional' Manx customs which were previously observed by their parents and grandparents. Again the custom may be considered as representing a symbol of one's own Manx identity and heritage and therefore as a 'badge of cultural identity'.

Conclusion

In conclusion, Manx folklore may be considered to be a tradition that is both changing and continuous in terms of its development over the past hundred or more years.

Certain aspects such as the *crosh cuirns* put up on May Eve, represent a tradition that has not altered at all in either form or practice throughout the time that it has been recorded. But although the execution of the practice has remained unaltered, the context in which it is performed and the reasons for which it is performed have changed dramatically. The original context and function of protection of one's home and livestock, thereby making it a rural and pastoral tradition, have been replaced as it has now become a symbol and declaration of an individual's cultural identity and allegiance. This is significant at a time when considerable public and political debate is taking place in the media over the question of Manx-born residents being a minority of the Island's population

In contrast the *mheillea* (harvest celebration) has undergone dramatic and significant changes over the past 200 years, in terms of its context, its apparent function and its participants. At a more fundamental level, although it has undergone superficial changes, it is still a celebration performed at the end of the harvest season where a significant proportion of a community can gather together. Therefore in comparison with May Eve where the practice stays the same but the context and function changes, the *mheillea* represents a tradition where the practice undergoes dramatic alteration and change but its function stays the same.

This pattern of continuity and change can be found throughout Manx folklore, in a wide variety of calendar customs, rites of passage and belief systems. As well as showing the dynamic nature of folklore and the role it plays within a society, it brings into question whether folklore has always been subject to ongoing evolution, that at times expresses itself as continuous development and at others to radical change. The degree to which these patterns can be traced over 100 or 200 years through recorded accounts and oral history, leads one to speculate as to how much change had previously taken place and gone unrecorded in past centuries. Even considering the major cultural and societal changes that have taken place over this period and the effect that they would have had on the development and expression of Manx folklore, previous centuries will have experienced some degree of continuity and change. Therefore the concept of a timeless and unchanging folklore tradition, that is considered to be dead or dying or irretrievably contaminated by foreign influence if it experiences or expresses any degree of change, is shown to be an unsustainable fallacy. Instead folklore is a dynamic entity and one that is forever regenerating itself, to thereby maintain its relevance and significance to the society in which it exists. This process of regeneration was both recognised and celebrated by the Manx in the proverb *Mannagh vow cliaghtey cliaghtey, nee cliaghtey coe* (if custom be not indulged with/ beget custom, custom will weep) but it also acts as a warning that apathy, rather than development, is folklore and culture's true enemy.

Bibliography

Baker M, 1974, *Folklore and Customs of Rural England.*

Cashen W, 1912, *Manx Folklore.*

Clague J, 1911, *Manx Reminiscences.*

Dundes A, 1980, *Interpreting Folklore.*

Evans Wentz W Y, 1911, *The Fairy Faith in Celtic Countries.*

Fenton A, 1978, *The Northern Isles: Orkney and Shetland.*

Fenton A, 1987, *Country Life in Scotland - Our Rural Past.*

Georges R A & Owen Jones M, 1995, *Folkloristics - An Introduction.*

Gill W W, 1932, *A Second Manx Scrapbook.*

Gill W W, 1963, *A Third Manx Scrapbook.*

Hole C, 1978, *A Dictionary of British Folk Customs.*

Hutton R, 1996, *The Stations of the Sun.*

Killip M, 1975, *The Folklore of the Isle of Man.*

Manx Folklife Survey (Oral History Archive, Manx National Heritage).

Moore A W, 1891, *The Folk-Lore of the Isle of Man* (reprint 1994, Llanerch Publishers).

Morrison S, 1911, *Manx Fairy Tales.*

Narváez P, 1997, 'Newfoundland Berry Pickers "In the Fairies": Maintaining Spatial, Temporal, and Moral Boundaries Through Legendry', in *The Good People – New Fairylore Essays* (ed. Narváez P).

Paton C I, 1942, *Manx Calendar Customs.*

Rhys J, 1901, *Celtic Folklore, Welsh and Manx.*

Roeder C, 1891, *'Folklore', Yn Lioar Manninagh* Vol I No. 9.

Roeder C, 1897, '*Contributions to the Folklore of the Isle of Man', Yn Lioar Manninagh* Vol III.

Roeder C, 1904, *Manx Notes and Queries.*

Rojcewicz P M, 1997, 'Between One Eye Blink and the Next: Fairies, UFOs and Problems of Knowledge', in *The Good People - New Fairylore Essays* (ed. Narváez P)

Simpson J & Roud S, 2000, *A Dictionary of English Folklore.*

Toelken B, 1996, *The Dynamics of Folklore.*

Train J, 1845, *History of the Isle of Man.*

'The Devil once a fiddler made': the connection between Manx, Scottish and Norwegian fiddle music

Fenella Crowe Bazin

Introduction

Even today, music is the principal cultural activity in the Isle of Man. No true Manx event, however large or small, is complete without a live performance of a song or two. So it is almost inevitable that my childhood experience of such a society nurtured my main research interest, which is to place music in its social, political and religious context. The results often offer an insight to the lives of the majority of the population whose cultural activities were otherwise relatively unrecorded. This paper is a summary of some preliminary research that looks at the problems of identifying one form of popular, secular, instrumental music-making in the Isle of Man before 1700. As there is very little documentation, much of what follows must be surmise but it is undoubtedly the basis for further discussion and work.

In the middle of the seventeenth century, two visitors to the Island published accounts of their impressions. Chaloner (1656: 5) and Clarke (1656: 111) commented that 'the Manx ... are much addicted to the Musick of the Violynes, so that there is scarce a family but more or lesse can play upon it.' To this Chaloner added, rather caustically, 'But as they are all ill composers, so are they bad players.'

The instrument they had heard was almost certainly not a modern violin. The 'violyne' was clearly well established in the Island, suggesting that this was an instrument with its roots in earlier times. The comment about the standards of playing would seem to bear this out. As gentlemen of culture, both writers would have been more accustomed to the gentler sounds of the courtly viol and the music of Monteverdi and Lully, then fashionable in London. Chaloner's criticism also suggests that the repertoire was unfamiliar to him, even bearing in mind the fact that novelty was more highly prized then than now. But whatever they had heard was recognisably an instrument that was somehow a member of the family of stringed, bowed instruments, although the sound might not have been to their taste. Chaloner also added the comment that 'it is strange that they should be singular in affecting this Instrument before others, their Neighbours: the Northern English; the Scots; the Highlanders, and the Irish, generally, affecting the Bag-Pipe.'

Why, when surrounded by countries famous for harps and pipes, does the Isle of Man apparently have no tradition linked with either instrument? The Irish use the harp on stamps, coins and Guinness, the Scots are world-famous for their bagpipes, while the northern English have the gentler Northumbrian pipes. The Welsh are principally renowned for their harp playing, although the *crwth*, which was really a bowed lyre, was a popular folk instrument with a 'harsh' tone (Baines 1983, 520). This description perhaps ties in with Chaloner's comment about the tonal quality of the Manx 'violyne'. There is only a single image on a Scandinavian-period cross (Kermode 1907, 69) that suggests harps might have been used in the Isle of Man but this rudimentary image could equally have been representative of an early *crwth*. Three hundred and fifty years ago the Manx were noted for fiddle music, at a time when there is little evidence for the instrument in any of the surrounding regions. Indeed, the modern violin was only introduced into southern England in the first half of the seventeenth century (Arnold 1983, 1930) and Johnson (1972, 111) suggests that the modern violin arrived in the Lowlands towards the end of the 1600s as a classical instrument before replacing the bagpipes as the most popular folk instrument. Purser (1992, 132, 136) confirms that the violin only gained a foothold in Scotland during the early 1700s. So it is fairly unlikely the modern instrument could have become sufficiently commonplace in the Isle of Man for a mid-seventeenth century commentator to be able to remark, 'there is scarce a family but more or lesse can play upon it'. As there is a lack of eyewitness descriptions, we must therefore turn to other types of evidence to try to discover what this tradition might have been.

Given the close trading and social links between Man and its neighbours during the whole of this period, a number of questions arise. Why were there no bagpipes and harps on the island? Why were 'violynes', whatever they were, not widespread in the surrounding regions? And why had the tradition before the eighteenth century apparently been so different in an island within sight of the surrounding countries?

These are questions that had long puzzled me. It was not until I read a history of Norwegian music (Grinde 1991) that I began to find some clues to a possible solution. Writing about the High Middle Ages, Grinde (1991, 13) notes that 'The instruments mentioned most frequently in old Norse literature are the fiddle and giga'. He also comments that 'Bagpipes, barrel organs and keyed harps were also well known in neighbouring countries during the middle ages but there is nothing to indicate that they were used in Norway' (Grinde 1991, 15). Given the strong Scandinavian elements of government, language, place-names and superstitions that have survived in the Isle of Man right up to the present day, is it not possible that a musical tradition familiar to Norway and Man had also continued for some hundreds of years?

In order to examine this theory, and in the absence of eyewitness accounts, it was necessary to turn to customs and traditions, folklore and, of course, the music itself.

Customs and traditions

There are numerous accounts of the fiddlers who travelled the length and breadth of the Island, carrying not only new songs but importantly, new stories and the local gossip. In the days before recorded music, anyone with a new song must have been the hero of the evening. In spite of the disapproval of the Church, dancing was popular. Waldron, in his *Description of the Isle of Man in 1726,* commented, in rather dismissive tones, 'Dancing, if I may call it so, jumping and turning round at least, to the fiddle and base-viol (sic), is their great diversion'.

Fiddle music played a part in every aspect of Manx life. No wedding was complete without music, and the fiddler was valued as highly as the parson (Clague 1911, 97). The musician's fee was known as the Unnysup[1]; dancing was kept up till a late hour and there was plenty of ale for everyone, which might possibly be one of the reasons that the Church frowned on dancing. The bridal couple were 'preceded by musick, who play all the while before them the tune 'The Black and Grey' and no other is ever used at weddings'. Manx historian A W Moore (1891, 157-159) comments that the 'Black and Grey' was 'a popular tune at the time of Charles II and it continued in vogue until the end of the eighteenth century'. It certainly appears in Playford, (Barlow 1985, 239) but there is no trace of this melody in the Manx nineteenth-century collections. Was this because the melody was so closely linked with the 'violyne' and had consequently disappeared with the introduction of the modern instrument? On the way to church, the fiddler might play on his own or, according to a 19th-century writer, be accompanied by a 'clarionet', or even a piper (Caine 1896, 4). The musicians went ahead of the bridegroom and his friends, who carried wands of willows to show they were more important than the bride and bridesmaids, who followed them. After the ceremony, the party would leave the church, this time led by the women (Moore 1891, 158). Nineteenth-century folklorist Dr Clague noted that 'in old times people came to the wedding on horseback, and sometimes there would be as many as sixty horses' (Clague 1911, 95). Similar customs were observed in Scotland (Johnson 1972, 112) and Norway, where the fiddler rode on horseback and was an important member of the bridal party.[2]

Fiddlers were often present at funerals too. It was usual for neighbours and relatives to sit through the night with the body; there was ale and tobacco and often a fiddler and singers to provide appropriate music (Clague 1911, 107).

But the fiddler really came into his own at Christmas. The traditional Manx Christmas lasted over a fortnight, beginning on 21 December and finishing with Twelfth Night. Only essential work was carried out, and it was a chance to relax. Every parish hired fiddlers at the public charge, and there was dancing and music every evening during the festival (Douglas nd, 25). This translation from the Manx of verses 19-21 from a seventeenth-century carval[3] describes the fiddler's role in the Christmas celebrations:

---

[1]There are several tunes with the title 'Unnysup' said by Miss A G Gilchrist to be a corruption of the term 'The hunt is up'.

[2]See Fig 2.

[3]A form of popular sacred song, usually sung in church on Christmas Eve after the officiating parson had left. Carvals could run into 30 or 40 verses. They often drew on biblical ideas and stories. A particular favourite was the story of the prodigal son. Before the late 18th century they were usually the province of

What great blessing will come upon us in the beginning of the New Year;
The fiddler coming before daybreak and enquiring "Are you alive?"
And calling, by their own names, all the household,
And filling every soul of them with the raptures of love.

The fiddler's wife comes early, with a face healthy and clean,
To get a brave cut of meat or a big present of wine,-
That is what they give to the fiddler for an offering or reward,-
When thou dost observe this thou art blest for ever.

She will leave the place happy in her heart,
With the big gifts which they have given her,
utting her blessing on the cattle and also on the calf,
When these blessings have been said, she will go, laden, home.[4]

The tradition seems to have continued into the 1800s, although an account of an incident in the middle of the nineteenth century suggests that the coming of the fiddler early on Christmas morning did not meet with the same rapturous joy. Mr. John Gell, a mason, was awakened by a well-known Douglas character, and commemorated the occasion in verse.

Cease, catgut scraper, thy vile trade,
My ears no longer tickle,
The Devil once a fiddler made,
And called him Tommy Nichol (Cowin 1902).

At the winter solstice in Shetland, fiddlers presented themselves at the doors of the houses, playing 'Da day dawis', a tune which according to musicologist John Purser had been 'long consecrated to Yule day, and is never played on any other occasion' (Purser 1992, 79). Our seventeenth-century Manx carval-writer noted that the fiddler's visit 'filled every soul of them with the raptures of love'; the Shetland commentator made a remarkably similar comment, writing that 'the interesting association of which (tune) thrills every soul with delight' (Purser 1992, 79).

Fiddle music and folklore

There is a rich vein of Manx folklore linked to music. Magical forces, if not resisted, could spirit people away to other worlds. Many of the stories were linked to fiddle

---

the educated clergy but were taken over in the 19th century by men who often had little education but felt strongly about their beliefs. This is a similar custom to the Welsh *plygain*.

[4]Isle of Man Examiner, 24.12.1926.

music which is perhaps to be expected, as the violin was the instrument in most common use. Strong supernatural powers were ascribed by the author of the carval to both the fiddler and his wife. That same supernatural quality is to be seen in 'Mylecharane's March', a remarkable stick-dance traditionally performed by a men's team on Old Christmas (6 January). At the close of the performance, the dancers:

linked in a circle around the fiddler, the sticks were drawn closer and closer around him until they 'cut off the fiddler's head' and he fell down 'dead'. Capering around the dancers came the *Laare Vane* (White Mare), a girl draped in a white sheet and holding a horse's head made of white-painted wood, with hinged jaws which snapped at any of the company. Finally, it 'raised' the fiddler and led him to a seat, where the *Laare Vane* sat down, in her lap the fiddler's head, which then became an oracle, answering questions mainly about marriage (Douglas nd, 27).

This is just one of the numerous occasions in Manx folklore in which the apartness of the fiddle player is emphasised and he is linked with powerful magical forces, both during life and after death. Such beliefs linger on. Tom Taggart, a well-known player of the cello, which he generally referred to as 'the fiddle' or 'Herself', died in the 1930s. After his death, the person who had moved into his cottage moved out again very swiftly, on the grounds that his playing kept her awake all night.[5]

Many of the stories probably have their roots in an ancient tradition, as they often refer to a people who were living underground. Parallels exist in the Hebrides (Kennedy-Fiaser 1921, xxi, 126-8), the Western Highlands (*Journal of Folklore* 1911, 228), as well as regions which also have a long fiddle tradition such as the Shetlands and parts of Scandinavia.[6] In Shetland, ferrytuns could be heard issuing from hills at night, although to hear the trows in the Hebrides playing and singing could cause a man to lose his wits (Saxby 1936, 65). These are all areas which have stories of tunes that were learned by listening to the music of the 'trows' or 'trolls', which could be heard drifting up through the earth from their underground dwellings (Lifton 1983, 49). Other stories may simply be explained away by the habit of many fiddlers of taking a drop too much to drink, combined with a vivid imagination. Such 'explanations' might also have been a means of giving greater status to a newly-composed tune.

Evidence for Scandinavian and Scottish influence in Manx music

For the strongest evidence linking Manx and Norwegian music we have to turn to the melodies themselves. Although those who heard them rarely remembered these wonderful magical tunes, there are a few examples of the elusive melodies heard by musicians as they made their way home late at night over the mountains. There are several sources for one particular Manx story (Gill 1932, 308-313). Three of the accounts agree on the principal element of the tale: the difficulty of remembering a fairy tune heard during a night-time journey through the hills near Ballaugh:

---

[5]Told to me by Miss Gwen Collister, a relative of Tom Taggart's, in 1996.
[6]I am indebted to Professor Crossley-Holland for drawing these to my attention.

Figure 1: Comparison of tune from Western Norway and the Manx melody
'*Bollan bane'*.

'Only one musician claimed to have remembered the tune long enough to get it home safely. Bill Pheric was coming home late one night across the mountains from Druidale and heard the fairies singing just as he was going over the river by the thorn tree that grows there. The tune they had was the '*Bollan bane*' [7], and he wanted to learn it from them, so he went back three times before he could pick it up and remember it, but after the third time he had it by heart. Just then, the sun got up and the fairies went away, for they always go at sunrise. He came home whistling the tune, and since then it has been popular and much played on the fiddle. Many people think that Bill Pheric invented the tune, but he hadn't, he got it from the fairies.'[8]

Apart from the obvious magical elements in this account - the crossing of water, a thorn tree, the recurrence of 'three' and the resumption of normality at sunrise - it is odd that such a good traditional musician as Bill Pheric should find it so difficult to memorise a melody. Maybe he was tired or inebriated, or both, or perhaps the story was simply a way of explaining the difficulty of learning a tune that was in an unfamiliar idiom.[9]

A fourth version places the story nearer Laxey and touches on the search for sheep lost in snow, another well-known story celebrated in song.[10]

There are at least two tunes with the same title. One has all the characteristics of an eighteenth- or nineteenth-century violin melody, with the spiccato technique, which appears in the first two bars and, again, towards the end. The other (Figure 1) is in a less familiar idiom and was sung to non-lexical words, which may be a remnant of an earlier, half-remembered language or a protective incantation. The tune was also used as part of a cante-fable[11], in which the narrator used the repetition of a short snatch of melody to punctuate events in the story. Only a few survive and those that do, all include references to the powers of a supernatural world that was believed to coexist in parallel with the everyday, humdrum life. I noted with interest that the Shetland

---

[7]In Moore, Morrison and Goodwin *Vocabulary of the Anglo-Manx Dialect*. On page 18, the *bollan bane* (the white wort) is said to be the mugwort *(Artemisia vulgaris)*. This is also known by the name *bollan seall'Eoin* (St John's plant) and is traditionally worn on Tynwald Day, St John's Day in the Old Calendar. It was believed to be a specific against the Evil Eye and witchcraft.

[8]Noted from Miss A M Crellin, Orrisdale in *Yn Liooar Manninagh* ii, 195.

[9]For a further discussion of this tune and its associated stories, see Gilchrist, A G in *Journal of the Folk-Song Society* 28 (December 1924) 107-9.

[10]'*Ny kirree fo'n niaghtey*' ('The sheep under the snow'), a story set in the hills above Laxey, which describes an unsuccessful, large-scale search for sheep buried during a sudden and harsh snowstorm.

[11]The French term is used by A G Gilchrist in her commentaries on Manx music in *Journal of the Folk Song Society*, 1924, 1925 and 1926.

Figure 2: Wedding Procession, Voss, Western Norway

musician Andrew Poleson sang the first line of a tune before striking it up on the fiddle.[12] Could this be a remnant of such cante-fables, or even, perhaps, the sagas?

A similar example from Bergen (Grinde 1991, 92-3) concerns a group of friends who hear wonderful music on a mountainside on Christmas Eve. The halling-type tune[13] (Figure 1) associated with this story bears a remarkable similarity to the *'Bollan Bane'*, both in its melodic shape and range, rhythmic pattern and phrasing.

The important social role of the fiddle-player is celebrated in a handsome bronze plaque in Voss, not far from Bergen (Figure 2). The melody reproduced on the plaque is a traditional wedding tune, which has a distinctive rhythmic pattern and melodic line (Figure 3).

There is a group of Manx tunes with very similar characteristics and which are, interestingly, rarely performed by Manx musicians today (Figure 3). The greatest similarity is the rhythmic pattern but the opening bar of the melody and the range of the tune overall are strikingly alike. Norwegian tunes often have unusual structural features, such as three-bar phrases, a pattern which is shared by 10% of the melodies contained in the principal Manx collection[14], and which rarely occurs in other folk-music of the British Isles. In this case, the tune from Voss has regular 4-bar phrases but the Manx mocking song *'Arrane ny mummeryn'* ('Mummer's song') has an irregular 11-bar structure. Another related Manx tune *'Bwoaill Baccagh'* shares the triple time signature and has 26 bars, broken into the following phrase pattern: 4, 4, 9, 4, 5. What appears to be a development (or debasement) of this variant is *'Booil Backel'*, which has been transformed into an 8-bar melody in duple time and is used as a popular courting dance with the title 'Return the blow'.

But these are not the only musical links between Mann, Scotland and Western Norway. Amongst the tunes collected by the late Mona Douglas is a cow-calling song

---

[12]'The fiddler and his art', *Scottish Tradition 9*, School of Scottish Studies, University of Edinburgh, CDTRAX 9009, 1993 Track 9.
[13]The halling is a lively Norwegian dance-tune in duple time.
[14]The Clague Notebooks: mss in the Manx National Heritage Library Mss 448A/449B.

Figure 3: The Voss wedding tune and 'Mummer's Song'

Figure 4: Cow calling song. Collected from Mrs Bridson, Glen Maye, by Mona Douglas

apparently still in use in the middle of the nineteenth century (Figure 4). The tune is thought by Professor Peter Crossley-Holland to be one of the few, if not the only, surviving example of the genre in Britain.[15] The *'Arrane Ghelby'* (the 'Dalby song', named by Sophia Morrison after the part of the Island where she collected it) has remarkable echoes of *'Et te lux oritur'*, music composed to celebrate the wedding of Princess Margaret of Scotland and King Erik II of Norway in 1281 (Purser 1992, 59). Although much abbreviated, the Manx version retains some characteristic features of the original, particularly the repetition and the higher register of the middle section, which originally coincided with the crowning of Erik and Margaret. Could this plainsong have been familiar to the monks in Rushen Abbey[16], or could it have arrived in the Island in its trouvère form, which is also known in Scotland? 'Dream' songs also appear in the Manx carval repertoire and there are echoes of dance songs (Krogseater 1982, 12) in the *'Mhelliah'*, a Manx harvest dance.

---

[15]Crossley-Holland, P, *Music from the Hollow Hills* Chap 10, Tale No 3 'Calling the Cattle' (Isle of Man) (unpublished copyright). Professor Crossley-Holland likens the song part to the *Jubilus pastorale*.

[16]The abbey in the south of the Island founded by the Norse king, Olaf I.

Although there are references to a few tunes in the eighteenth century, the earliest collections of Manx tunes date from the nineteenth century, of which the most comprehensive is in the Clague Notebooks. Most of the melodies in this collection move by step, smoothing out irregular intervals that appear in related tunes from England, Scotland, Wales and Ireland (Bazin 1995, 43-9). Another group of Manx tunes from the Clague Notebooks feature not the smooth stepwise movement, but are based on a pattern of thirds, fifths and octaves, a characteristic often found in the Norwegian folk tradition[17], as well as in medieval church music of northern Britain.[18] The mixture of major and minor thirds found in a triad could well have led to the tonal ambiguity sometimes found in Manx music, with an oscillation (if not a confusion) between modes, whether major, minor, Aeolian or Dorian. Tunes often appear in more than one guise,[19] or move between two modes.[20] Still other remnants seem to have survived, including melodies that use the 'prid' scale found widely in the music of Western Norway.

By the end of the eighteenth century it is fairly clear that Manx fiddle music was in step with that in the surrounding countries. The merchant classes in the Isle of Man had adopted lifestyles and cultural pursuits indistinguishable from their partners and colleagues in Britain and further afield. The modern violin was employed by musicians who were as familiar with the music of the countryside as that of the concert hall, equally happily playing from the latest tune-books as from the score of a Handel oratorio. The earlier style of 'violyne' playing was probably overlaid by more 'modern' music. But pockets of the old style remained, with tunes that had perhaps survived from the time of the Scandinavian rule.

By the beginning of the twentieth century vestiges of the old style of fiddle playing had all but disappeared, surviving only in the late nineteenth-century collections of folklore and music, and in occasional, tantalising references by early commentators. New, mainstream styles had taken over, driven by the Island's economy, which was based mainly on the burgeoning tourist industry. But these, too, made use of the old Manx tunes, for example in the compositions of Haydn Wood, himself a violinist of some note, and his older brother Harry, who was for fifty years one of the most important figures in the popular music scene in the Isle of Man. However, it seems that small pockets of the tradition survived in remoter rural areas. With a reawakened interest in Manx music from the 1970s, new styles have developed, based on the traditional body of material but borrowing modern styles and techniques to produce an exhilarating new 'tradition' with a life of its own. Many modern musicians in the Isle of Man have been greatly influenced by Irish music. Young Manx instrumentalists could well find inspiration in exploring the other equally rich styles that have close historical links with the Isle of Man, such as Scotland and Western Norway.

---

[17]And used by Greig in, for example, 'Morning' from the Peer Gynt Suite.
[18]A famous example is the 12th-century Hymn to St Magnus which uses the interval of a third both in the melodic line and in the part-writing (Purser 49 and De Geer, I: 'Music and the Twelfth Century Orkney Earldom: A Cultural Crossroads in Musicological Perspective' in B E Crawford (ed) *St Magnus Cathedral and Orkney's Twelfth-Century Renaissance* (Aberdeen, University Press, 1988) 242.
[19]'Mylecharaine' is a particularly interesting example. See Bazin 'Mylecharaine: a call to nationhood' Folksong tradition and revival: Centenary Conference of the English Folk Song Society Sheffield, July 1998. Awaiting publication but lodged as a ms in the Manx National Heritage Library.
[20]See *'Haink sooreydepr nish gys dorrys ven-treoghe'* ('The suitor came to the widow's door') in Bazin 1995, 428.

This paper is simply the first step into a discussion of the pre-eighteenth-century instrumental tradition in the Isle of Man. I feel that the evidence contained in the customs and traditions, the folklore and especially the musical examples are sufficient to pursue and enrich our understanding of Manx musical history.

References

Arnold D, 1983, (ed.), *The New Oxford Companion to Music,* Vol 2, 1930. (Oxford, Oxford University Press).

Baines A, 1983, in *The New Oxford Companion to Music,* Vol 1, 520, D Arnold (ed.), (Oxford/New York, Oxford University Press).

Bazin F C, 1995, *Music in the Isle of Man up to 1896.* PhD thesis. Copies available in the Manx National Heritage Library and the University of Liverpool Library.

Caine H, 1896, *The Deemster* (London, Chatto and Windus).

Chaloner J, 1656, *A short treatise on the Isle of Man in Daniel King's Vale Royall,* (London, John Streeter).

Clague J, 1911, *Manx Reminiscences,* (Isle of Man, M J Backwell).

Clarke S, 1656, *A Mirror or Lookinge-Glass both for the Saints and Sinners wherein is Recorded, as Gods Great Goodness to the one, so His Seveare Iudgment's Against the Other, wherevnto is added a Geographicall Description of all the knowne world as allso of the Chiefest City's Both Ancient and modern &c.* (London, R Gaywood, 3rd edition).

Cowin J, 1902, *Reminiscences of a Notable Manx Citizen* (Isle of Man, Clucas and Fargher).

Douglas M, nd, *This is Ellan Vannin* (Isle of Man, Isle of Man Weekly Times).

Gill W W, 1932, *A Second Manx Scrapbook* (London, Arrowsmith).

Grinde N, 1991, *The History of Norwegian Music* (Translated by Halverson W H and Sateren L B): (Lincoln and London, University of Nebraska Press).

Johnson D, 1972, *Music and Society in Lowland Scotland in the Eighteenth Century,* (London, Oxford University Press).

Kennedy-Fraser M, 1921, *Songs of the Hebrides,* Vol 3.

Kermode P M C, 1907, *Manx Crosses,* (London, Bemrose and Sons Ltd).

Krogseater J, 1982, Folk-dancing in Norway (Oslo, Tanum-North).

Lifton S, 1983, *The listeners guide to folk music* (Dorset, Blandford Press).

Moore A W, 1891, *The Folklore of the Isle of Man* (IOM, Brown & Sons; London, D Nutt).

Purser J, 1992, *Scotland's Music,* (Edinburgh, Mainstream Publishing Co Ltd).

Saxby J M E, 1936, *Shetland Tradition and Lore* (Edinburgh, Grant and Murray).

Waldron G, 1864, 'Description of the Isle of Man in 1726' in *The Manx Society Vol* XI.

The Isle of Man - In the British Isles but not ruled by Britain: A modern peculiarity from ancient occurrences

Sybil Sharpe

Introduction

In this chapter, I attempt to explore some issues regarding the relationship between the United Kingdom government and Tynwald. This is a preliminary exploration undertaken in a limited time and all that I profess to do is to point to some avenues for further research and debate. There are several views on this conundrum. I contend that, under one such, it can be argued that Westminster is in an even weaker position of supremacy in relation to the Isle of Man legislature than it is in relation to dominion states such as Canada. Any analogy between Tynwald and the newly devolved Assemblies and the Scottish Parliament is erroneously drawn. Further, under the majority of views held, Westminster has no power to coerce compliance either with European Union law (including freedom of movement and employment of member state residents) nor with United Kingdom taxation provisions whether imposed by H. M. government or through compliance with European Union membership.

The Manx Legislative Process

Before considering the origins of the Manx legislature, it might be helpful for those who have no knowledge whatsoever of this jurisdiction for me to give a short overview of law-making in Man. Tynwald consists of the House of Keys (a directly elected chamber of 24 members) and a second chamber, the Legislative Council, (at present consisting of eight members elected by Tynwald, the Bishop of Sodor and Man, the Attorney General and the President of Tynwald). There were proposals in the

Constitution Bill 2000, now withdrawn, to increase the membership of the Keys to 33 and from this directly elected number for eight members to be elected by Keys to the Legislative Council. This Council would also have included the Bishop, the Attorney General and the President, though the former two officers would not have had a vote[1]. An earlier Bill to provide for a popularly elected second chamber also failed[2]. The Island does not have a political party system, the Members of Keys standing overwhelmingly as independents rather than on any party ticket. Legislation passes through both chambers in a way that is not dissimilar to that currently prevailing in the United Kingdom. The two chambers sit separately to consider primary legislation and together for other purposes as Tynwald Court[3]. Both Government and Private Members' Bills and any amendments thereto are usually drafted by draftsmen in the Attorney General's Office. The Home Office (perhaps a constitutionally contentious choice of advisor) frequently had a consultative role in this process. The Lord Chancellor's Department took over this role from the Home Office in June 2001. Legislation passes through four separate stages. The first is a first reading and formal introduction to the Bill. The second is a debate on the substance[4]. The third stage involves the consideration of individual clauses within the Bill. Such consideration may be by the whole House or may be referred to a Committee. Amendments must be effected by the House. The third reading is the final stage. The Bill then moves from the Keys to the Legislative Council and essentially the same stages are gone through by the second chamber although it is usually by means of a less formal and speedier process. If there is disagreement between Keys and the Council which cannot be resolved by a 'conference' between both chambers, under section 10 of the Isle of Man Constitution Act 1961, a Bill may become law under a system analogous to the Parliament Acts procedure in the United Kingdom. An absolute majority of Tynwald Court is necessary before the Royal Assent may be given. Assent (of which more later) is normally[5] given through delegated power to the Lieutenant Governor. There is a final requirement before a Bill can become law. This requirement grounds the previous procedures in their historic origin. An Act must be promulgated on Tynwald Day (5th July) at Tynwald Hill in both English and Manx to those assembled[6].

The Origins and Survival of Tynwald

The early history of Man is shrouded in as many mists as those that regularly envelope the island. The original celtic population was invaded by the Norse from the middle of

---

[1]The Constitution Bill 2000 fell at the Clauses stage on 23rd January 2001.

[2]The Constitution Bill 1999. See also the Report of the Select Committee on the Constitution Bill (November 2000).

[3]The Constitution Bill 2000 clause 8 would have provided for Council and the Keys to vote 'as one body'. By clause 9, where a Bill was rejected by one chamber, an affirmative vote by an absolute majority of Tynwald (not less than 17 elected members) would have been necessary for it to pass.

[4]There is a little used procedure whereby an individual who has a personal interest that will be adversely affected by a Bill (such interest being over and above that of the general public) he may appear in person or through counsel at this stage. He may also be heard at the 'clauses' stage.

[5]Royal Assent to Legislation (Isle of Man) Order 1981. An Act takes effect when the Royal Assent is announced to Tynwald by the President.

[6]Promulgation Act 1988. The promulgation must be certified by the Lieutenant Governor, the President of Tynwald and the Speaker of the House of Keys.

the 9th century and for four hundred years there was a process of gradual assimilation. Nordic customs became embedded in the legislative and judicial systems. One feature of this system was that a selected body of freemen should be consulted and that no judgement without their consent was valid. This differed from the Celtic practice where the King consulted his Chiefs and merely declared his decision to freemen. Tynwald was a derivative of the Icelandic "folk-moot". Decisions on law would be proclaimed from a hill by a law speaker sitting with the King in court and worthy freemen. The assembly was both judicial and executive in function. Advice on the law was taken from 'deemsters' (those learned in the law). The selected freemen numbered 24 and became known as the Keys[7]. The deemsters became (and still are) the judges in the superior courts of law. They were, until the late 16th century, elected by the people. Though members of the Council, they never acted in an executive capacity. Although the composition of the Keys as an elected body varied over the centuries according to the degree of control exercised by the Kings (later the Lords) of Man, (Moore 1900, Gell 1867)[8] there is a longer continuous history of defined legislative procedure and of democracy in the island than can be said to exist in respect of the United Kingdom.

The Island together with the Hebrides (the southern islands as in 'Sodor and Man') was held by the Kings of Man under allegiance to the King of Norway. It seems that allegiance was then transferred to the English King John, a transfer that, arguably, proved not to be a good long-term move for the people of Man! In the thirteenth century, Harold II, King of Man, was accepted as an absolute monarch by the English Crown. This is evidenced by the issue of a licence to Harold to be given safe conduct to enter England with leave of the Crown, such a document only being issued to a "monarch" or "absolute prince" (Gell 1983). The island continued as a kingdom owing allegiance, but the feudal lord was either England or Scotland, depending on respective fortunes in the power struggle between the two countries. The Kingship of Man passed by inheritance to the first Earl of Salisbury, his grant by Edward III making no reference to homage or service to the Crown (Gell 1983). The Isle of Man was later claimed by the Duke of Lancaster (later Henry IV) although whether this was by conquest has been disputed (Gell 1983)[9]. Henry vested the Kingship of Man in Sir John Stanley for a homage of 'two falcons'. The Stanley family became the dynastic rulers of Man and in 1460 Thomas II took the title 'Lord of Man' in preference to 'King of Man'. Due to the frequent absences of the rulers, their 'substitutes' in the form of Lieutenants (later titled Governors) exercised most of the prerogatives of the Lords. This prerogative power was guided by the advice of the Tynwald Council and the deemsters. In 1765, the Isle of Man Purchase Act revested sovereignty in the Crown. It is important to note, however, that the Crown acquired no greater powers than had belonged to the previous proprietors. The constitution was not changed in any way and any assumption of a right on the part of the Westminster Parliament to legislate for the island must be seen in the political context of the time. The colonies were proving troublesome as witnessed by the American Declaration of Independence in 1776.

---

[7]Moore (1900 vol i) states that the word Keys may come from the Scandinavian word 'keise' meaning 'chosen' or from an English pronunciation of the Manx Gaelic for four and twenty. It might also have had a figurative meaning viz. that by which a difficulty is explained.

[8]The Keys was eventually confirmed as an elective body by statute in 1866 and its judicial appellate power was abolished.

[9]It may be that the title was acquired other than by inheritance, but not 'by conquest'.

Revenues extracted from the empire were not as readily forthcoming as before. It is no surprise therefore that the first legislation passed by the imperial Parliament after revestment related to customs duties. The previous Lord, the Duke of Atholl, had possessed no power to impose customs duties or to legislate without the authority of Tynwald (Moore 1900, vol ii)[10]. The requirement of lawmaking, the passing of laws by a Lieutenant or Governor of the Lord on the advice of the Council and the deemsters, continued in a statutorily embodied form. That statute of 1417 was never repealed by Westminster. Indeed, Tynwald only repealed the substance of that Act (though not the Indenture itself) in the Pre-Vestment Written laws (Ascertainment) Act 1978 (Farrant 1990)[11].

The Difference between Tynwald, the Devolved Parliaments and the Parliaments of the Dominions

It can be seen that, since its inception, Tynwald has at no time been abolished and that it owes its legitimacy not to Westminster, but to an earlier tradition. Any analogy that may be made between it and the parliaments of other jurisdictions that were once within the Empire is, arguably, misplaced. Australia and Canada, for example, are of course independent members of the Commonwealth, though still, at present, owing allegiance to the British Monarch. Both jurisdictions have a constitution originating in statute; the Commonwealth of Australia Constitution Act 1900 and the British North America Act 1867 (amended by the Constitution Act 1982) respectively. The legislative authority in these nations, therefore, originates from Westminster and the federal Parliaments that now function on the two-chamber paradigm are its progeny. Somewhat incongruously, section 4 of the Statute of Westminster 1931 effectively gave legislative autonomy to the 'Dominions'.[12] Section 4 states that no Act of Parliament of the United Kingdom

'shall be deemed to extend to a Dominion as part of the law of that Dominion, unless it is expressly declared in the Act that the Dominion requested, and consented to the enactment thereof.'

Despite academic debate as to whether section 4 is in any way legally entrenched, or whether it effectively is so by reason of political reality[13], there is no doubt that it has allowed those jurisdictions to develop as independent nations. Further, not only did

---

[10]Even James I confirmed the continuance of customary laws by letters patent dated 1609. See also the transcript of a lecture delivered by the Clerk of Tynwald (Professor Bates) to the Friends of Peel Cathedral on 30/10/1998. Starting with the Isle of Man Customs, Harbours and Public Purposes Act 1866, the Isle of Man regained, on an incremental basis, control over taxation, internal expenditure and all other insular matters.

[11]The statute provided for a written compact (indenture) between the Commissioners for the King and the Keys and deemsters.

[12]The preamble to the Act and sect. 1 which applied it to the Dominions of Canada, Australia, New Zealand, South Africa, the Irish Free State and Newfoundland.

[13]See British Coal Corporation v R [1935] AC 500. The British Courts would enforce such legislation, but undoubtedly the Dominion courts would not. See also R v Ndblovu 1968(4) SA 515 where the Rhodesian High Court endorsed UDI in the face of the Southern Rhodesia Act 1965. It has also been pointed out that the literal wording of sect.4 does not require actual assent, merely a declaration to that effect, see Manuel v A-G [1983] Ch 107.

section 4 prevent Westminster from passing unwanted legislation in respect of the named Dominions, section 3 of the Act gave 'full power' to each of the Dominion Parliaments to make laws having extra territorial provision. It therefore enabled valid non-domestic legislation to be enacted. There is, of course, a political rather then a legal reason why such autonomy was accorded by this statute. The government of the United Kingdom was divesting itself of its imperial commitments. The Isle of Man did not benefit from the releasing of these commitments since it was never a colony, but a separate Kingdom. The paradox is that, whilst the Dominions have clear authority to pursue a policy of legislative autonomy, the Isle of Man is in a more complex position because no legislation has ever been enacted governing the limits of the powers between the two governments (Horner 1987).

The recent trend to rank Tynwald with the newly devolved United Kingdom Assemblies or the Scottish Parliament in any analysis of its situation is clearly wide of the mark. The Assemblies and the Scottish Parliament are governed by separate Acts and have different and distinct limitations on their powers[14]. The history of all three United Kingdom constituents is one of either conquest, absorption or an Act of Union resulting in the merging of their legislative identities with Westminster. The limitations imposed on the powers of the three reflects this history. The Welsh Assembly, generally, has no more than subordinate power viz. that conferred upon the Secretary of State. The Northern Ireland Assembly has a legislative competence limited by 'excepted' matters and by requirements to uphold European Union Law and the Human Rights Act 1998. Legislation must not discriminate against any person or class of persons. The excepted matters include international relations, nationality and immigration and taxes. Reserved matters (requiring the consent of the Secretary of State) include criminal law and the penal system and the maintaining of order. The Scotland Act 1998 again gives legislative competence subject to a list of 'reserved' matters and to a requirement that European Union law and the Human Rights Act are not infringed. Schedule 5 sets out the 'reserved' matters which include taxes, monetary policy and financial services, immigration and nationality, transport (whether by road, rail or air) the transmission and distribution of oil, gas and electricity and employment and industrial relations. Thus, even the Scottish Parliament has constraints upon its powers in respect of matters that Tynwald would regard as its domestic preserve. Further, and very importantly, the Isle of Man is not within the European Union and is therefore only bound by such regulations as apply to it in respect of the special trade and customs relationship that results from Protocol 3 to the Act of Accession. There is no requirement to observe E.U. treaties on the free movement of persons and services. The island receives no E.U. funding and makes no contribution thereto. The autonomy of Man is supported by a national coinage and by the recognition of its territorial waters.

---

[14]The Government of Wales Act 1998, the Northern Ireland Act 1998 and the Scotland Act 1998.

The Conundrum – Whether Tynwald or Westminster is Ultimately Supreme in Respect of Legislation Affecting the Isle of Man?

In the foregoing sections, I have given a very brief outline of the historical and contextual constitutional position of the Isle of Man legislature. This leads us to the heart of the problem. This problem is the relative authority of the two legislatures. The issue is not merely an academic one because although frequently the interests of the two jurisdictions coincide there are occasions when they do not. Two illustrations of possible future 'irreconcilable differences' (taxation and the right of residence) are mentioned in the following section. There are two parts to the puzzle. The first is whether Westminster can legislate for Man. The second is whether Tynwald can legislate without the approval of Westminster.

It is clear that the claim of Westminster to legislate for the Isle of Man is based upon the absence of evidence of any positive objection to the enforcement of such legislation rather than to any positive authority granting this power. Certainly, there is a body of Manx judicial opinion that before revestment an English statute did not bind the island (Gell 1983). English jurists conceded that a statute did not extend to the Isle of Man unless 'it is specifically so named'[15]. Coke referred to the 'peculiar laws and customs of the island'[16]. He cites, as an example of the non application of English law, Calvin's Case determined in 1608. This case is said to hold that the widow of the Second Earl was unable to claim dower on the island because the Statutes *de donis* of Uses and Wills was a general Act and had no enforceability in Man. It has been argued by Gell (1983) that even this analysis is, strictly, an *obiter* one, there never having been, at that time, an Act of Parliament that professed to extend to the island. However, the view that English legislation could bind the island if it was so intended (regardless of whether that intent was expressly declared on the face of the statute or was inferred from its content) has been advanced by Edge[17]. He considers that even before revestment this was the situation. There appears to be little authority to support this contention, however, and what there is may well be ambiguous[18]. What is certainly more clear is that after 1765, there was an assumption made by the English legislature that it could bind the Isle of Man in respect of customs revenue and that this assumption was made for blatantly self-serving purposes. As Blackstone stated [19]

'The distinct jurisdiction of this little subordinate royalty being found inconvenient for the purposes of public justice, and for the revenue, (it afforded commodious asylum for debtors, outlaws and smugglers) authority was given to the Treasury by Statute – to purchase the interest of the then proprietors for the use of the Crown.'

The enforceability of legislation that was for the benefit of the United Kingdom was conveniently assumed on other matters as well, such as service in the Imperial Militia

---

[15]Wood's Institutes of the Laws of England 1772 and Blackstone Commentaries vol.i.

[16]Coke's Institutes the 1st and 4th parts.

[17]'David Goliath and Supremacy: The Isle of Man and the Sovereignty of the United Kingdom Parliament' [1995] *Anglo-American Law Review* 1.

[18]The Petition for Redress brought by the heirs of William Christian is, arguably, unclear authority in this matter because of the wording of the Act of Indemnity. The Act refers to 'the dominions'.

[19]Blackstone Commentaries vol i.

(Edge 1997). What seems to have occurred is a less than subtle change in the relationship between the Island and the English Crown. Horner (1987) points out that after 1688, the British Monarchy had, *de facto*, been subordinated to the Westminster Parliament and that the Isle of Man metamorphosed from a territory owing allegiance into a dependent territory. In the context of a burgeoning colonial empire, this meant that those statutes deemed to be 'imperial' in nature were applied to the Isle of Man. The regaining of autonomy occurred from the mid 19th century onwards and coincided with the collapse of the Empire. The political climate, rather than legal legitimacy, had allowed the British government to assume legislative competence for Man. According to the Home Office[20], views expressed in the Stonham Report in 1969 and *obiter dicta* case law [21], the United Kingdom by convention will refrain from legislating in respect of insular matters without consent.

Even if the United Kingdom government accepts that this is the case and no longer argues that it refrains from such legislation by reason of 'good practice' only, a convention is not a very safe basis upon which to escape imposed legislation. Despite statements to the contrary made by academic writers such as Jennings[22] and Mitchell[23], there is a strong body of opinion that holds that there is a distinction of importance between laws and conventions. Munro[24] backs Dicey in this debate and points out that no analogy can be made between customary laws and conventions. Customary law has become part of the common law or has been incorporated into statute. A convention, however, does not become law simply by reason of long observance. Thus, judges have refused to enforce conventions in the courts. The most pertinent example of judicial refusal to enforce convention is seen in Canadian case law. In the well known authority of *In Reference re Resolution to Amend the Constitution*[25] it was said that, unless a convention had been adopted into statute, it could not become law regardless of the importance of its subject matter. It is true, of course that the more significant the convention which it is sought to breach, the less likely it is that it will be *politically* possible to do so. The more recent case of *Osborne v Canada (Treasury Board)*[26] confirmed that conventions form part of the constitution in 'the broader political sense' but are legally unenforceable and, further, that a statute is not exempt from scrutiny under the Charter of Fundamental Rights and Freedoms merely because it upholds a constitutional convention. Of course, political expediency dictates that the United Kingdom government would not readily defy any supposed convention not to legislate for the island on insular matters without consent. However, there may well be future conflicts ahead where the international obligations of the United Kingdom 'overflow' into the domestic arena in the Isle of Man. Pressures placed on the British government to comply with the obligations under the Maastricht Treaty and the Treaty Of Amsterdam will probably mean that matters such as crime, justice and the movement of persons within the EU area are increasingly determined by a central body of

---

[20]Review of Financial Regulation in the Crown Dependencies Home Office (1998) Cm 4109-iv.
[21]Re Tucker (A Bankrupt) (1985) 11 Manx Law Bulletin 33.
[22]The Law and the Constitution (1959).
[23]Constitutional Law (1968).
[24]Studies in Constitutional Law 2nd ed. (1999).
[25][1981] 1 SCR 753.
[26][1991] 2 SCR.

Ministers rather than by national parliaments (Colvin and Noorlander 1998). Taxation is already rearing its head as a contentious issue between Tynwald and Westminster. It is likely that pressures toward a homogenised European taxation system will grow. There is a slight difference of opinion regarding the status of international treaties. Edge (1997) considers that international treaties extend to the Island by virtue of the sovereignty exercised by the British Crown unless a reservation is made. On the other hand Professor Bates, the previous Clerk of Tynwald, believes that a treaty must be expressly extended to the Island on ratification. However, as stated above, Man is not a member of the EU and, so far, has escaped the implementation of Union law [27]. Whether this will continue to be the case could depend upon whether political pressure is placed upon the British government to enact legislation that brings Manx law in line with that prevailing in the United Kingdom which itself is subject to the primacy of Community law [28].

Should such a scenario ever arise, it would, I submit, be preferable to argue that the legislation is unenforceable because any assumption by the British government of the right to pass laws without the consent of Tynwald is erroneous and without historical foundation. Acquiescence in a mistaken exercise of power over many years does not legitimate that power. The current arrangement, whereby Tynwald enacts its own domestic legislation in parallel to the United Kingdom [29] rather than consenting to the extended application of Westminster statutes, is less than satisfactory. An arrangement that depends upon some alleged 'concession' by an imperial parliament is not a secure one. This has been demonstrated by the few occasions when a certain amount of compulsion was placed upon Tynwald to legislate in line with the sexual and penal norms prevailing in the United Kingdom and mandated under the European Convention on Human Rights.[30] The question of whether the individual statutes thereby enacted should have existed in any civilised democracy is not the issue here. The issue is the possibility of future conflict and legislative capacity. An argument can be put forward that the right claimed by Westminster to pass legislation on behalf of the Island, even legislation affecting international obligations, is actually without legal foundation. There is a need to reopen the statement made in *In the Matter of CB Radio Distributors* (Gell 1983) that it was 'now too late' to question that right 'at any rate in this court'.

The second part of the conundrum is whether Tynwald may legislate unconstrained by the wider interests of the United Kingdom. To this question there is clearer answer, but even this answer is complicated by the requirement of Royal Assent. Edge is of the

---

[27]DHSS v Barr and Montrose Ltd. (1990-2) Manx Law Reports 243. Manx law, which requires non-nationals to obtain a work permit, is not void as a discriminatory practice since EU law does not apply. The Residence Bill 2000 is likely to become law later this year. This Act will limit the right of residence on Man. Once the population reaches what is regarded as a critical level, existing residents, those who have established a home on the Island, those born in Man and spouses, divorcees, widows and children of residents or those born here will be entitled to unconditional registration. Others will have to apply for conditional registration and such registration will be granted on terms and only when a sufficient connection with or benefit to the Island is demonstrated.

[28]Van Gend en Loos Case 26/62 [1963] ECR 1; Costa v ENEL. Case 6/64 1964] ECR 585 and R v Secretary of State for Transport ex p. Factorame (no.2) [1991] AC 603.

[29]As in the case of the United Kingdom Human Rights Act 1998.

[30]The Criminal Justice (Penalties etc.) Act 1993 finally removed birching as a penalty, although since the case of Tyrer v UK it had never been implemented as a sentence by the judiciary. The Sexual Offences Act 1992 decriminalised consensual adult homosexual activity.

view that Tynwald may legislate to abrogate or to make any insular and/or international law even if this is contrary to the Imperial law of Great Britain. The only limitation (since Man owes allegiance to the English Sovereign) is that Tynwald may have no power to place the Crown in breach of international obligations (Edge 1997). Whilst, prior to the Bill of Rights of 1688, Manx interests might have conflicted with the international obligations of the Crown in person, the position is now more complicated. Any residual Crown prerogative that exists in respect of making treaties or deploying armed forces is exercised on the advice of government ministers. It is increasingly difficult to distinguish the impact of foreign policy (which is effectively now a matter for the British government) from the impact of domestic policy in a society that is rapidly becoming a global one. Ultimately therefore, the ability of Tynwald to exercise unconstrained legislative power must depend upon the grant of royal assent, such assent, currently, being a necessary step before the promulgation of any statute. There has been much debate as to how and when this assent should be given and, I submit, some of this debate is not crucial to the instant issue. However, without wishing to 'lose the plot', I consider it necessary to make some further comment on this and to discuss a precedent from another jurisdiction to suggest that, *in extremis,* even the lack of royal assent might not invalidate a Manx statute so far as the judiciary of the Island is concerned.

The Royal Assent

Historically, consent to Tynwald Bills was given by the King and, later, the renamed Lord of Man. It was only after revestment that the Sovereign attained this power (Cain 1992). From 1813 onwards, assent was exercised on the advice of the Privy Council and the practice of submitting Bills to the Privy Council continued until 1981. As a consequence of expressed desire for greater self-determination, the Royal Assent to Legislation Isle of Man Order (1981) was passed[31]. This Order, in Article 2, delegated to the Lieutenant-Governor the powers exercisable by Queen in Council. The power is not limited by subject matter, but it does not apply when the Lieutenant-Governor considers consent must be reserved under Article 3 [32], or when he is so directed by the Secretary of State under Article 4. However, the crucial issue must inevitably be when such assent might be refused, by whomsoever it is exercised. Professor Bates has argued that the need for assent, if not completely abolished, should be restricted to defence and external relations [33]. This would bring the need for assent in line with the reserved powers under the 1981 Order, the only other significant matters currently requiring reservation being nationality and the constitutional relationship between the two countries. Professor Bates views the current process of bargaining in respect of the content of legislation as a questionable exercise of prerogative power. Horner (1987) considers that there is no convention (parallel to that in the United Kingdom) requiring that assent will not be refused. The lack of any clear authority for the situations that

---

[31]Made by prerogative order of the P.C. 23rd September 1981.

[32]Article 3 refers to matters 'which in the opinion of the Lieutenant Governor deal wholly or partly with defence, international relations, nationality and citizenship and the constitutional relationship between the United Kingdom and the Isle of Man'. It also covers matters affecting the Royal prerogative or HM Queen in her private capacity.

[33]Lecture to The Friends of Peel Cathedral (1998).

might lead to the refusal of assent has led to speculation, based on past instances and future predictions, as to when this crisis might arise. In evidence to the Stonham Report, the Home Office referred to the possibility of a statute having 'unacceptable repercussions' outside the Island as one such situation. This is a pretty vague and subjective criterion. What is 'unacceptable' and to whom must it be so? One suspects that the answer is that 'unacceptable' means politically uncomfortable for the United Kingdom government's international image. One example might be any legislation that would clearly infringe the International Covenant on Civil and Political Rights 1966. This would certainly be a breach of the international obligations of the Crown since the United Nations requires periodic reports in respect of compliance by dependent jurisdictions[34]. However, such obvious treaty violations apart, it is hard to see the legal justification for refusing assent simply because a statute might embarrass the United Kingdom or prove inconvenient to its external policy objectives. The remaining examples then given by the Home Office included the deleterious effect of proposed legislation on the Island. This is, arguably, of no relevance whatsoever to the question of assent. Once Tynwald has debated and passed a Bill, it is a paternalistic and unwarranted interference with autonomy for a foreign government to advise what is and what is not in the national interest. It is also now accepted that the fact that Manx law and domestic English law would be in conflict is no necessary reason for assent to be refused (Edge 1997).

Whether consent is given is, therefore, very much an exercise of discretion governed by political factors rather than by legal circumscription. As the 21st century functions at an increasingly global level, the pressure for centralisation of control among nations vies with the liberal tradition of supporting the autonomy and identity of smaller countries. It seems that the European Union itself embodies an aspect of this conflict. The greater autonomy granted to the British regions through devolved parliaments must be seen in the context of their overall subjugation to European Directives and the impact upon them of European Union Treaties. The Isle of Man, however, has no legal obligation to conform to such a system and legally (as well as morally) the United Kingdom should allow the Island to legislate in ways that further the interests, both national and international, of its residents. The United Nations Declaration On The Granting Of Independence To Colonial Countries And Peoples 1960 stated that territories should become self-governing and that all powers should be transferred to their peoples 'without conditions or reservations, in accordance with their freely expressed will and desire'. It seems there is an argument founded in international law, that, regardless of the reservation concerning the constitutional relationship of Man and the United Kingdom, the Crown should assent to any future Tynwald statute seeking a release from the dependency status of Man.

It would take a crisis in political relations for such a situation to arise and, of course, there would have to be a situation where the advantages of dependency were outweighed by the disadvantages, but it is not an entirely fanciful possibility. The recent arguments over fiscal policy are but one area of tension. I submit that there might be others, such as freedom of movement, arising in the future. It is stated government policy to promote and defend the Island's internal autonomy and to work towards greater autonomy in international affairs.

---

[34]See the Fifth Report by the Crown Dependencies of the United Kingdom Under Article 40 of the ICPR (August 1999).

Should the Island declare unilateral independence and should Royal Assent, on the advice of Ministers, be refused what would be the legal consequence? It is possible that the immediate response from Westminster might be to pass an Act permitting it to legislate directly for the Island, even though this would be a new statutory assertion of power rather than a reassertion of a pre-existing statutory right. There is a precedent of sorts because, in 1965, the Southern Rhodesia Act was passed in a situation of unilateral independence declared by Mr. Smith. The Privy Council recognised the validity of that statute and stated that it had full effect in Southern Rhodesia[35]. However, the theory of parliamentary supremacy and the actuality are rather different. The Rhodesian courts refused to recognise the Westminster Act and continued to apply the law of the illegal regime[36]. This may have been a country that was geographically much further removed from Great Britain than is the Isle of Man. Nonetheless, if Manx deemsters proceeded to enforce Manx made law and ignored Westminster legislation, it seems unlikely that a military invasion would be mounted. Despite the flouting of the Royal prerogative that would inevitably have occurred, political reality might well suggest that the model of independence adopted by the Commonwealth Monarchies owing allegiance to the Queen would be finally accepted by the United Kingdom. I submit that if and when this should occur is a matter of political feasibility rather than of legal incapacity.

Conclusion

In this overview I have attempted to demonstrate that there is a basis for an argument that the United Kingdom has erroneously assumed legislative competence in respect of the Isle of Man and that there may be an historical basis for contending that Westminster cannot validly legislate for Tynwald even by express extension. Further research is needed to establish that the acquiescence of deemsters in applying any such legislation after revestment was borne of political duress rather than based on legal enforceability. In respect of Tynwald's own legislative powers, there is clearly no restriction on such exercise other than the obtaining of the consent of the Lord of Man; such assent powers now being transferred to the Crown and forming part of the Royal Prerogative. Whilst the Isle of Man is still a dependency, Tynwald cannot legislate to place the United Kingdom in breach of its obligations under international law. However, refusal of assent should not be used as a means to promote imperial interests in opposition to those of the Island, since this would be a breach of the United Nations Declaration on rights of self-determination. Further research analysing the differences between the emergence of the Commonwealth countries as independent states and the current situation of Man might be useful. Such an analysis would show that, historically, Man has a greater claim to autonomy than the Dominions, such claim being as of right and not as the result of a Westminster statute. Due to its geographical proximity to the United Kingdom, Man never received recognition as an international power and it may now be timely to re-examine the place of the Island within the global community.

---

[35]Madzimbamuto v Lardner-Burke [1969] AC 654.
[36]Dhlamini v Carter (1968)(2) SA 464 and R v Nadlovu (1968)(4) SA515.

Bibliography

Cain T W, 1992, 'Royal Assent to Acts of Tynwald', Manx Law Bulletin, 113.

Colvin M and Noorlander P, 1998, 'Human Rights and Accountability after the Treaty of Amsterdam', European Human Rights Law Review, 191.

Edge P, 1997, 'Public Law', Manx Law Society.

Farrant R D, 1990, 'The Constitution of Man', Manx Law Bulletin, 86.

Gell J, 1867, Manx Society, vol xii.

Gell J, 1983, 'In the Matter of CB Radio Distributors Ltd. (Staff of Govt.)', Manx Law Reports, 351.

Horner A, 1987, in *Constitutions of Dependencies and Special Sovereignties*, ed. Blaustein (Ocean, New York).

Moore A W, 1900, *History of the Isle of Man* (Douglas).

Securing the Future of Manx Gaelic

Philip Gawne

Introduction

Against all odds, Manx Gaelic has clawed itself back from the verge of extinction over the past thirty years. It is more than surprising that a language declared dead by academics and rejected by the Manx community some thirty years ago is rapidly growing in popularity, has steadily increasing numbers of speakers and has recently received substantial Government backing through the introduction of Manx Gaelic medium education in September 2001.

This chapter offers an explanation for the remarkable change in fortunes for Manx and chronicles the first attempts at language planning undertaken by the Manx Government in the mid 1980s and 1990s. It is, however, first appropriate to contextualise these developments with a brief overview of the historical development of the Manx language.[1]

It appears that distinctions between Scottish, Irish and Manx Gaelic began to emerge in the 13th to 14th century during the tumultuous period following the collapse of the Norse kingdom of Mann and the Isles and prior to the long settled period of English control through the Stanleys. The first written evidence for the existence of Manx Gaelic as a language or dialect separate from the other Gaelic languages appears as late as 1611 with Bishop Phillips' translation of the Book of Common Prayer (Moore 1893). It is generally accepted that Phillips' orthography formed the basis for the split between Manx and its larger linguistic neighbours, Irish and Scottish Gaelic and that this split was later cemented by the extensive biblical and religious translations of Bishop Wilson. This view was however challenged by Dr Nicholas Williams of University College, Dublin in his Ned Maddrell Memorial Lecture, 'Aspects of the history of

---

[1] Abbreviations
DoE Isle of Man Department of Education.
GU *Report of the Select Committee on the Greater Use of Manx Gaelic, Tynwald (18/06/85).*
T7 *Report of Proceedings of Tynwald Court* (Isle of Man Government, 12th December 1984).

Manx' (1998 unpublished), in which he cites the similarities between early written Manx and that of the Book of the Dean of Lismore as evidence that Manx orthography was brought to Mann from Scotland in the 16th century. With the exception of the Stanley stronghold in Castletown, Manx Gaelic was universally spoken in Mann until the 1765 Revestment Act by which the Duke of Atholl sold the Isle of Man to the British Crown. This led to the collapse of the Manx economy and significant emigration requiring the previously relatively isolated Manx people to use English at the expense of their native tongue.

The move to English was accelerated by immigration from North West England (1790-814) and the emergence in the 1830s of mass tourism in the Isle of Man. Although the 19th Century began with the overwhelming majority of residents speaking Manx, by the time of the 1901 census, the number of speakers had fallen to 4,419 – only 8.1% of the population. By 1921 the figures had fallen to around 1.5% and they continued to decline until the 1961 census when only 165 people (0.34%) spoke the language. Despite a slight improvement by 1971 (up to 0.52%) the language appeared doomed and when the last traditional native speaker, Ned Maddrell, died in 1974, many academics declared the Manx language to be extinct. Indeed, no question on Manx was asked in the 1981 census. From this desperate position, the 1991 census made surprising reading: 740 people were recorded as being able to speak, read or write Manx - around 1% of the population. This has risen to 2.2% in the 2001 census.

Manx was not officially taught in the schools and many people believed that it had no practical use in the modern world, so why did these people choose to learn Manx, bearing in mind that prior to 1991 there was little support available to adult learners? The Isle of Man Act 1958 heralded the beginning of more than two decades of significant constitutional reform which saw a democratic, responsible Manx government emerge from the shadows of British colonial rule. The 1950s and early sixties had been a time of high unemployment in Mann, so the Manx Government, keen to exercise some of its newly acquired powers, in the sixties and seventies, introduced changes to the tax system aimed at attracting new residents to the Isle of Man (Kermode 2001).

The new resident policies led to massive social and cultural upheaval with population growth of 13% in the sixties followed by a 21% growth in the seventies. The arrival of so many outsiders placed a severe strain on the close-knit traditional Manx communities and saw the rapid growth of nationalist politics. By the end of the 1970s Mec Vannin (the Manx Nationalist Party) came very close to winning a number of seats in the House of Keys. Following the initial shock caused by the arrival of so many new residents, many Manx people were searching for a sense of identity and purpose. Urged on by the common perception that Government and new residents alike were treating the Manx as second-class citizens, a number of Manx people and some incomers looked to the Manx language and its associated culture to re-establish a strong Manx identity (Gawne 2000a, 20-32; Gawne 2000b, 139-143).

With the confidence gained from Mann's growing constitutional independence perhaps influenced by the upsurge in popular support for the nationalist cause, the ideas of moderate nationalism began to be accepted by mainstream politicians. With an increasing and already significant vocal minority supporting the Manx language and culture, Charles Cain, Member of the House of Keys (MHK) for Ramsey, placed the following motion before Tynwald (Cain, Tynwald Proceedings, T7 17).

Tynwald is of the opinion:

(1) That Manx Gaelic should be supported and encouraged by all agencies of Government and Boards of Tynwald so far as they are practically able.

(2) That all official oaths and declarations should be able to be made in Manx Gaelic or English at the option of the person making any such oath or declaration.

(3) That all documents expressed in Manx Gaelic shall have equal official and legal standing as documents expressed in English.

(4) That where places, roads or streets are bilingually named in English and Manx Gaelic, the use of the Manx name should have the same official and legal standing as the use of the English name.

The motion was put to Tynwald on Wednesday 12th December 1984, and directly followed Tynwald's agreement of a declaratory resolution that: '1986 be designated Manx Heritage Year' (Kerruish, Tynwald Proceedings, T7 16-17). Charles Kerruish, Speaker of the House of Keys (SHK), had defended this resolution by asserting that 'this Government and recent Governments have shown an astonishing disregard for the need to both preserve and promote that (Manx) Heritage'.

In commending his motion on the language to Tynwald, Charles Cain declared that his motion: '... is not here to enforce any set of cultural values. What it does is to enable a Manxman to use his own language with pride and to express his own nationality without being made to feel second rate' (Cain T7 19). Referring to the second part of his motion he said: '... Are Gaelic speakers therefore to take it that the use of the language on Tynwald Day is merely a sop to the peasants, or merely a tourist gimmick? Either way it is an insult to our culture and to our forebears. Either it is an official language or it is not, and for myself I feel it is only right that any Manxman should have the right to take official oaths in the Manx Gaelic language' (Cain T7 19-20).

Mr Cain concluded by summarising his view as follows: 'This debate is in general about how this court regards its cultural heritage as embodied in the Manx language. Is it worth fostering or not? Is the Manx language something important to our cultural heritage or not? I believe it is, and I believe that by supporting this resolution it is the least that you can do' (Cain T7 20).

Only Eddie Lowey, Member of the Legislative Council (MLC) spoke against the motion: '... I do not believe that there is any pressure from within the Island for this and I am not going to be branded less of a patriot to the Isle of Man as a Manxman because I do not happen to speak Manx Gaelic or, even more important, understand it. That may be wicked of me, it may be disloyal in some eyes; I do not particularly believe it is' (Lowey T7 21). Mr Lowey concluded by giving us an insight into the main concern of those who were not in favour of supporting the language: 'I do not accept in total my good friend from Ramsey's prognostication that somehow a country is less of a country if it does not have its own language. It may be in someone's eyes essential. I would disagree with that; I would say it may be desirable, but at what cost? I am not certain that cost is an acceptable one at this moment in time ...' (Lowey T7 21).

Mr Cain received support from the Speaker, with Dominic Delaney MHK finally making the following remarks which in essence describe the desired outcome of the motion: '... as far as I am concerned, ... probably one of the major things we will do in the life of this Government is get some backbone to the Isle of Man, if we can do it by this way, even though members might never even be able to speak a word of Manx I know that maybe my children or my grandchildren might have the opportunity and encouragement to do so' (Delaney T7 22). An amendment to the motion was moved and carried – that the resolution be referred to a Committee for consideration and report. Four MHKs, Messers Cain, Maddrell and Moore and Mrs Christian, and one MLC, Mr Lowey were elected on to what was soon to become the Select Committee on the Greater Use of Manx Gaelic.

The Select Committee on the Greater Use of Manx Gaelic

The Select Committee spent six months considering the motion seeking evidence from interested parties either directly or through advertisements in the press. The bulk of evidence from the general public was from individuals and societies who wished to see greater use of Manx, fourteen of the seventeen letters received being strongly supportive of Mr Cain's motion.

Of the three letters opposing the motion, two show considerable opposition if not hostility towards the proposals. The first from the Isle of Man Bank uses alarmist rhetoric to suggest that every Bank branch, shop and business in Man would be forced to employ Manx speakers if the motion were carried. The second letter from a private member of the public launches a blistering attack on: '... an apparent attempt ... being made by a small vociferous and almost totally unrepresentative minority to give greater emphasis to Manx Gaelic to an extent that it could affect detrimentally the economic well-being of the whole Island'. He concluded by saying: 'From private discussion I have had throughout the Island, I believe there is an overwhelming majority who have little or no concern for the Manx language' (Oates GU).

The Committee received a mixed response from nineteen Government agencies and officials. Deemster Luft and the IoM Post Office Authority in particular provided very negative responses to the motion. However, in general those opposed to the proposals did at least support the sentiment of the motion. Their opposition centred rather on the lack of staff available to provide translations, the potential costs of producing all forms and leaflets in Manx and English, and delays in customer service if business were to be allowed to be conducted through Manx.

In total, fourteen Government respondents expressed some degree of opposition, though twelve of these conceded that there were some merits in the motion. Those in favour generally expressed some sympathy to the preservation of the language and most were in favour of bilingual signs, letter heads and notices. The Board of Education explained that its policy was for Manx heritage and the environment to be studied at primary schools with the teaching of Manx as an optional subject. It also was planning to introduce a Manx studies course at one secondary school (though this never fully materialised) and was supporting an O-level course in Manx at the College of Further Education.

Undoubtedly the most positive response came from the Manx Museum and National Trust (latterly known as Manx National Heritage), which offered overwhelming support for Mr Cain's motion. The Trust pointed out that: 'while accepting that Manx speakers represent a small minority of the community, it is a growing minority and the fact that indigenous language acts as a badge of cultural identity elevates the importance of Manx above its current minority status'. The Trust wished to go further than the original motion stating that the Trust: '... while supporting the principle of the resolution, would favour a clear, unambiguous and positive statutory declaration of general application to the effect that the Manx language has the same legal status in the Isle of Man as the English language' (Harrison GU).

The Report of the Select Committee on the Greater Use of Manx Gaelic was presented to Tynwald on the 10th July 1985 and approved without further debate. In the general observations at the beginning of the Report it set out the following statement of philosophy which was fundamental to its consideration of the four sections of Mr Cain's original motion: '... the use of Manx Gaelic should be encouraged wherever possible and practicable'. In conclusion the committee reported that: '... until a more significant proportion of the population is familiar with the language, its integration into day to day life, particularly in Government, will perforce be limited' (GU 2.3 and 7.2). The committee pressed for the introduction of more Manx studies courses in schools but was keen to stress that it did not wish to force Manx down the throats of a reluctant population.

The recommendations of the Report approved by Tynwald were as follows:

(a) Tynwald declares its intent that the preservation and promotion of the Manx Gaelic should be an objective of the Isle of Man Government.

(b) The Board of Education in conjunction with the Manx Heritage Foundation should provide foundation courses in Manx studies for all pupils in both primary and secondary schools with opportunities for further specific courses on a voluntary basis and to that end should also provide courses for teachers. We also recommend that an O-level course be created in Manx studies.

(c) Boards and Departments should use bi-lingual signs for offices, vehicles and on notepaper and should, wherever possible and practical, make greater use of the Manx Gaelic insofar as this can be done without increasing costs or reducing efflciency.

(d) The Ceremonial Oaths entered in the *Liber Juramentorum* should be capable of being taken in Manx Gaelic provided certain conditions are fulfilled and appropriate legislation introduced where necessary.

(e) The Manx Heritage Foundation should establish a voluntary Manx Language Advisory Commission.

(f) The use of bi-lingual documentation should not be discouraged provided such use does not deleteriously affect commercial activity or the expeditious administration of justice.

(g) Street name signs and village and town boundary signs should be bi-lingual except where the traditional Manx name is the accepted form (GU 7.3).

Outcomes: first attempt at language planning

The approval by Tynwald of these recommendations provided the first significant attempt at language planning by Government. Regrettably, no agency was identified to ensure that these recommendations were acted upon. Despite the lack of consideration of an implementation strategy, this report established some important principles not least that Tynwald believe that support of Manx Gaelic should be an objective of the Manx Government.

Most of the recommendations of the report have been acted upon in one form or another though importantly the proviso that support should be given only where there are no significant cost implications has limited the implementation of recommendations to at best the minimum level suggested. It could be argued that recommendation (a) led to the establishment of the Gaelic Broadcasting Committee, although this is more widely credited to the persistence of Peter Karran MHK, a keen supporter of the language and founder of Caarjyn ny Gaelgey (friends of the Manx language). The Gaelic Broadcasting Committee (Bing Ymskeaylley Gaelgagh) was established following an amendment to the Broadcasting Act and since its formation has been very effective in bringing more Manx Gaelic broadcasts to Manx Radio. Unfortunately, the committee's narrow brief excludes support for TV, video and film, so limiting its overall potential.

Undoubtedly the aspiration of recommendation (a) has helped encourage the growth of Government support for Manx, but it is also true that agencies, societies and individuals have had to work hard even to attain the modest compliance of Government to the 1985 Report's recommendations. In the late 1980s there was further nationalist unrest prompted once more by the popular view that incomers, particularly those in the finance sector, were taking control of the Isle of Man and destroying Manx culture and identity. In 1990, the year following the imprisonment of three nationalists for burning down luxury homes, Government commissioned a Gallup survey on the Quality of Life in the Isle of Man which found that 36% of respondents wished to see Manx taught in schools. This significant finding came at the same time as the Department of Education (DoE) was being approached by the Manx Language Working Party, among others, to have Manx introduced into the school system. So, in January 1992, nearly seven years after Tynwald approved recommendation (b), after significant nationalist unrest and considerable lobbying by the Manx Heritage Foundation and the Manx Language Working Party, the Manx Language Programme was introduced by the DoE, with the first official Manx classes being held in September 1992.

In December 1995 the DoE produced a report on the Future Development of the Manx Language, which was received by Tynwald [2] (see below). It explained that:

Following a decision by the Council of Ministers, a Manx Language Officer (funded by the Manx Heritage Foundation for two years) and two peripatetic Manx teachers (funded by DoE) were appointed. They took up their posts in January 1992 in order to introduce the formal teaching of the language in schools. A decision was taken to offer a 'taster' Manx course to all pupils aged seven and over (including secondary school pupils), ... Pupils would take Manx for a nominal half-hour per week on an optional basis ... (DoE).

---

[2]*The Future Development of the Manx Language - A Report to Tynwald,* (December 1995) 6.1.1.

To date the Manx Language Programme has been well supported with somewhere between 20-40 % of all school children attending optional Manx lessons at some time during their school years. The DoE has enhanced its Manx language provision in recent years by increasing its staff by one to three teachers and a Manx Language Officer, and by introducing the Teisht Chadjin Ghaelgagh (GCSE equivalent in Manx Gaelic). So more than ten years after Tynwald approval, recommendation (b) was more or less achieved at least in relation to the Manx language, if not for Manx studies. Even though the delay in introducing specific Manx language courses on a voluntary basis was undoubtedly unnecessary, it cannot be overestimated how significant this introduction was. For nearly ten years now, large numbers of children in Man have been given access to the language of the country in which they live. Children enjoy their Manx lessons and importantly many of them are vociferous in upholding their right to learn Manx Gaelic. It seems that the reasons given by the select committee for limiting the support given to the language are being superseded, as more and more children are leaving school with Manx and a more significant proportion of the population is becoming familiar with the language.

Recommendation (c) was enthusiastically adopted by most Government agencies, at least in terms of bilingual headed paper and signs on vehicles, though there are still a few who have chosen not to do this. Adoption of bilingual signs for offices and buildings has not been so well supported, as the aspiration to make greater use of the language without increasing costs was self-defeating. Despite this, the official use of Manx by Government Departments has done much to raise the perceived status of the language.

During the summer of 2001, over sixteen years after it was first approved, recommendation (d) calling for the Ceremonial Oaths to be available in Manx was finally achieved. Despite it having been possible for some oaths to be taken in Manx for a number of years, such as the oath taken by Members of the House of Keys, the production of translations of oaths for the remaining offices recommended in the 1985 Report was only completed in July 2001.

The Manx Heritage Foundation established Coonceil ny Gaelgey, the Manx Language Advisory Council in 1986 as agreed in recommendation (e) of the 1985 Report. However, Coonceil ny Gaelgey confines itself to the production of authoritative translations and the production of new words where gaps in the language appear. It does not advise on the development and promotion of Manx, nor does it advise on the teaching of Manx, both of which were suggested in the Report.

Recommendation (f) has had a mixed response. Some Manx is used in documentation - most significantly by the IoM Water Authority, however, the specific use of Manx on bank notes, coins and stamps has not been addressed. The successful issue of stamps for Heritage Year 1986 and for the centenary of Yn Cheshaght Ghailckagh, the Manx Language Society 1999 are notable exceptions to this. Recently an amendment placed by Peter Karran MHK to a Banking Act passing through Tynwald led to the requirement that all banks accept cheques written in the Manx language.

Recommendation (g) has received a similarly mixed response. Recently Douglas Corporation has undertaken an extensive exercise to replace all its street and road signs with bilingual ones. In sharp contrast, other local authorities such as Castletown have removed bilingual signs and replaced them with versions in English only.

So the recommendations of the 1985 Report, though haphazard and somewhat limited in their implementation, have largely been acted upon and on the whole they have led to considerable improvements in support for, and in the status of, the Manx language.

Second phase of language planning

Following the successful introduction by DoE of its Manx language teaching programme in 1992 an effort was made to update and strengthen the 1985 recommendations with a DoE Report to Tynwald on the Future Development of the Manx Language. It appeared in December 1995 and was primarily written by the DoE's Manx Language Officer, Dr Brian Stowell. It focussed on recommendations for extending the Manx language provision offered by the DoE as well as highlighting areas to be addressed by other government and non government agencies.

Dr Stowell expressed some concern – privately at the time and more publicly since – that the report asked for more than Tynwald and the general public would accept, indeed, that it sought more than was practically achievable. The retention in the report, by senior DoE officials, of an ambitious recommendation for recruitment of teachers and an insistence by certain politicians that the entire report be placed before Tynwald, meant that a motion for the report's approval was convincingly defeated. An amendment to the motion, which called for Tynwald approval of the report's main recommendations, but not the controversial recommendation to recruit 9.3 teachers over 5 years, was defeated by only one vote with the report eventually being received by Tynwald. While this defeat meant that the report has no official status, it was significant in that nearly half the members of Tynwald were prepared to back all but one of its extensive range of recommendations for language development.

The DoE Report, Government's second attempt at serious language planning, is being used by DoE as a guide to Manx Language development and policy. Many of its recommendations have been implemented: a GCSE equivalent course has been introduced, and work to produce an A-level equivalent is well under way; the new Manx Education Bill provides greater security for Manx in the curriculum; a Manx Medium class was introduced in September 2001. These, and other less significant aspects of the report have been successfully implemented. Unfortunately, little or no action has been taken to introduce effective teacher training or to address the understaffing of the Manx language programme, leaving the hub of Manx language development at significant risk.

Help from Gaelic Scotland – Grass Roots Development

In February 1996, a few months after Tynwald received the DoE Report, Chris Sheard and Phil Gawne visited a number of Scottish Gaelic development agencies in Inverness and the Isle of Skye. Chris, who was leader of Manx Gaelic playgroup Yn Chied Chesmayd, organised the visit with help from Finlay MacLeod of CNSA, the Scottish Gaelic Pre-school Council, and Margaret MacIver of Gaelic Development agency, CnaG. The visit inspired the formation of Mooinjer Veggey (MV), the Manx pre-school organisation, which was established within a year of this trip (Gawne 2000a).

MV has provided some of the most exciting Manx language developments in recent years.[3] By July 2001, 3% of children starting school in the Isle of Man had been to one of MV's groups, which aim to bring children from non Manx speaking homes to fluency in understanding and semi-speaker level in Manx Gaelic. MV's greatest success has been in providing easy access to Manx Gaelic for young families, people who previously were not attracted to the language. From its inception in January 1997 involving five enthusiastic families who were already committed to supporting Manx language and culture, MV has grown to the extent that in September 2001 it provided a Manx pre-school service for over 80 families, most of whom had little or no initial contact with Manx. Whereas Manx Gaelic had primarily been a male dominated pursuit, MV has also been successful in encouraging women to access the Manx language by providing child-care jobs for around twelve part time staff. These successes are all the more remarkable in that, unlike the situation in the United Kingdom, where pre-school groups are primarily Government funded, MV has only recently been successful in attracting large scale Government support (50% for year ending 31.8.01), with fees paid by parents making up a significant amount of MV's income.

The second important grass roots development to emerge following the trip to Scotland was the Manx Gaelic festival, Feailley Ghaelgagh (FG). The first FG was run in November 1996 with the aim of promoting the value and importance of the language throughout the Isle of Man. The week long festival is now a recognised feature of Manx cultural life and has been particularly successful in persuading business and Government sectors to use the language. FG includes concerts, ceilis, workshops and exhibitions for the general public as well as specific events for Manx speakers. Whilst it attracts around 800 people to specific events during the week, it also becomes a focus for many businesses and Government departments to use simple Manx greetings. Extensive advertising in the newspapers and on the radio ensure that most people in the country are aware of the language.

Third phase of language planning

Another significant development which came out of the trip to Scotland was the establishment of the part-time post of Manx Language Development Officer (a post currently held by the writer). Due to the overwhelming demand for Manx lessons in the schools, the DoE Manx Language Officer's time was soon primarily focussed on the schools language programme. Advice from workers in the Scottish Gaelic movement made clear that there was a huge amount of development work needed in other domains: in pre-school, for adult learners and in general promotion. The DoE officer clearly did not have the time to deal with these areas. Yn Cheshaght Ghailckagh was soon convinced of the need for an additional Manx language officer (this was also recommended in the DoE report - 1995). Following an approach to the Manx Heritage Foundation by Yn Cheshaght Ghailckagh the part time post of yn Greinneyder (Manx Language Development Officer) was established in April 1998, jointly funded by the Manx Heritage Foundation and Manx National Heritage.

---

[3]Mooinjer Veggey websites: http://www.mooinjerveggey.esmartstudent.com
http://www.mooinjerveggey.iomonline.co.im

The primary purpose of this post was the production of a language development plan – Government's third Manx language planning document. In essence the plan was devised to ensure that existing demand for Manx services is met as well as to ensure an ample supply of competent Manx Gaelic speakers well into the future. The main recommendations are based on sound language planning ideas from Wales, Scotland and Ireland. The most crucial development area identified by the plan is the provision of quality Manx Gaelic medium education. This is essential if Manx is ever to re-establish itself as the competently spoken, regularly used language of a significant part of our community. The other key recommendations of the report include greater financial support for Manx pre-school groups and, to address current Manx language needs, the establishment of a one-year-to-fluency Manx immersion course and the establishment of a full time development and support service.

The Manx Language Development Programme, approved by the Manx Heritage Foundation and Manx National Heritage in December 2000, has provided additional impetus to the development of the Manx language and already a number of its key recommendations have been implemented. The programme is being used by the Manx Heritage Foundation as a basis for its support of the Manx Gaelic language and the approval of the programme has led to the establishment of Bing ny Gaelgey an inter departmental language development committee involving the Department of Education, Manx Heritage Foundation and Manx National Heritage. There are many areas identified by the programme which need to be addressed, not least the continued marketing and promotion of Manx Gaelic throughout the Isle of Man. Undoubtedly the areas which will have the most significant effect on the future of the language are adequate teacher training and the development of quality teaching resources. There is every sign that Bing ny Gaelgey and its member organisations will provide the necessary support and funding to ensure that these areas are properly addressed.

A Linguistic and Cultural Phoenix

Clearly the death and rebirth of Manx Gaelic can be strongly linked with the social and cultural turmoil which affected the Isle of Man for much of the 1970s and 1980s. Nationalist direct action and electoral success during these decades represented a distillation of wide felt misgivings over the decline in traditional life and loss of Manx identity. Perhaps spurred on initially as a reaction to nationalist activities, Government has shown increasing willingness to support Manx Gaelic with the late 1990s seeing a reluctant recruit converted to an unreserved enthusiast.

To many Manx people the language can never be a replacement for the traditional Manx way of life which has been so comprehensively undermined by the immigration of the past three decades. There is, however, a growing acceptance that it is one of only a handful of unique aspects of Manxness which can be used to ensure that a form of Manx identity survives into the future. As traditional Manxness is perceived to be further eroded and the proportion of Manx born residents on the Isle of Man continues to decline, this role of the Manx Gaelic language, in providing a new, all inclusive, Manx identity, looks set to expand for many years to come. With this strong need for the language established and the foundations for linguistic development largely in place, the future security of Manx Gaelic looks better than it has for centuries.

Bibliography

Broderick G, 1996, 'Language Decline and Language Revival in the Isle of Man', unpublished *Ned Maddrell Memorial Lecture, 28 November 1996.*

Gawne P, 2000a, 'Development of the Manx Nation - An Epitome of Inter-Celtic Cultural Contacts', *Congress 99, (Celtic Congress Scotland, 2000), p. 20-32.*

Gawne P, 2000b, ' Aithne na nGael: Life after Death' in McCoy G (ed.), *Gaelic Identities, (Belfast: Ultach Trust/Institute of Irish Studies, Queen's University, Belfast), pp. 139-143.*

Gawne P, 2000c, *Jannoo Shickyr Traa ry-heet y Ghaelg - Securing the future for Manx, A Manx Language Development Programme for the Manx Heritage Foundation and Manx National Heritage.*

Kermode D, 2001, 'Offshore Island Politics: the constitutional and political development of the Isle of Man in the twentieth century'. *Centre for Manx Studies Monograph 5, pp 239-254. (Liverpool University Press).*

Moore A W, 1893, The Book of Common Prayer in Manx Gaelic, Douglas, Isle of Man: Hart at OUP for the Manx Society. Vol XXXII *of the Manx Society.*

Thomson R and Pilgrim A, *Outline of Manx Language and Literature, Yn Cheshaght Ghailckagh.*

Isle of Man Government Reports, Report of Proceedings of Tynwald Court, (Douglas, Isle of Man, 12th December 1984).

Report of the Select Committee on the Greater Use of Manx Gaelic, Tynwald, (18th June 1985).

Isle of Man Department of Education, The Future Development of the Manx Language - A report to Tynwald, (December 1995).

Gallup Survey of the Quality of Life, Isle of Man (1990).